The Financial Issues
of the
New International
Economic Order

Pergamon Titles of Related Interest

UNITAR-CEESTEM Library on NIEO

Related Journals*

*Free specimen copies available upon request.

PERGAMON
POLICY
STUDIES

ON THE NEW INTERNATIONAL
ECONOMIC ORDER

The Financial Issues of the New International Economic Order

Edited by
Jorge Lozoya
A.K. Bhattacharya

A volume in the New International
Economic Order (NIEO) Library
Published for UNITAR and the
Center for Economic and Social
Studies of the Third World (CEESTEM)

Pergamon Press

NEW YORK • OXFORD • TORONTO • SYDNEY • FRANKFURT • PARIS

Pergamon Press Offices:

U.S.A.   Pergamon Press Inc., Maxwell House, Fairview Park,
                     Elmsford, New York 10523, U.S.A.

U.K.   Pergamon Press Ltd., Headington Hill Hall,
                     Oxford OX3 0BW, England

CANADA   Pergamon of Canada, Ltd. Suite 104, 150 Consumers Road,
                     Willowdale, Ontario M2J 1P9, Canada

AUSTRALIA   Pergamon Press (Aust.) Pty. Ltd., P.O. Box 544,
                     Potts Point, NSW 2011, Australia

FRANCE   Pergamon Press SARL, 24 rue des Ecoles,
                     75240 Paris, Cedex 05, France

**FEDERAL REPUBLIC   Pergamon Press GmbH, Hammerweg 6, Postfach 1305,
OF GERMANY**   6242 Kronberg/Schönberg, Federal Republic of Germany

Library of Congress Cataloging in Publication Data

Main entry under title:

The Financial issues of the new international
    economic order
(Pergamon policy studies on the new international
    economic order)
Bibliography: p
    Includes index.
    1. International finance. I. Lozoya, Jorge
Alberto. II. Bhattacharya, Anindya K. III. Series.
HG3881.F52   332.4'5   79-29709
ISBN 0-08-025121-8

Printed in the United States of America

Contents

List of
Tables and
Figures

Preface to the UNITAR-CEESTEM NIEO Library

The present volume is one in a series of 17 books which make up the UNITAR-CEESTEM NIEO Library. While each volume covers a specific aspect of the issues that comprise the New International Economic Order and can be read independently of the others, it seems useful to provide a brief introduction to outline the scope of the entire undertaking and put this volume in its proper context.

In the winter of 1976-77, UNITAR (the United Nations Institute for Training and Research) initiated with CEESTEM (the Centro de Estudios Economicos y Sociales del Tercer Mundo, Mexico) a series of inquiries into problems and opportunities associated with the establishment of the New International Economic Order (NIEO). Both institutions agreed that the NIEO constituted one of the highest priority items on the international agenda, and that independent, objective and scholarly investigation of its objectives, obstacles, opportunities, and indicated strategies may be of great value both to the decision makers directly concerned with the negotiation of the issues, and to the international community at large. The UNITAR-CEESTEM NIEO Library is a result of the research that was undertaken by the central professional staffs of the institutes, and by their jointly formed international network of collaborators and consultants.

What are some of the reasons behind this assessment of the importance of the NIEO in contemporary economic and world affairs? Although most people know that the world economy is encountering serious difficulties on both national and international levels, few people outside a small circle of experts realize the seriousness of the problems and the breadth of their scope. Contrary to some current perceptions, the NIEO is neither a passing pressure of the poor countries on

the rich, nor merely a demand for more aid and assistance.   It
is a process which has deep historical precedents, and an
undisputed historical significance.
    We need not go back further than the end of World War II
to find an entire array of historical events which set the stage
for the later emergence of the call for the NIEO. While these
events   arose   from   their   own   historical   antecedents,   they
themselves produced the setting for the breakdown of the
post-war economic system, and the widening gap between rich
and poor nations.
    The   first   and   perhaps   most   decisive   event   was   the
liberation of the oppressed peoples of Africa and Asia, in the
great wave of decolonization that swept the world in the years
following World War II.   The newly independent states were
said to be sovereign and equal to all other states, old and
new,   large   and   small.   Their   admittance   to   the   U.N.
underscored this.   However, the fresh political and juridical
status of the new countries was far from matched by their
actual economic conditions.   The majority felt that their de
jure political colonization ended only to be replaced by a de
facto economic colonization.
    The   historical   process   which   gave   the   majority   of   the
world's population the status of citizens of sovereign and equal
states,   but   left   them   at   the   same   time   in   a   situation   of
economic   underdevelopment   and   dependence,   triggered   the
"revolution of rising expectations".   Desires for rapid economic
growth led Third World governments into ambitious plans and
programmes   of   national   development.   Most   of   the   plans
envisaged a quick repetition of the industrial growth processes
of the developed world, following a path already long trodden
by the countries of Latin America.   When the unintended
side-effects of traditional patterns of industrialization became
evident -- uncontrolled growth of cities, relative neglect of
rural areas and agriculture, threats to the environment, and
the increasing stratification of people in modern and traditional
sectors,   often   with   serious   damage   to   social   structure   and
cohesion   --   many   of   the   original   development   strategies
underwent modification.   The goal of rapid economic growth
was not surrendered, however.   Quantitative growth targets
were formally included in the official development strategies of
the First and Second U.N. Development Decades (for the 1960s
and the 1970s, respectively).
    However, the mid-term review of the achievement of the
Second Development Decade's goals showed mixed results.   The
greatest   disappointment   came   in   the   area   of   agricultural
production and official development aid.   On the average, the
U.N. official development aid targets have not even been half
achieved.   At the same time service charges on past loans
began to put enormous pressures on developing countries'

balance of payment, and world poverty showed no signs of diminishing. There was insufficient progress in commodity trade, inadequate access to the markets of developed countries, particularly for agricultural products; tariffs have escalated, especially for semi-processed and processed products, and new tariff and nontariff restrictions were introduced by many developed countries on a number of items, including textiles and leather goods. The plight of the least developed, island and land-locked developing countries, gave rise to additional concern. While some progress was achieved, for example, through the introduction of a generalized system of preferences by the developed countries, and the proposals of the Tokyo Declaration concerning multilateral trade negotiations, the negative developments weighed more heavily in the balance and created widespread dissatisfaction in the developing world.

Another set of factors came into play as well. This was the sudden and unexpected rise of Third World economic and political power. The Middle East oil embargo of 1972-73, and the subsequent fourfold increase in the price of oil created a world energy crisis. It affected all oil-importing nations, developed as well as developing. It also exhibited the dependence of the developed countries on the developing world for several major natural resources, and proved the ability of the Third World to wield economic and political power effectively. The consequences included rises in the price of food, due to the increased cost of chemical fertilizers, and further tensions between producers and consumers of raw materials. But the OPEC-type exercise of Third World economic and political power proved unable to improve the condition of the developing countries as a whole. Despite significantly higher gross resource flows from the oil-exporting to the oil-importing developing countries, the economic plight of the latter worsened due to the higher cost of energy. Developed countries found themselves beset by economic problems of their own, including not only higher oil prices but inflation, unemployment, and unused industrial capacity. Economic rates of growth slowed, while in most countries balance of payment deficits grew. Even where surpluses could still be generated, concerns focused on the domestic economy, and the political will to increase levels of aid and assistance to the Third World faltered.

Compounding the economic difficulties of the developed nations were signs of breakdown in the international monetary system which affected all countries, developed as well as developing. Amidst growing tensions between the United States, Japan, and the European Community over matters of trade, the Bretton Woods system collapsed and gave rise to a system of floating exchange rates. The value of the U.S.

dollar began to erode, creating serious difficulties for those countries which, like most of the Third World, held their reserves in dollars. The creation of Special Drawing Rights provided some access to foreign exchange independently of dollar holdings, but such access favored the countries already developed, and the rest remained seriously dissatisfied with the workings of the international monetary system. It became evident that some of the fundamental tenets of the post-war world economy were being called into question, and indeed that some had already collapsed.

The NIEO made its appearance as an international political issue in the context of this series of events. Encouraged by the success of OPEC but fearful of splintering Third World solidarity through the newly won wealth of a few of its countries, Presidents Boumedienne of Algeria and Echeverria of Mexico, among others, called for structural reforms in the international economic system. Their governments' initiative resulted in the adoption of such major U.N. resolutions as those of the Sixth and Seventh Special Session, and the Charter of Economic Rights and Duties of States. These in turn provided the impetus for a long series of declarations, resolutions, position papers and studies on various NIEO issues by the United Nations system and the international community at large.

The coming together of these historical factors was not purely coincidental. The wave of decolonization was the culmination of a long-term historical process of democratization, and the rise of the concept of universal rights for individuals and societies. It led, in turn, to a mounting desire for rapid industrialization by the newly independent countries. This met with major frustrations. But as economic interdependence intensified, as trade and markets expanded, and access to energy and raw materials became crucial to the developed world's giant economic machinery, the concentration of economic power itself was modified. It was no longer wielded by a few powerful governments but also fell into the hands of oil exporting nations and transnational corporations.

The historical process which gave birth to a host of independent nation-states placed into sharp relief the inequities of the previous economic system, and provided some of the developing countries with fresh degrees of economic leverage. Since they not only control the supply of a number of important fuels and raw materials but also absorb about 25 percent of the developed world's exports, their demands can no longer be ignored. And they insist that a healthy growth in the world economy cannot be brought about within the framework of the existing economic system.

When the General Assembly, in December, 1977 called for another Special Session in 1980 to assess progress in the establishment of the NIEO, it took a decisive step in bringing the North-South debate to the Organization, where it belongs. It created an ongoing forum for discussions and negotiation in the interim through the Committee of the Whole, which during 1978 managed to define its role and function despite earlier disagreements. Together with the work of the bodies charged with the preparation of the International Development Strategy for the Third United Nations Development Decade, the Organization created the fora for substantive progress in the area of restructuring the economic relations of developed and developing countries. Faced with mounting pressures on national economics in all parts of the world, the international community now finds itself facing a watershed decision: to make use of these fora, or to continue to use mainly bi-lateral and sectoral corrective measures to mitigate tensions while entrusting the resolution of problems to the mechanisms of the free market.

This decision is intimately linked to an entire array of basic questions. Among them:

The question of cost and benefit. Who will have to bear the burden of instituting NIEO and will the results be worth the sacrifices? Will benefits really accrue to the poor people to help fulfill their basic needs and will developing countries be made truly more self-reliant -- or will the main beneficiaries be the already rich elites? Will the developed countries also benefit from NIEO (a positive-sum game) or will it mainly mean the redistribution of the current stock of wealth from them to the developing countries (a zero-sum game)?

The question of legitimacy. Is the free market the basic mechanism of world trade and the best vehicle of development, or is it merely a convenient fiction to cover up the current unjust manipulations of the major economic groups?

The question of morality. Do the rich countries have a moral obligation to help the poor, and especially the poorest? Does this responsibility extend to those countries who had no historical part in the creation of poverty in the third world?

The question of political feasibility. How strongly will different organized groups in society support or oppose governmental policies aimed at the achievement of the NIEO --and how much solidarity exists in these domains internationally, among the developing and the developed countries themselves?

It is unrealistic to expect that real progress will be made on specific NIEO issues (such as official development aid, technical assistance, debt renegotiation, removal of tariff barriers, technical cooperation among developing countries, the link between SDRs and development, voting power in the World Bank and IMF, transfers of technology, regulation of transnational corporations, a system of consultations on industrialization, and restructuring the economic and social

sectors of the United Nations) so long as the basic issues are
not resolved and a consensus does not emerge concerning
them. The NIEO can be achieved if, and only if, it is perceived that its benefits are universal and can reach all segments of the world's population (especially the neediest); if it
is held that its costs do not exceed its benefits; if its regulatory mechanisms are seen to be legitimate; if some real
sense of moral responsibility exists among members of the
human community, and if sufficient political support is
available nationally as well as internationally for the indicated
measures. If one or more of these preconditions are not met,
the NIEO will not be achieved; Member States will continue to
practice the existing, predominantly piecemeal, ad hoc and
mainly bilateral modes of adjusting to stresses and reaching
compromises.

The basic purpose of the UNITAR-CEESTEM NIEO Library
is to provide an independent and objective assessment of these
issues, and to report its findings in time for the historic
events of 1980: the Special Session of the General Assembly
devoted to the assessment of progress toward the NIEO, and
the immediately following regular session, during which the
International Development Strategy for the 1980s and beyond
(the U.N.'s Third Development Decade) is to be debated and
adopted. It would clearly be an enormous waste of time and
effort to enter into these negotiations without forming a clear
idea of the issues that bear on their success. But reporting
on them is not a simple matter of using insight and intuition;
it requires painstaking and organized empirical research. The
requirement is to identify the forces that operate for or
against the NIEO in all parts of the world. Intuitive answers
concerning its cost and benefits, legitimacy, morality, and
political feasibility occur to all persons knowledgeable in these
areas, but such answers tend to vary and are thus not
sufficiently reliable. Expert research on the current obstacles
and opportunities associated with the NIEO in the different
regions of the world, and with respect to the diverse sectors
of the world economy, needs to be conducted. The results of
such research may shed some much needed light on the
chances of success in establishing a new international economic
order generally, and on the types of objectives and modes of
negotiations that, in the positive case, could lead to it
specifically. For although it is unlikely that a dominant
consensus already exists in the world concerning the cost and
benefit, legitimacy, morality, and political feasibility of the
NIEO (if it did exist, the international community would
probably not be experiencing the sense of frustration it has
today), the precise estimation of costs versus benefits,
legitimacy versus illegitimacy, morality versus indifference,
and political feasibility versus futility by different societal

groups could reveal highly differentiated potentials for achieving a dominant consensus in the future. Today's chaotic welter of opinions and pressures concerning the NIEO need not remain such, but could crystallize into a decisive mood favoring or opposing it. To those who object to such analysis on the grounds that economic theory, rather than wide-ranging socio-political considerations, must serve to decide the fate of NIEO, we may reply that economic theory, while relevant, is in itself over generous: it can often prove both sides of conflicting positions. Since both sides in a dispute can marshal some variety of economic theory in their defense, and no common criteria exist for assessing the relative merits of all theories, economic rationality as conveyed by economic theories becomes marginal in the negotiating process. We need to go one step deeper, inquiring into the reasons particular theories are summoned to defend particular points of view, as well as measuring the intensity of commitment to these viewpoints and the negotiating power of the parties subscribing to them.

Thus, the focus of the UNITAR-CEESTEM Library is not a given economic theory, but the perceptions and opinions underlying the positions taken by diverse actors. The configuration and strength of these perceptions and opinions will ultimately determine whether negotiations in the area of the NIEO can be successful, and if so, which strategies will have optimum chances of success.

The Library contains volumes arranged in three different series. First, there is a series of overview studies. These provide background, context, and basic reference data. They include a volume defining and classifying the principal objectives of the NIEO as agreed or debated in the United Nations and other major international fora; a volume giving an overview and assessment of alternative viewpoints on the NIEO espoused by various nongovernmental groups and researchers and different parts of the world; a third defining the most critical obstacles confronting the establishment of the NIEO; a fourth dealing with the specific problems of food and agriculture as they are debated in the framework of the United Nations. A fifth volume suggests the basic strategies which appear indicated and appropriate to accelerate progress toward the NIEO; and a final volume communicates the results of the associated UNITAR-CEESTEM International Opinion Survey of Decision-Makers and Experts on the crucial questions of the NIEO.

The second series contains geographic studies. Volumes in this series review the positions and postures of national governments and the attitudes of business, labor, the public media, and the opinion of the population at large in various nations and regions of the world. Individual volumes focus on the United States and Canada, on Western Europe, on Eastern Europe including the Soviet Union, on Asia including

Australia, on Latin America, and on Africa and the Middle East.

The third series of the NIEO Library is devoted to functional studies. Here experts give their views and assessments of such issues as the possible and the desirable structure of the world economy; of the patterns and problems of international trade and industrial development; of international financial matters, and of the associated political and institutional, as well as social and cultural problems and opportunities.

Among them, the seventeen volumes of the Library cover practically all the principal issues encountered in efforts to establish a New International Economic Order, through in-depth discussion by independent investigators, coming from different societies in different parts of the world.

The UNITAR-CEESTEM NIEO Library offers wide-ranging analyses, and sometimes divergent viewpoints, on a broad range of topics. It does not offer simplistic solutions, nor advocate one viewpoint indiscriminately over others. It seeks to illuminate the range and complexity of the issues, provide clarification of individual items, and to lend a sense of the vastness and significance of the NIEO as a whole.

It is the hope of all of us, researchers and consultants of the UNITAR-CEESTEM project on the NIEO, that our results, published as the NIEO Library, may render some service to the decisionmaker and negotiator who must cope with the problems of the international economic order, as well as to the student of international economic and world affairs, interested in further research on these topics. It is our view that the NIEO is a historically necessary, and humanly and politically appropriate attempt to create a world order that is sustainable for generations, equitable for all, and capable of meeting the most urgent needs and demands of the peoples and nations of the world community.

Ervin Laszlo
Project Director

Introduction

The UNITAR–CEESTEM policy studies series on the New International Economic Order (NIEO) examines obstacles and opportunities associated with current efforts to create a new and more equitable world economic order. This volume deals with the establishment of the NIEO in the international monetary-financial arena. It focuses on long-term require- ments for a better functioning of the international financial system within the famework of a NIEO, rather than on the immediate tactics that various actors may wish to pursue. The editors assume that a discussion of principal, long-term goals is helpful in reviewing day-to-day strategies for bringing about a New International Economic Order.

The major themes addressed in this volume are the international monetary system, external debt, private bank financing and capital markets, and petrodollars and collective self-reliance. Reflecting the real world divergence of views, the positions of the authors vary on fundamental strategies required to bring about changes in structural relations between the developed and developing countries, as well as on specific issues, such as the role of private lenders vis-a-vis official sources of finance and the management of risks in- volved in lending to developing countries. In particular, there is still a broad divergence of opinion on intermediate and long-term goals for implementing a NIEO in the financial arena. However, certain approaches are held in common by almost all authors, especially in areas related to the obstacles in the way of the establishment of a NIEO, and in relation to general strategies needed to bring about an increasing transfer of resources from the developed to the developing countries.

In the area of the international monetary system, concern is expressed over the acute instability in the present international order owing to the interlinked issues of balance-of-payments adjustment, international liquidity, and the lack of confidence in the role of the U.S. dollar as the chief medium for international transactions and reserves. The persistent and consistent balance-of-payments deficit of the United States leads to a growing crisis of confidence in the value of the U.S. dollar, thereby creating exchange rate turmoil all over the world. The so-called "Triffin dilemma" - deficit financing by the United States to meet the growing liquidity needs of the world and the consequent erosion of confidence in the value of the U.S. dollar - constitutes a basic element of instability in the current international monetary system. The dollar dependence of the international economy has jeopardized the smooth functioning of international trade and payments, thereby making the attainment of NIEO objectives (such as the narrowing of the gap between rich and poor nations, the acceleration of growth and progress in developing countries, and the achievement of a just and equitable system in international relations) difficult, if not impossible. This instability in the international monetary system, coupled with other problems (such as the persistence of inflationary pressures, the slowdown in the pace of domestic expansion of major economies, high unemployment rates and rising oil prices) poses a formidable obstacle to the achievement of NIEO objectives, and developing countries which do not participate adequately in major international monetary and financial decisions, nevertheless, continue to be adversely affected by the existing international-financial order.

In the area of the policies and operations of the International Monetary Fund (IMF), profound dissatisfaction is voiced concerning structure, functioning, policy orientation, and actual operations of the IMF. There is a strong feeling that the existing power structure of the IMF does not properly reflect the changed power relations of the world economy today. Neither the United States, nor the European Economic Community, nor Japan is capable of imposing hegemony on each other or on the international system as a whole. The IMF has become irrelevant to the needs of major industrial powers and, by default, has turned into an instrument for the domination of economies of developing countries by the Group of Ten. It is unable to impose the rules of the game equitably on all participants in the international monetary system. It continues to place much of the blame on deficit nations, while being helpless to shape the destiny of surplus countries. The IMF has proved incapable of counteracting the acute imbalances in the world economy after the oil price hikes, or of neutralizing the massive financial expansion of private commercial banks in the international arena. The recycling of surplus petrodollars through the commerical banking system is a product of the crisis of the international monetary order, and a result of the conscious separation between industrial and financial power among nations maintained deliberately through the workings of the present international monetary system. It is paradoxical that the IMF was not only unable to control private financing growth, but it even increased its own lendable resources, thereby creating greater international liquidity. In this context of excess liquidity in the private banking sector, it is difficult to conceive the possibility of creating greater official financial flows to developing countries, including the possibility of using the Special Drawing Rights/Aid "link" as a development financing mechanism.

As evidenced particularly by the Latin American experience, the IMF policy of insistence on orthodox methods of balance-of-payments adjustment (such as demand contraction, wage control, and exchange rate adjustment) does not correct structural imbalances in a permanent manner, but, rather, leads to "stop-go" development. The IMF does not take adequate account of the structural differences between developed and developing countries, nor of the need for import substitution policies in developing economies. The IMF policy of putting pressure on deficit countries by way of standardized stabilization methods overlooks the structural factors behind balance-of-payments disequilibrium in developing societies (such as dependence on critical imports of intermediate and capital goods, exchange gap, and so on) and does not solve the problem of adjustment of external payments imbalance in the context of economic growth. Rather, it limits the possibilities for economic development of the Third World and, thus, contributes to depressing the world economy at large. In the context of underdevelopment, adjustment policies for external disequilibrium impinge on growth processes and structural changes. Promoting the latter requires an integrated focus, which is currently missing from the conventional stabilization policies of the IMF, due largely to the rigid distinction maintained between "temporary" balance-of-payments financing support and long-term capital investment needs. Clearly, the IMF will not effectively support NIEO objectives as long as its policy orientation is not radically modified to make it more representative of the needs and aspirations of developing societies.

On external debt, concern is expressed over both the unprecedented growth in the absolute value of the external debt of developing countries as a group and the crushing burden of servicing such debt. The current foreign exchange needs of many developing countries are being met at the cost of a mounting external debt, which increases their dependence on external creditors and commits their future monetary reserves in advance. In recent years, the financial flows to developing countries have become increasingly more "privatized," limiting the possibilities of control of this process by national and international monetary authorities. While excess liquidity in the private sector implies greater access to private funds by developing countries and greater flexibility to confront balance-of-payments deficits, it also means more debt and more vulnerability of borrowers in the future. The question of financial "discipline" is increasingly being counterposed to the imperatives of economic growth in the Third World.

Since much of the external debt problem of the developing world is due to structural imbalances inherent in the present system of international trade (both in the price structure and the regional distribution of trade among nations), renegotiation of rescheduling of the current debt will be merely a short-term palliative, unless these measures are accompanied by longer-term measures, such as the removal of barriers to a better system of trade for developing countries and the improvement of the existing official assistance performance of major industrial countries. The question of the relationship between the lenders' risk premium and borrowers' growth performance must be reformulated to take into consideration, especially, those developing economies that have a lower growth rate over time and, therefore, face a more serious debt problem in the future.

On private bank financing of development, there is agreement among the authors that the international financial markets provide highly restricted access to developing countries, especially in the long-term capital market segment. While there is no deliberate pattern of discrimination against developing countries as such, national regulations (such as queue system, government authorization for foreign issues, ceilings on foreign issues, and restrictions on foreign security purchases by national institutional investors), in fact, prevent freer access by foreigners in general to national capital markets. The main obstacle to greater access of developing countries to the national and international capital markets is, however, attitudinal rather than institutional. The "high risk" image of developing country borrowers, the relative unfamiliarity of such borrowers to private lenders, and a stricter and more conservative "country risk" assessment standard than that prevailing in the medium-term credit market pose formidable obstacles to improving the access of developing countries to external capital markets. The predictable and unfortunate upshot is a high degree of country concentration of private bank lending to the developing world. Three quarters of Eurocurrency credits extended to developing countries are concentrated in a handful of nations, and foreign and international bond markets are similarly restricted to selected countries. The "low income" countries, by contrast, receive less that two percent of annual Eurocurrency credits extended to the developing world, and they obtain no bond financing at all. Altogether, bond issues comprise less than

20 per cent of total external funds raised by developing countries as a group in the international financial markets.

As regards problematic effects of massive private bank financing of development needs, concern is voiced over the rapid pace of growth of the Eurocurrency market away from national controls, its impact on domestic inflation, management of domestic monetary policy, debt-service burden in stagnant economies, and the increasing dependency of those economies vis-a-vis a few large transnational banks. Since more than 40 per cent of the total external debt of developing countries as a group is owed to the private sector, the debt-service payment burden is all the more acute for those "high income" and "middle income" developing countries that borrowed the most from the private sector during the decade of the 1970s. Debt-service payments in the face of domestic chaos or stagnation can be a crushing burden leading to unacceptable powers of external decision making in the economic and political life of developing countries.

On the issue of petrodollar recycling, it is felt that the OPEC nations are losing out on the current methods utilized to recycle surplus oil revenues. The existing pattern of the use of surplus OPEC funds reveals a heavy cost on OPEC by way of imported inflation, inappropriate choice of technology, overcommitment of defense expenditures, and negative rates of return on commerical investments abroad. The actual returns on OPEC assets held in developed countries are below the current rate of inflation on export prices of industrialized countries and the increase in import prices for OPEC. In addition to this market risk, OPEC assets abroad are becoming increasingly vulnerable to the stability of economic activity, money and capital markets, and external currency values of the developed world, not to mention the possible threat of freezing their assets in the absence of political "goodwill" between OPEC and developed nations.

The real cost of the transfer of resources from the West to OPEC is being borne by nonoil developing countries that are paying for both higher OPEC oil prices and the resulting higher import prices from developed countries. Clearly, the time has come for a thorough review of the current uses of OPEC surplus funds with a view to channeling greater amounts of petrodollars to developing countries by way of primary recycling. Surplus OPEC funds could play a critical role in the developing unexploited natural resources and manpower reservoirs in the Third World. By the same token, the latter would be less prone to discriminate against OPEC interests compared to Western countries.

The main area of disagreement among authors in this volume centers on the role of the private sector in financing development. Some are suspicious of the motivations of private lenders as well as of the contributions of private financing to

development. The overwhelming feeling in Latin America is
that private lenders acquire too much weight in influencing the
direction of the borrowing country's development planning, and
that this dependence on private credits should be reduced
through an improvement in the terms of trade and the existing flow of official resource transfer. Other authors, by
contrast, view private financial flows more favorably, in terms
of excess liquidity in the private banking sector, the declining
trend in official resource transfer, low real interest rates on
private bank loans and credits, lengthening maturities of
private credits, and the historic record of a relatively
nonpolitical nature of private bank financing, especially in the
Far East.

Several major policy recommendations emerge in this
volume. As far as the international monetary system is
concerned, it needs fundamental reform, if the present crisis
and the injustices of the system are to be overcome. A
Central World Bank should be created to issue an international
currency valued on a group of raw materials and heeding the
principles of the NIEO, rather than reflecting the present
power structure. This new currency ought to be issued and
distributed in accordance with needs rather than with voting
power or quotas. The onus of adjustment of external
imbalance should be placed on surplus countries rather than
those in deficit. Regional "lenders of last resort" should be
instituted through swap arrangements that regional groups
could use.

If the NIEO is to become a reality, it must involve a
radical redistribution of global reserves based on need and
without having to satisfy some outside criteria of a subjective
character. Such resources should be available to a needy
country unconditionally and automatically. A new approach to
the adjustment of balance-of-payments disequilibrium should be
formulated, taking into account the need for sustained
economic growth and for avoiding structural bottlenecks. Such
an approach requires a relative price policy to selectively
divert demand, and a supply policy to grant incentives to the
production and investment in tradable goods and services.
Additional financial suuport to promote the latter goal should
be provided by regional and interregional development banks.

Requests for debt relief should be based on the greatest
need for those countries that are not growing fast enough to
service their external debt. Some form of debt relief should
also be based on cultural practices in different parts of the
world. Renewed appeals for increases in Official Development
Assistance (ODA) should be based on timing of the business
cycle wherein larger amounts of ODA should be given during
periods of recession in developed countries. ODA should also
be linked to a tax on the world's free resources, such as
space and the sea, and to a tax on military spending.

As regards improving the access of developing countries to private financial markets, a variety of schemes - guarantees, insurance, underwriting, cofinancing, and rationalization of national official regulations - could be undertaken to implement a plan of action. The "minimum regulation - maximum incentive" policies of countries in the Asia-Pacific region should be carefully examined to see what can be done to attract private financing.

On OPEC funds, there ought to be much greater primary recycling of surplus petrodollars to developing countries instead of the present practice of secondary recycling through international banks and international organizations. Some of the main areas in which surplus OPEC funds could be utilized are minerals, food, forest resources, manufacturing industry, commodity price stabilization, and regional capital markets. A permanent secretariat for the South along the lines of OECD should be established to accomplish this task of utilizing OPEC funds to promote greater collective self-reliance among developing countries. In conclusion, the present international monetary and financial order is clearly unsatisfactory and needs fundamental reforms. A radical change in the existing system is called for to serve the critical NIEO objective of a more equitable set of relations among countries in varying stages of development. The implementation of the measures listed in this volume would require political will and coordinated action on the part of all countries - developing, oil exporting, and industrialized. Hopefully, this volume will contribute toward an understanding of the policy actions that must be undertaken if there is to be real and appreciable progress in the establishment of a New International Economic Order.

The editors wish to acknowledge the continuing support of Davidson Nicol, Executive General of UNITAR, and of B. F. Osorio-Tafall, Director General of the Center for Economic and Social Studies of the Third World (CESSTW), as well as the enthusiastic leadership of Ervin Laszlo along with the realization of the UNITAR-CEESTEM Project.

I
The International Monetary System

1 Transfer of Financial Resources and the NIEO

Jaime Estevez

The upheavals that took place in the international economy at the begininning of the decade of the 1970s have led to an evolution in political and economic analysis, somewhat similar to that provoked in every society by the crisis of the 1930s. In fact, just as the latter generated the conviction that it was necessary for the State to take a leading role in the national economy, so today there is an almost unanimous awareness of mankind's need for more responsible direction of the world economy.

The basic resolutions adopted by the United Nations General Assembly in 1974 expressed this awareness: the Declaration and Programme of Action for the Establishment of a New International Economic Order, and the Charter of Economic Rights and Duties of States. That same year, what had seemed almost impossible was accomplished in the monetary and financial sector: the agreement of the International Monetary Fund (IMF) Committee of Twenty (Committee for the Reform of the International Monetary System and Related Questions) on the fundamental orientations for a qualitative reshaping of the international monetary system. The decision was directed to stimulating trade growth and world employment and to promoting economic development, converting Special Drawing Rights (SDRs) into the main reserve asset, and fomenting a greater net flow of real resources to developing countries.

From this perspective, the general sequence of events in the last five years has been quite disappointing. In the monetary and financial sector, most of the reforms have remained on paper. This has meant that the problems and difficulties, foreseen in the last decade and experienced at the beginning of the present one, have become much worse, notably reducing the room for maneuver and threatening to make the global situation unmanageable. Progress in the establishment of a new order in the financial area seems today more difficult to achieve than five years ago, for the following reasons.

First, if the consensus of 1974 has not been carried out, it is not because of a technical deficiency or lack of debate. That consensus was the result of more than fifteen years of arguing; negotiations, both private and public, took place among government experts as well as academic specialists from all over the world. A second "technical" round of debates could do little to increase the likelihood that the measures agreed upon will, for sure, be put into effect.

Second, the very serious deterioration of the international monetary and financial situation has made many people doubt that even the 1974 agreements could be now adhered to. In fact, there is an ever stronger conviction that the present development aid system, the international monetary system, and the international monetary and financial organizations are not only institutional obstacles to the measures proposed, but make the global functioning of the international economy more difficult, and make the central objectives of the New International Economic Order (NIEO) impossible to carry out. The objectives referred to are the attainment of equity in international relations; recognition of the sovereign and inalienable right of all States to choose their own economic, political, social, and cultural system; speeding up of economic growth in the developing countries; doing away with the gap between industrial and developing countries; and so on.

Thus, the present crisis can only be overcome through the qualitative reform of international financial and monetary relations and of their institutional system, evidently unjust and now unworkable.

NEW TRENDS OF FINANCIAL ASSISTANCE FOR DEVELOPMENT

Financial assistance for development is a relatively new concept. Before World War II, there were various forms for noncommerical transfers, including cooperation and aid among allies, and between the metropolises and their colonies. The first post-war experience of financial aid flows between politically independent countries for the purpose of stimulating economic development occurred under the Marshall Plan. The efficacy of this plan in speeding the rapid economic recovery of Western Europe, and also benefiting the "donating" economy, greatly contributed to generating a certain indiscriminate aid cult. Based on a particular theoretical conception of the development-underdevelopment problem, this cult emphasized capital availability as a key element vis-a-vis a low internal capital accumulation capacity, and advocated

external capital as a solution be it in the form of direct
investment or credits.

In accordance with this logic, the developed capitalist
countries and the international monetary and credit
organizations have severely limited access to credit in the case
of those who put significant obstacles in the way of direct
foreign investment. The developing countries themselves
accepted this approach and set out, as a fundamental demand,
a substantial increase in transfer of financial resources in
their favor.

In this framework, various resolutions (among them the
International Development Strategy of the U.N. Second Decade)
compelled the industrialized countries to increase the net flow
of financial resources to the developing countries. The global
goal was for the developed countries to contribute a sum
equivalent to one percent of their gross national product
(GNP) to the LDC. It was further specified that transfers
with a high grant element or Official Development Assistance
(ODA) ought to reach 0.7 percent of the GNP of the industrialized countries. The Programme of Action for the Establishment of the NIEO emphasized the importance of carrying
out these quantitative goals. It also emphasized the need to
improve the transfer conditions, in order to increase the
official element, thus fulfilling the objectives of the International Development Strategy. Experience has shown, however, that the global goal of one percent is unrealistic and
largely counterproductive; and that, within the present international economic order, the ODA increase to a rate of 0.7
percent of the industrialized countries' GNP is impossible.

As was foreseen in the discussion which led to the 1974
resolutions, one of the most dramatic changes has been the
critical increase in the already chronic external debt of the
developing countries. Between 1975 and 1977 alone, the nonoil
developing countries accumulated a global current account
deficit of around 110 billion dollars. This deficit was
temporarily financed through the notable increase in the total
net flows of financial resources to developing countries from 35
billion dollars in 1973 to 64.4 billion in 1977, not including the
transfers made by the socialist countries. This near doubling
of net flows is explained by greater credit and direct
investment availability made possible by the expansion of
international liquidity and by the use of a significant part of
the OPEC surplus.

The notable increase in the total flow of resources has
basically resulted from the increase in the transfer of private
resources in commercial terms. From 1975 to 1977, the
developing countries obtained a net annual average in excess
of 12 billion dollars from the financial markets. Also, the
nonconcessionary private financial flows of DAC members to the
developing countries increased from 8 billion dollars yearly in

1973-74 to an average of 23 billion in 1975-77. (DAC is the
Development Assistance Committee of the Organization for
Economic Cooperation and Development, based in Paris and
comprising the 18 members of the OECD: United States,
Japan, Germany, France, United Kingdom, Italy, Canada,
Australia, Austria, Belgium, Denmark, Ireland, Luxembourg,
Netherlands, New Zealand, Norway, Sweden, and Switzerland.)
    From the flows which directly or indirectly can be called
aid, only the allocations from the OPEC countries to the
developing countries have meant a substantial new contribution. In 1977, these net flows rose to nine billion dollars,
two-thirds of which were on concessionary terms, which is
equivalent to 40 percent of assistance for development
granted by all the DAC members. By contrast, among the
total net financial flows from the DAC members to developing
countries, the relative importance of those considered ODA, as
well as other official transfers and private grants, has been
greatly reduced. In 1973-74 these represented 63 percent of
total net flows, while in 1975-77 they reached only an average
of 44 percent.

Table 1.1. Net Financial Flows from DAC Members to
Developing Countries
(Annual average in millions of U.S. dollars)

	1973-74	Percent	1975-76-77	Percent
Concessionary:	10,335	46.2	14,004	33.7
ODA Private grants	1,291	5.8	1,415	3.4
Other Official	2,325	10.4	3,114	7.5
Other Private:				
Direct investment	2,922	13.1	9,439	22.7
Bilateral and multilateral portfolio	3,634	16.3	8,067	19.4
Export credit	1,841	8.2	5,568	13.4
TOTAL	22,347	100.0	41,608	100.0

Source: IMF Survey, July 25, 1977 and July 24, 1978.

The grants, loans, and contributions considered as ODA have increased, on average, their grant component. In 1976, this reached 88.9 percent, clearly exceeding the norm of 84 percent established by the DAC members in 1972. This phenomenon reflects a more than proportional increase in grants as well as the fact that the average interest rate of credits in concessionary grants has risen less than that of commercial credits.

In nominal terms, the ODA amounts granted by the DAC countries increased fractionally, but decreased in relative terms with respect to the total flow of resources from DAC countries to developing countries, as well as with respect to the GNP of industrialized countries. If, in the 1965-67 three year period, these flows totaled 57 percent of the flows coming from the DAC members, ten years later (in the 1975-77 three year period), they made up only 33 percent. In GNP terms, only Sweden, the Netherlands, and Norway have complied with the goal of 0.7 percent. For the DAC members as a group, the ODA/GNP relation has decreased from 0.42 percent in 1965-67 to 0.31 percent in 1977, which is one of the two lowest values since statistics in these matters became available in 1950. According to World Bank estimates, what is most probable is that this ratio will continue to decrease, reaching a mere 0.28 percent by the end of the decade.

The phenomena analyzed (the notable increase in the total of nominal flows and the strong relative diminution of concessionary assistance) has resulted in a structural deterioration in the external payments of the Third World. The external debt, with or without public guarantee, which developing countries had accumulated up to 1969 was a little over 50 billion dollars. In the first four years of this decade, this debt doubled, reaching a sum of more than 100 billion in 1973, and in the following three years it doubled again, reaching 202.5 billion by the end of 1976. The magnitude of this debt threatens to destroy the growth possibilities of developing countries and produce an overall crisis in the international system of payments. The figures correspond to dollars of each year. It is difficult to determine a deflationary mechanism which will adequately reflect, for the Third World taken as a whole, the debt's evolution (and that of transfers) in real terms, first, because inflation affects the different countries in diverse ways; second, because of the large variety of terms and conditions of the debt. In any case, according to IMF calculating between 1973 and 1976, the developing countries' total debt, in constant dollars, increased by more than 40 percent.

What is of greater concern than the size of the debt is the accelerated deterioration of its terms. The phenomena analyzed have meant a large increase in the private share of the debt. The outstanding debt with public guarantee (disbursed) vis-a-vis private creditors has systematically increased in relative importance, rising from 32.2 percent in 1970, to 36.5 percent in 1973, and to 45.3 percent in 1976. There are no equivalent data on credits of private origin and destination without public guarantee, but information presently available indicates that for the nonoil developing countries this kind of debt has grown from 29.3 billion dollars in 1974 to 46.8 billion in 1977.

This situation has very serious consequences. The international bank market continues to be strongly concentrated, dominated by fewer than 50 banks. Among these banks, some 12 United States banks and their foreign branches are creditors for more than half of the private credit resources. This has given them great decision making power with respect to the developing countries' economic life.

Secondly, the private nature of the debt has brought about a systematic increase in the nominal interest rates. Between 1970 and 1976, interest payments almost quadrupled, reaching a sum of 7.1 billion dollars. In terms of the total debt, interest rates went from 3.5 percent in 1970 to 4.4. percent in 1976. The rise in interest rates has coincided with a decrease in growth rates in the GNP of the nonoil developing countries. These growth rates were, on the average, below 4.5 percent from 1975 to 1977. This implies that an increasing proportion of the potential resources of accumulation had to be transfered abroad. In turn, this phenomenon implies that the interest rates of new private credits are, on the average, twice as high as the growth in the gross national product of the nonoil developing countries. This makes the payment of credits extremely difficult; and, what is more serious, it tends to favor thier use in speculative dealings.

Thirdly, the private nature of the debt has increased its debtor concentration. The only countries with access to the bond market and that benefit most from international bank credits are oil-exporting developing countries with fairly high relative incomes. In 1975, of 96 developing countries, 17 had received 71 percent of the credits still owed, and the first seven were responsible for 45.4 percent of the outstanding debt.

Amortization payments have steadily increased, although relatively less than those corresponding to interest, rising from 4 billion in 1970 to 11 billion dollars in 1978. Consequently, from the total, the payments for debt servicing in 1970 represented 30 percent and in 1976, 39 percent. On the other hand, the debt servicing of the nonoil developing countries was 8.4 percent of their exports in 1974, in 1975 it was 9.9 percent, and in 1976 nearly 10.0 percent.

It is not surprising, therefore, that the problems of the developing countries' external debt and, more generally, the issue of development financing have taken a primary place in the discussions between rich and poor countries. The results of development financing do away with the naive criterion cf some twelve years ago which saw a panacea in the increase of financial flows to developing countries. The problems of development have been seen as more structural and complex and not solely due to insufficient capital. The global consideration of the functioning of international economic relations has acquired great importance, as well as the character of the internal economic, social, and political structures of the Third World countries.

The decisive problem of the effective destination of the flow of resources received by the developing countries, together with the deterioration in the terms of granting credits, gives rise to legitimate doubts on the final utility of the present system of development assistance.

The steep rise in oil prices is hardly an imitable example and, even if it were, it could end up being negative for a considerable number of developing countries. Nevertheless, it has served to reiterate and bring to the public eye the simple truth that the deficit problems in balance of payments and the external debt are only the financial manifestation of existing imbalances in the relative prices of products and in the structure of international trade relations. The current account deficits of nonoil developing countries are determined by causes beyond their control. Furthermore, no change in the existing situtation is foreseen in the near future. Thus, beyond what can be achieved in the field of development assistance, if substantial progress is not made in the establishment of at least the principal measures considered in the United Nations resolutions pertaining to the NIEO, the already critical financial situation of Third World countries will necessarily tend to worsen. This will affect their development perspectives and will obstruct the possibilities of overcoming the recession difficulties of the industrial countries.

The present imbalances in the international monetary system favor the development of the dangerous tendencies pointed out. Competition to acquire the largest share of the many surplus liquid resources and persistent world inflation oblige the international banks to turn to clients prepared to pay growing rates of interest.

The developing countries, faced with a drastic reduction in their pace of growth, tend to rely on the private capital market and have turned into an important source of absorption for these liquid masses, a large part of which (11 billion dollars) is redeposited as reserves in international banks, demanding again the search for new clients by private banks.

For its part, the IMF has shown itself structurally incapable of ordering and channeling the system. It continues to place all the emphasis on obliging the underdeveloped countries with deficits to overcome the imbalances, while being able to control the persistent surplus of others.

The pressure on those with deficits results in a severe limitation on their development possibilities, and contributes to depressing the world economy, without an effective solution being given to problems that are structural. On the contrary, an equivalent pressure on surplus countries, oriented to giving impulse to an increase in their acquisitions in developing countries, would have more positive effects on these countries' financial imbalances and would substantially help their economic development.

THE ACTUAL PERSPECTIVES OF THE 1974 PROPOSALS

The United Nations resolution of 1974 proposed the adoption of important measures oriented to promoting the highest possible net transfer to developing countries. This was to be carried out through the reduction in the present value of the external debt, and the search for alternative sources of development finance.

A first proposal, strongly supported by a sector of the developing countries and incorporated into the Programme of Action, was for the renegotiation of the external debt with a view to its annulment, moratorium, or readjustment; and subsidies for interest payments, promoting, in particular, the adoption of urgent measures to mitigate the negative consequences of the burden of the external debt contracted in unfavorable conditions. Although less explicit, the proposal was present in the International Development for the Second Decade, when the need was put forward to foresee and avoid the crisis caused by the debt through refinancing and the redistribution of its servicing.

Many industrialized countries have announced their decision to convert part of the official loans into grants. The largest issuers of official credits, the United States and France, have still not decided how great the reduction will be. The nine countries that made public their decision have jointly agreed to annul a total sum of 6.2 billion, representing 3 percent of the external debt of the nonoil developing countries. However, in the case of countries with lower income - they are the main beneficiaries - the annulment represents around 13 percent of their outstanding debt.

The amounts renegotiated in the last ten years do not represent more than 4 percent of the total public and private external debt of the nonoil developing countries. In general, renegotiations have taken the form of a slow and complicated process in which the debtor countries have found themselves in a doubly disadvantageous position; first, because negotiations are only made when they are in an extremely critical balance of payments situation which allows them no room for maneuver; and second, because they confront renegotiation individually, while creditors are organized.

It is practically impossible for the industrial countries to accept an abolition or substantial renegotiation of the accumulated debt. This is even more the case when an important segment of Third World countries (those with easy access to the international capital market) fears that this will endanger their prestige as debtors. In any case, if a measure of this kind were to be generally and indiscriminately adopted, it would benefit the countries with a high or medium income more than those poor countries that have, until now, received little aid.

A second proposal, put forward by the Charter of Economic Rights and Duties of the States, is that of substantially reducing military expenditure, achieving a general and total disarmament, and directing these available funds to promoting economic and social development. This initiative would be of great importance in bringing about the alternative use of resources, but there is little possibility of its being converted into an effective source of development finance for some years to come. This is due to the fact that the degree of armament expenditure depends on structural conditions which are not likely to change in the short term; on the other hand, there is nothing to guarantee that its reduction will effectively imply an increase in development transfers.

The third and most concrete proposal to increase resource transfer to the developing countries has been that of linking the creation of international liquidity with development financing. The strategy of the Second Decade for Development proposed that the possibility of establishing a link between the allocation of new reserves assets and the additional financing of development should be considered. The Programme of Action was much more emphatic, requiring the undelayed creation of a link between SDRs and development financing. This proposal was originally made at a time when the international economy needed to create considerable financial resources, it being fully feasible in technical terms that this would result in a substantial transfer of resources to developing countries.

In spite of the fact that the developed countries formally accepted the agreement that credit reserves would be centrally created, in practical terms, they have been reluctant to sacrifice this source of wealth. After arduous negotiations, an agreement was obtained to create liquidity in the form of SDRs for a total of 9.3 billion SDRs between 1970 and 1974. However, concomitantly, the developed countries unilaterally expanded reserves in national currencies to what is equivalent to 92.3 billion SDRs. Of the SDRs issued, seven billion were granted to the developed countries and only 2.3 billion to Third World nations.

From 1974 to the first half of 1978, new issues of SDRs were not authorized, since the industrialized countries and the IMF argued that greater liquidity was not required. Nevertheless, from the end of 1974 to the end of 1977, foreign exchange reserves grew to the equivalent of 74 billion SDRs. At the end of 1978, in the IMF-World Bank joint annual assembly, the developing countries reiterated that SDRs ought to be substituted for the United States dollar as reserve assets; an agreement was then obtained on a new issue of SDRs for 12 billion in a period of three years.

Nevertheless, the excess liquidity presently existing makes it impossible to fulfill the objective of converting SDRs into the main reserve asset, without first developing an adequate formula to withdraw an important percentage of the dollars presently used as international currency. The IMF has undertaken the task of studying and giving impulse to a substitution mechanism of dollars for SDRs. However, this does not seem to give any results, because the Fund continues to be unable to prevent the increase in the U.S. balance of payments deficits. It is important that the mechanisms adopted do not simply mean the financing of United States past deficits by the international community. An alternative method, within the present system of SDR allocation, would be one in which countries whose national currencies have been used as reserves are refused any increase in these reserves that has not been approved by the international community, and, what is more, are obliged to direct the SDRs received to buying their holdings.

After the 1974 resolutions, considering the relative failure of the proposals made, a fourth suggestion began to take shape. It deals with the establishment of a kind of world tributary system, which would apply international rates in the use of the universal common heritage (such as sea and outerspace resources), taxes on nonrenewable resources and the assets of the transnational corporations, devolution to the country of origin of the taxes collected on incomes of the experts and professionals coming from less developed countries, etc. Measures of this kind, as pointed out by the RIO Report, could mean that at least half of the transfers of resources will have an automatic basis during the next decade.

Various other instruments and measures could be suggested to transfer resources to the developing countries. Nevertheless, experience shows that it is difficult for industrial countries to voluntarily accept a more automatic system of international transfer of resources to developing countries, even when this could be highly convenient for them in the medium term, since it would stimulate a new expansive period in the world economy.

THE INSTITUTIONAL NATURE OF DEVELOPMENT
ASSISTANCE AND THE NIEO

In the years immediately prior to the adoption of the resolution on the NIEO, an evident decrease had taken place in the authority and relative importance of the IMF and the World Bank. On the one hand, the industrial countries increasingly made their own basic economic decisions completely independent of the IMF. For example, the establishment, in May 1968, of the double gold market, the devaluation of the franc in 1969, dollar-gold inconvertibility in 1971, and the Smithsonian Agreement in December of the same year were all unilateral decisions or decisions taken within the "Group of Ten." On the other hand, the vast expansion of the private supply of credits offered the developing countries expensive but plentiful and independent financing. Thus, the stand-by credits granted decreased by an annual average of 1.8 billion SDRs in 1968-70 to 0.4 billion in 1971-73, the lowest amounts since 1957.

It is, thus, understandable why the 1974 resolutions did not set out the need to qualitatively reform the IMF as a central measure; rather, they proposed a greater participation of the developing countries in its decisions and an examination of the lending policies to improve its practices, taking into consideration the particular situation of every developing country.

Since 1976, a change has occurred in relative importance of these institutions, and particularly the IMF. Not only has the expansion of private credit begun to reach a limit; the sharp increase in the total debt, with the subsequent inability of developing countries to pay, has led the private banks to demand an agreement between the IMF and the debtor country as a prior requirement for the granting of new credits and the refinancing of old ones. This was indirectly expressed in a strong recovery of stand-by credits in 1976, on top of the resources granted to the developing countries through the oil facility. To confirm the renewed importance of the IMF, it is enough to observe the attention the mass media are, again, dedicating to its conflicts with different governments. All this leads one to think that in the 1980s the Fund and the Bank will be of decisive importance in the monetary system's evolution, and in the internal political and economic options of the developing countries.

Unfortunately, the objectives and the spirit which move the IMF and the World Bank are anachronistic. These institutions were set up as an integral part of the Bretton Woods agreements in 1944, to contribute to solving the grave problems presented by the destroyed yet developed economies of Western Europe. In that context, the concerns of the Third

World were totally absent. Its problems were not dealt with, and the proposal to stipulate the need for a greater intervention in favor of developing countries was expressly rejected. Thirty-five years later, none of the pillars of the international monetary system agreed upon in 1944 remain (i.e. gold standard, dollar-gold convertibility, role of the dollar as the sole dominant currency, principal of stable exchange rates). The sole survivors are the World Bank and the IMF.

The IMF was created with the explicit object of being a guarantor for the "good conduct" code in international monetary matters and as a short-term stabilizing financing mechanism. Without changing its objectives or its conduct models, the IMF was later converted into the main monetary and financial authority of the entire world economy. The loss, in recent years, of most of the authority it enjoyed with respect to the industrial countries has converted the IMF into an institution dedicated to supervising the developing countries, but without assuming the changes in conduct which the problems of the Third World would imply. Thus, the IMF stabilization model is useful only when the problems are effectively due to an excess of internal global demand. In the industrial countries, this can correspond to a cyclical phase and, at times, to errors in the kind of monetary and fiscal policy applied. It may, then, be useful to temporarily reduce demand to activate later growth. On the contrary, in developing countries the main attention should be paid to the other side of the equation: insufficiency of supply.

Some year ago, Latin American economic thought developed an alternative conception, insufficient in many ways, but useful as an instrument of analysis. It highlighted the structural problems behind inflationary pressures and imbalances in balance of payments. A policy which, in a permanent way, tends to be based on credit restrictions, limitation of fiscal expenditure, and greater freedom in imports can not be useful to solve the imbalances to be found in developing countries. Rather, this policy tends to be counterproductive. The elimination or liberalization of exchange controls, suitable in the case of developed economies, becomes an obstacle in developing countries, unable to compete with the production of industrialized powers. In order that this does not result in serious balance of payment deficits, the Fund appplies great pressure to contain internal demand, for which its antiinflationary programs are based on a substantial restraint on fiscal expenditure and salaries. Cases are unknown of a control on prices recommended by the IMF.

It is difficult to expect a substantial modification of the IMF through secondary changes in the distribution of voting power or in its internal regulations. The decision of the developing countries to overcome regional subdivision and constitute the "Group of Twenty-four" has probably been the most important transformation of the IMF's internal structure in recent years. Although this changes the weight and style of actions taken within the IMF, it is a limited change which keeps the developing countries in a subordinate and secondary role. At the same time, the relatively greater weight of Saudi Arabia can counteract the positive effects and accentuate the IMF's conservative policies. The IMF and the World Bank will not be instrumental in effectively favoring the establishment of the NIEO as long as the system which grants internal power to those with economic power in the world economy is not modified.

Unless it is decided to entrust the functioning of the world financial and monetary order to the altruism of the rich nations, or the claim is maintained that economic decisions are of a strictly technical nature unrelated to reasons and interests of economical and political power, the countries of the Third World must insist that the IMF and the World Bank turn into what they should always have been: organizations truly dependent on the United Nations.

It is difficult to be enthusiastic about the possibility of imposing such an objective, but this also implies that we cannot be optimistic about the world economy in the next decade. In this sense, the developing countries' only alternative is to diminish the power and importance of the IMF and the World Bank. They must increase, as far as possible, mutual cooperation in order to obtain better negotiation capabilities in international trade and finance.

2 External Disequilibrium in Developing Countries and the Adjustment Process: The Need for a New IMF Approach and Policies*

Rene Villarreal

International finance institutions are of a dualistic nature. On the one hand, different articles of agreement set down a series of reciprocal privileges between the signatories of the accords, which, in turn, represent commercial and international payments' benefits; but, on the other, obligations imply a lesser degree of freedom in the design and application of trade and exchange policies by members.

The particular set of rules and agreements that govern commerical, financial, and monetary relations among countries determine what could be called an "international economic order." Most transactions that any country carries out with another fall under the control of multilateral institutions. Many economists have argued that there is a pronounced asymmetry in the international economic order. They attribute this disparity to the bias of these institutions' policies in favor of industrialized countries, which would explain why a new international economic order (NIEO) has been proposed.

The aim of this chapter is to analyze the role of adjustment policies applied to balance of payments disequilibria in the present-day international economic context, and the means by which finance institutions are able to introduce these policies in member countries. The study focuses on the relevance and impact of these policies for developing countries. An appropriate sample was taken in order to examine empirical evidence of how well adjustment policies worked out in Latin America during the 1965-1975 period. The purpose is to show that the approach of international finance institutions - the

---

*The author wishes to thank Miguel A. Olea and Susana Ross for their contribution in preparing this essay.

International Monetary fund in particular - is not adequate to solve the problem of external disequilibria, given the nature of the problems faced by the developing countries. For them, the adjustment problem is of utmost importance since, unlike industrial countries, the level of foreign trade and net inflow of foreign capital determine, to a great extent, their level of production and economic growth. The historical experience of developing countries has shown that when devaluation is used, deliberately or forcably, as an adjustment mechanism, often it has not been able to correct the disequilibrium, or, when it does, it is only on a temporary basis. There are several factors behind this failure, and perhaps one of the most important factors is the IMF's erroneous treatment of the disequilibrium problem in developing countries, based on applying orthodox balance of payments theory. After due analysis of the origins and causes of disequilibrium in developing countries, the study proposes a scheme for a new IMF approach and adjustment policies, based on the structuralist understanding of the balance of payments.

THE IMF'S APPROACH

The Theoretical Framework

It is important to distinguish between balance of payments and devaluation theories. Orthodox balance of payments theory does not generally set forth the difference in a clear manner, and it is precisely here that part of the problem is to be found in establishing adjustment policies. A balance of payments theory, basically, should provide the answers to two questions: what is the origin of the external disequilibirum, and what are the best adjustment policies and mechanisms for correcting the disequilibrium?

Orthodox balance of payments theory is concerned with the adjustment policies and process when an economy has an external disequilibrium, without concerning itself with the origin of the imbalance. Thus, the theory directly analyzes adjustment mechanisms for the disequilibrium according to a regime of fixed exchange rates or through variations in the exchange rate.(1) However, if there is no clear, explicit diagnosis as to the origin of the illness (external disequilibrium), how can we establish whether or not the prescription (adjustment policies) is really the correct one? Undoubtedly, the symptoms are evident as a result of a growing deficit in the balance on current account, an outflow of reserves, an excess of expenditures over income, and so on. Nevertheless, how do we know whether the adjustment mechanisms and policies will cure the illness or only the symptoms?

As Richard Cooper says, theory "has been more concerned with the process of adjustment back to equilibrium than the characteristics of the new equilibrium - indeed the new equilibrium is often the same as the initial one."(2) In other words, even though the approach might be of a "dynamic nature" (with particular emphasis on the adjustment process), primary interest focuses on comparative statics, which is outside the context of economic growth. Therefore, it is worth considering whether, once this new equilibrium is reached, the economy can renew sustained growth without incurring, once again, external disequilibrium? The paradigm of orthodox balance of payments theory does not pose this question.

Although orthodox balance of payments theory is incomplete in the sense that it lacks an explicit analysis of the different causes or origins of external disequilibria, through different approaches or theories of devaluation we can infer the type of origin they implicitly assume.

The theories of devaluation as an adjustment mechanism for external disequilibrium represent four approaches that are more complementary than mutually exclusive, for what they do is place greater emphasis on specific aspects of the adjustment process: on relative prices and response due to the elasticity of exports and imports (elasticity approach), on the effect of income and absorption (absorption approach), and on the equilibrium between demand and supply of money (monetarist approach). A fourth approach argues that the analysis of balance of payments adjustment policies and programs should be carried out with a "heterodox" interpretation that blends the other three lines of theory.(3) The elasticity approach assumes that the origin of the disequilibrium is an overvaluation of costs and prices; therefore, an adjustment policy would require a change in relative costs and prices. The absorption approach assumes that the origin of the disequilibrium is an ex-ante excess of absorption with respect to income overspending; therefore, adjustment requires contractionary monetary and fiscal policies. The monetarist approach assumes that the origin of the disequilibrium is an ex-ante excess flow supply of money; therefore, here, too, a contractionary monetary policy is required to make the adjustment. These are all aspects of the orthodox approach.

However, the structuralist or heterodox approach is required in developing countries. It does not overlook the fact that the problem of disequilibrium may be acute or may only become evident when there is a maladjustment in relative costs and prices, such as in the case of an excess of absorption or demand with respect to income. Nevertheless, in developing countries, the origin of external disequilibrium is eminently structural in nature and is due to intrinsic maladjustments in the growth and foreign trade processes. In

this approach, relative price adjustment policies (devaluation)
should be considered jointly with an expansionary but selective
demand policy and, at the same time, with a "supply policy"
that directly stimulates production and investment in export
and import substitution sectors.

The importance of properly diagnosing the origin of the
disequilibrium was recognized in the IMF by J.J. Polak in 1948
and by E.M. Bernstein in 1958, but later forgotten both in
theory and in practice. In 1948, Polak questioned "whether
exchange depreciation will bring equilibrium in the balance of
payments," and he suggested "the mechanism by which it will
achieve this equilibrium, depends to a considerable degree on
the cause of the disequilibrium."(4)

The monetarist approach that has recently been
developed, in academic circles as well as by the IMF research
group, explicitly recognizes that the origin of the
disequilibrium is an ex-ante excess flow supply of money.
Devaluation theories have developed under the perspective of
the neoclassic and neo-Keynesian schools, within a frame of
reference based on the experience of the adjustment processes
and the particular characteristics of developed economies.
According to Latin American economic thought, the
structuralist approach to the balance of payments, which had
its origin in the work of J.F. Noyola (1948), ECLA (1956),
and more recently R. Villarreal (1976), offers an alternative
approach to orthodox theory, emphasizing that, in order to
evaluate the effectiveness of devaluation or any other type of
policy (as an adjustment process of external disequilibrium), it
is necessary not only to make a diagnosis of the cause of this
imbalance, but to place it within the framework of the growth
process in developing countries.(5)

A fundamental conclusion in a recent UNCTAD study
stresses the importance, when determining the appropriate
volume of assistance and the conditions required for its
provision, of distinguishing between those elements in a
balance of payments deficit for which the developing country is
itself responsible, and those that are due to factors outside its
control. This is important because it affects the speed of
adjustment required for the provision of the assistance, which
might entail high costs for a developing country when the
elements in the deficit are beyond its control.(6) The
orthodox devaluation approach used by IMF as an adjustment
policy is analyzed in the following paragraphs, while the
heterodox or structuralist approach is explained in the final
section of this chapter.

The Orthodox Approach

The elasticity approach

The elasticity approach to devaluation stems from the definition
of disequilibrium as the deficit in the balance on current
account (Bca), which is the difference between exports (X)
and imports (M) of goods and services (Bca = X - M). It
emphasizes the need for a significant elasticity in the balance
on current account with respect to variations in the exchange
rate, so that a devaluation can be effective in reducing the
deficit in the Bca.

    The Marshall-Lerner condition specifies that if the sum of
the demand elasticities of imports and exports is greater than
one (ηx + ηm > 1), devaluation of the exchange rate will
correct the disequilibrium, given that 1) elasticities of supply
of imports and exports are infinitely elastic, and 2) trade is
balanced initially. This devaluation approach implies the
application of a Marshallian analysis of partial equilibrium in
the export and import markets of goods and services.
Devaluation is the instrument by which the relative prices of
tradable goods are increased. The imbalance is, in essence, a
maladjustment of relative prices with respect to the prevailing
exchange rate, due to an overvaluation of costs and prices.

The absorption approach

The income-absorption approach to devaluation, proposed by
Sidney Alexander, is a macroeconomic anlaysis of general
equilibrium which stresses the aggregates of the economy by
distinguishing and establishing the relationship between income
(Y), absorption (A), consumption (C), investment (I), and
government expenditure (G) and the balance on current
account (Bca = X - M).(7) That is to say:

    (1) Y = C + I + G + X - M

    (2) Y - (C + I + G) = X - M

    (3) Y - A = Bca

    (4) y - a = bca

    Equation (3) indicates that, if the balance on current
account (Bca) shows a deficit, it is because absorption (A) is
greater than income (Y). In terms of variations (equation 4),
it means that the change in bca is equal to the difference of
goods and services in the economy. In order for a devaluation
to correct the disequilibrium in Bca, it is necessary - and
independent of the demand elasticity of exports and imports -

for income to increase more than absorption. In the specific case in which the economy is at full employment and, therefore, income cannot increase, absorption (A), necessarily, has to decrease for devaluation to be effective as an adjustment mechanism. This is precisely one of the central elements of this approach.

Alexander's approach emphasizes the effects of devaluation on income and absorption. The author recognizes two possible effects which have been induced or are indirectly derived from devaluation with regard to income: the effect of idle resources and the effect of terms of trade.

The effect of idle resources states that, "the principal effect of a devaluation on income is associated with the increased exports of the devaluing country and the induced stimulation of domestic demand through the familiar multiplier relationship, provided there are unemployed resources....The net effect of the recovery of income and production on the foreign balance is not the total amount of additional production induced, but merely the difference between that amount and the induced increase in absorption."(8) On the other hand, at least under unemployment conditions, it can be expected that a devaluation will bring about a favorable effect on production and employment.

The terms-of-trade effect refers to the deterioration of export prices in foreign exchange with respect to import prices. This effect is of little importance for developing countries, which are generally "small countries" and cannot influence price fixing for exports and imports in the international market.

Alexander believes that there are three direct effects of devaluation on absorption: those of real monetary balances, income redistribution, and monetary illusion.

> In general, then, many of the effects of a de-
> valuation on the balance of payments through the
> direct absorption effects may be expected to be
> transitory and non-proportional....Under conditions
> of full employment, the favorable direct absorption
> effects are likely to be weak. It would seem to be
> much more effective to operate on absorption directly
> through monetary and credit policy-limitation of gov-
> ernment expenditures, of private investment and,
> possibly, of private consumption.(9)

Under the income-absorption approach, if the economy is at full employment and the direct effect of absorption is limited and transitory, it is more advisable to use contractionary monetary and fiscal policies than to directly reduce absorption, thus improving the current account as much as possible. This approach implicitly assumes that the origin of the disequilibrium is an ex-ante excess absorption over income, that is, overspending.

The monetarist approach

The monetary approach to devaluation is almost the same as the income-absorption approach under conditions of full employment, but it exclusively emphasizes monetary mechanisms. According to this approach the partial balance which is in disequilibrium is the reserve balance and "not the subsequent imbalances" in the current account which are underlined in both the elasticity and the income-absorption approaches.

For advocates of the monetary approach, external disequilibrium or deficit in the reserve balance has its origin in the ex-ante excess flow of the money supply.

The monetary approach to the balance of payments of an open economy coincides with the monetary approach of a closed economy, which is based on the rehabilitation of the quantity theory of money. In turn, this theory is based on the classical quantity equation of exchange (MV = PQ), which states that the supply of money in the economy (M), multiplied by the income velocity (V) is equal to the index of the price level (P), multiplied by the real product (Q). What really converts the equation of exchange - a mere tautology - into the quantity theory of the balance of payments are the assumptions of constancy of 'V,' 'P,' and 'Q' established by the monetarist advocates:(10)

1. The economy is at full employment and, therefore, Q is given and cannot increase.
2. The country is a small one and, therefore, its economy faces a parametric set of prices and interest rates determined in the world market. This implies that the domestic rate of inflation cannot be different from the international rates, and there can be only transitory fluctuations.
3. Income velocity is a certain type of stable function (basically a constant determined institutionally).

Thus, the monetarist thesis on the origin of the balance of payments disequilibrium in the modern version of the quantity theory (where m + v = p + q)(11) would state the following:

> If the growth rate of the money supply (m) is greater than world inflation (p), plus the growth rate of the real national product (q), minus income velocity (v), that is, if m > p + q - v, there will be a monetary maladjustment that will show up as a disequilibrium in the balance of payments through an outflow of international reserves.(12)

In other words, it is just as straightforward as the simple
expression of the monetarist thesis for a closed economy on
internal disequilibrium (inflation) which states there is 'too
much money to buy too few goods.' For an open economy, we
could say that the situation is the following: there is too much
money to buy domestic goods, and/or services, and/or assets,
which increases the demand for foreign exchange. Since this
demand will bring pressures for a devaluation in the exchange
rate, the monetary authority will sell foreign exchange, thus
reducing the level of reserves in the Central Bank, which, in
turn, will cause a deficit in the reserve balance.
    Given the simplicity of the monetary approach for
diagnosing the origin of the disequilibrium as an exclusive
phenomenon of an 'ex-ante excess flow supply of money,' it is
to be expected that policy recommendations (the prescription),
with reagard to an analysis of devaluation as an adjustment
mechanism, will also be simple. With respect to this, Harry
Johnson says that,

> ....in the specific case of devaluation, the policy
> amounts to increasing the nominal amount of money
> demanded, through the effect of the increase in do-
> mestic prices consequent on devaluation in reducing
> the real value of the existing money stock by mone-
> tary policy at an unchanged exchange rate; and the
> policy will be effective only to the extent that the
> reduction of real balances through devaluation is not
> offset by domestic credit creation.(13)

In other words, if devaluation is combined with a contractionary monetary policy, the policy will be effective.
    The monetary approach can be considered a special case
of the income-absorption approach, differing in that the former
refers to a disequilibrium in the reserve balance and not in
the balance on current account. The monetary approach is the
specific case of the income-absorption approach under conditions of full employment (income does not vary due to the
effects of idle resources and/or terms of trade). In this case,
devaluation will not affect income, and the effect of real
monetary balances would be considered as the only important
direct impact on absorption. In essence, the adjustment
mechanism of devaluation according to the monetary approach
would be the following: an increase in prices due to the
devaluation - keeping credit expansion constant - would reduce
the real monetary balances held by the public, who
consequently would increase their demand for money to adjust
real monetary balances; therefore, the ex-ante excess supply
of money would be cancelled out by an increase in the demand
for money, and, in this manner, the deficit in the balance of
reserves would be reduced.

It is important to observe that the monetary approach to
devaluation establishes, in principle, an adjustment mechanism
for external disequilibrium through contraction of aggregate
demand.   Imports decrease, not because they have been substituted by internal production, but due to the monetary
contraction of aggregate demand. Exports can increase by
"freeing" internal goods and services that potentially, if they
are competitive, can be exported. They do not increase due to
an increase in production of this sector. It is clear that in
the monetary approach to the balance of payments, developed
in the 1960s in academic circles and by the IMF research
group, adjustment to disequilibrium is only carried out through
contraction in demand and economic activity and outside the
context of economic growth.

Origins of the IMF's Monetary Approach to
the Balance of Payments

The monetary approach to the balance of payments has its
roots in David Hume's writings (1752) on the classical specie-
flow mechanism.   Since World War II, members of the Chicago
School - headed by Milton Friedman - have rehabilitated the
quantity theory of money. During the past decade, Robert
Mundell and Harry Johnson introduced the monetary approach
to the balance of payments in academic circles. The research
group of the IMF - under the direction of J.J. Polak - has
developed its own approach, both in theory and in practice.
The IMF's research group recognizes that its monetary
approach first arose while analyzing the problems of developing
countries, for the following four reasons:

First, in the 1950's, many less developed countries lacked the detailed national income and product
accounts necessary for an analysis of national income
and balance of payments determination along Keynes-
ian, or income-absorption, lines; nor was it feasible
to apply the elasticities approach in an adequate
manner....
Second, the nature of the Fund's work on balance of payments problems of member countries made
it desirable to have available a framework for quantitative analysis that was suffciently manageable (in
the days before long-distance access to computers)
to be serviceable during staff missions to foreign
capitals....
The third reason is more fundamental. Less
developed countries typically have a simpler financial
structure than do more developed countries. In the
absence of well developed asset markets and financial

instruments, there are relatively few alternatives to
either holding funds in monetary form or spending
them on domestic or foreign goods and services or
on foreign financial instruments. In these circumstances, the implication for the external balance of a
difference between the amount of money newly supplied through domestic credit creation and the
additional amount that residents wish to hold is more
obtrusive than it is in countries with a more complex
financial structure....
    Finally, a monetary framework for analyzing the
balance of payments effects of economic policy was
particularly appropriate for many developing countries, particularly in Latin America, in which control
over domestic credit was in fact relied on as a major
instrument - perhaps the most important one - of
demand management and balance of payments control.... The Fund's approach to monetary management - or, as it came to be called, to financial
programming - for the purpose of achieving balance
of payments equilibrium evolved during the 1950s,
initially in staff work on Latin American member
countries. It emerged from the need to discuss with
the authorities of a member requesting financial
assistance from the Fund the adequacy of the policy
program proposed by them and the quantitative conditions ("credit ceilings") under which the member
would continue to have access to the Fund's resources made available in a stand-by arrangement.(14)

Based on the preceding remarks, it can be concluded that in
the IMF's monetarist approach there is no explicit analysis of
the origin or evolution of the external disequilibrium in developing countries, but, rather, a supposition of the effectiveness of one adjustment mechanism - the contraction of the
money supply - which determines that the origin of the deficit
is essentially a monetary maladjustment. Thus, the adjustment
mechanism is pragmatic during the state of implementation and
the conclusion implicitly valid for the origin of the deficit as
well.
    This approach is considered "monetarist" and not
"monetary" to avoid any confusion which might arise regarding
the focus of the academic approach and the IMF's. Frenkel
and Johnson have argued that their approach to the balance of
payments is monetary as opposed to monetarist, given that,

    the monetary approach to the balance of payments
    asserts neither that monetary mismanagement is the
    only cause, nor that monetary policy change is the

only possible cure for balance of payments problems;
it does suggest, however, that monetary processes
will bring about a cure of some kind - not necessarily very attractive - unless frustrated by
deliberate monetary policy action.(15)

In his last articles, Harry Johnson clearly changed his point of
view and took an explicit monetarist position by recognizing
that all disequilibria in the balance of payments are essentially
monetary and that all can be corrected through the management of a monetary policy:

All balance of payments disequilibria are
monetary in essence. So-called "structural" deficits
or surpluses, such as the deficits described as "inevitable" for "underdeveloped" economies simply
cannot exist, unless one includes in the concept of
"structure" an unalterable propensity of governments
to rely on inflationary finance of development programmes that should be accepted and paid for by
contributions of aid from more developed countries....All balance of payments disequilibria could be
handled by the use of domestic monetary policy.(16)

IMF's Approach to the Origin of the
External Disequilibrium

During the last twenty years, the approach to external
imbalance adopted by the IMF attributes the origin of the
disequilibrium to a maladjustment of relative prices or costs
and/or overspending in the economy, due to an ex-ante excess
flow of the money supply. For these reasons, "both approaches (the IMF's and the academic one) consider the
balance of payments to be an essentially monetary phenomenon
and stress the importance of the demand for money and of the
money supply process in an open economy."(17)
    Hence, the IMF approach is basically monetarist, even
though it recognizes two other specific cases of disequilibrium:
temporary and structural. When the imbalance is caused by
circumstances beyond the control of the country, such as
adverse climatic conditions or a cyclical drop in world demand,
the Fund recognizes that it is a temporary disequilibrium. To
assist member countries in this situation, the IMF has
established the Export-Earnings Compensatory Financing
Facility. Access to these resources does not have such
conditionality as does access to the higher credit tranches and
Extended Fund Facility. The Extended Facility was established
in 1974 to help those member countries that face an external
disequilibrium whose origin can be found in "structural mal-

adjustments" in costs and prices, production and foreign
trade (a concept which has not been clearly defined). Use of
this financial facility assumes the same monetarist prescription,
as members can make use of the financial assistance for a
longer period of time and for greater amounts than under
stand-by arrangements, in exchange for following a
stabilization program with stronger contractionary policies. In
other words, in theory and in practice, the IMF believes that
the root of a disequilibrium is a monetary maladjustment that
requires the application of a monetary prescription during a
short or medium-term adjustment period.

                IMF's Approach to Adjustment Policies

Adjustment policies are stipulated in the stabilization program
the member country submits to the IMF for approval and
access to financial resources. In general, it includes a
package of policies on devaluation, liberalization, and demand
contraction to correct disequilibria of relative prices and costs
and of overinvestment due to an ex-ante excess flow supply of
money. The implementing mechanism or operative instrument is
based on a stand-by arrangement and, more recently, on an
extended arrangement.
        The adjustment policies implicit in the IMF approach
constitute the mechanism designed to correct distortions in
relative costs or prices both in the domestic economy and in
its relationship with the world. These policies assume that the
free market price mechanism will be the most efficient and
effective one available to reallocate resources toward the
production of tradable goods that will bring about an
adjustment in the trade balance. The following package of
policies is usually recommended:

Relative costs and price policy (devaluation and liberalization)

Devaluation of the exchange rate. This measure is aimed at
raising the relative prices of tradable versus nontradable
goods. The implicit assumption is that the elasticity of the
balance on current account will make it respond favorably to
variations in the exchange rate.

Exchange, commercial, and domestic price control liberalization.
In general, devaluation of the exchange rate is accompanied by
an exchange liberalization policy that forces the country to
eliminate exchange controls, including multiple rates of
exchange. Commerical liberalization implies elimination of
quantitative controls on trade and, in some cases, reduction
of tariff protection. In a parallel fashion, it includes clauses
that imply elimination of controls on domestic commerce to

further reduce obstacles for resource reallocation to these
sectors through the price mechanism which, after devaluation,
will be more profitable.

Salary control. Salaries should increase at a lower rate than
they do in the main countries with which trade is carried on.
The reasoning behind this policy is to avoid nullifying the
advantage of relative costs which theoretically stems from an
exchange-rate devaluation. It is interesting to observe that
salaries are the only cost item which is subject to control.

Policy to contract aggregate demand

Monetary policy. In general, the package of monetary
measures includes a program of credit restriction and/or
increases in the interest rate by increasing the reserve
requirements in the banking system (the minimum reserve
requirements) and other measures of a monetary nature, such
as increases in the rediscount rate of the Central Bank and
the sale of treasury bonds in the domestic market. In
addition, there is a limit imposed on the issue of monetary
liabilities by the Central Bank.

Fiscal policy. The fiscal program places special emphasis on a
reduction of the public sector's deficit, basically, by restricting current expenditures. In general, limitations are placed
on the hiring of government personnel and stringent control
systems are designed for administrative expenditures by the
government and public sector enterprises. In drastic cases,
the stand-by or extended arrangement stipulates changes in
the tax system in an effort to increase tax collection, thereby
decreasing the population's purchasing power and increasing
the public sector resources to finance the deficit.

External and internal financing policy. Demand reduction
programs extend their scope of action to financing the
exchange and savings-investment gaps by restricting the
borrowing of the public sector, both externally and internally,
and to setting minimum requirements in the level of reserves.
    It is important that the rigidity of the stabilization
program depends on the seriousness of the external
disequilibrium, which is determined by comparing the quota of
the country in need of financial assistance with the level of its
disequilibrium. The fact that a country is industrialized or
developing does not imply any differential treatment.
Theoretically, the Fund will demand of a surplus country the
same stringent adjustment measures (appreciation of the
exchange rate and a policy of demand expansion), but past
evidence shows that, in practice, the burden of adjustment
measures has fallen on deficit countries.

IMF's Approach to Adjustment Mechanisms

The Fund's basic instrument to implement an adjustment program is known as a stand-by arrangement and, in recent years, an extended arrangement. Both cover financial assistance in support of a stabilization program that consists of a detailed program of adjustment policies, whose characteristics depend on the level of use of the Fund's resources and the time the member country expects to use them. An agreement does not always require an exchange-rate adjustment, since only in those cases that were considered to be a "fundamental" disequilibrium under the Bretton Woods system - that is, when the deficit could not be "reasonably" financed through the use of reserves or external financing - did it include a clause on devaluation of the exchange rate. It is worth remembering that, since 1973, many Latin American countries fixed their exchange parity with respect to a strong currency. As a result, disequilibria of a fundamental nature continue to exist de facto in these countries.

The combination of policies in the program is a function of the level of use of the upper credit tranches and of the permanent facilities in the Fund's General Resources Department. Table 2.1 shows facilities and possible cumulative arrangements in different tranches. These arrangements are expressed as a percentage of the member's quota, since availability of financing for a member country's adjustment depends directly on its capital subscription to the Fund.

Table 2.1. Amounts Available under Supplementary
Financing Facility*
(percent of quota)

	Use of ordinary resources	Supplementary Financing
Regular tranches	100	102.5
First credit tranche	25	12.5
Second credit tranche	25	30.0
Third credit tranche	25	30.0
Fourth credit tranche	25	30.0
Extended Facility	140	140.0

*In special circumstances, resources beyond these limits could be made available.

Source: IMF Survey, September 18, 1978 (The Fund Under the Second Amendment: A Supplement), p. 295.

As these arrangements represent a higher percentage of the quota, conditionality becomes stricter (table 2.2). The reserve tranche is the only one which can be used without conditionality, but, even in this case, the need for financing for balance of payments reasons must be proved.

The objective of the Supplementary Financing Facility is to supply additional financing in combination with use of the Fund's resources - through stand-by or extended agreements - to those countries that face severe and disproportionate disequilibria which go beyond their quotas (table 2.1).

EMPIRICAL EVIDENCE FOR LATIN AMERICA

The policies and instruments the IMF uses to fulfill its executive role in the adjustment process are consistent with the theoretical approaches. Thus, in order to evaluate operativeness of these instruments in developing countries, careful analysis of the experience in correcting their particular disequilibria becomes necessary.

In order to analyze empirical evidence for Latin America regarding the effects of devaluation and complementary stabilization policy on the balance of payments, a sample was taken of the countries that devaluated at least once during the 1965-1975 period. For some countries that devaluated during this period, there is not available reliable statistical data, in which case they were not included in the sample. There are, in all, some 50 devaluations fitting into this category. Brazil and Colombia were not included in the analysis since they had a system of minidevaluations or sliding exchange rates whose effects are quite different from those of a sudden devaluation of considerable magnitude.

The objective was to show how the adjustment policy of devaluation and stabilization - as it is conceived and implemented under the conditional agreements which provide access to the IMF's resources - permit the member country only a temporary improvement in the balance of payments. This happens not because of a channeling of resources to the export sector or to import substitution, but rather because of a decrease in imports as a result of a reducton in the growth rate of the real product and a decrease in the investment level that commits future productive capacity.

The central hypothesis tested in the empirical analysis was that the Latin American experience in the adjustment process proves that their economics do not respond to orthodox adjustment mechanisms or to the IMF's policies concerning external disequilibria for the following reasons: Effect on relative prices. Measures aimed at reallocating resources and reducing absorption due to changes in the

Table 2.2.   Cumulative Purchases
(percent of quotas)

	Present Position		With Supplementary Financing Facility	
	Tranche Policy	Extended Facility	Tranche Policy	Extended Facility
Reserve tranche	25.0	25.0	25.0	25.0
Credit tranches				
4 X 25	100.0	–	100.0	–
1 X 25	–	25.0	–	25.0
Extended Facility	–	140.0	–	140.0
Supplementary financing[1]				
1 X 12.5; 3 X 30	–	–	102.5	–
With Extended Facility	–	–	–	140.0
Subtotal	125.0	190.0	227.5	330.0
Compensatory financing	75.0	75.0	75.0	75.0
Buffer stock	50.0	50.0	50.0	50.0
Cumulative total[2]	250.0	315.0	352.5	455.0

[1]Under special circumstances, a stand-by arrangement may be approved for purchases beyond these limits and the normal limitations under tranche policy; in such cases, purchases will be made with supplementary financing.   The amount of such additional finance will be quantified in relation to a member's need and the adequacy of its program.

[2]In addition, some members have used oil facility drawings.   The average use by these members was equal to 75 percent of quota.

Source: IMF Survey, September 18, 1978 (The Fund Under the Second Amendment: A Supplement), p. 290.

economy's relative prices via devaluation have extremely limited
effects, given the rigidity of the productive apparatus and
the structural bottlenecks that characterize Latin American
economies.

Effect on income.   Adjustment of the external sector
through stabilization policy does not occur as a result of an
increase in exports and a greater substitution of imports but,
rather, becaue of an internal economic recession. The monetary
and fiscal contraction is excessive, since it does not take into
account the devaluation's own contractionist effect in developing countries.

Recurrent effect.   Adjustment in most cases is only
temporary and, therefore, the problem of disequilibrium is
recurring and cyclical. Shortly after using devaluation and
demand reduction policy as an adjustment mechanism, the
balance of payments deteriorates once again. In principle,
this is due to trying to cure the symptoms and not the
disease.

In order to prove the previous hypothesis, different
statistical instruments were used. The sample that includes 34
variations in the exchange rate in Latin American countries
from 1965 to 1975 was taken as a starting point.

                    Results of the Empirical Test

Effects of devaluation

Cross-section least-squares linear regression analysis was used
to analyze the incidence of variations in the exchange rate on
different transactions included in the balance of payments.
The independent variable was the percentage change in the
exchange rate and the dependent variables were the main items
found in the balance of payments - exports, imports, trade
balance, and current accounts balance - with lags of one or
two years.

Since the devaluations under consideration took place
during different times of the year, we selected the exchange
rate values at the end of the year for all countries. This
naturally introduced a bias in the sample in favor of those
countries which devalued closer to the end of the year, but
for a large sample, this bias is not very significant.

The general form of the adjusted equations is linear:
$\Delta\%$ of dependent variable = constant + beta
                    ($\Delta\%$ of exchange rate)
where:
dependent variable = particular transaction of the balance of
                    payments; and
        Beta   = slope of the regression line
                   = elasticity of the dependent variable with
                    respect to the exchange rate.

Each one of the dependent variables - exports and imports of merchandise, and the values of the trade balance and the current account - was run as a function of changes in the exchange rate. As the quantities are expressed in percentage changes, the beta coefficients of the regression represent the elasticity of the dependent variable with respect to the exchange rate.

Estimated coefficients for the export and import functions of merchandise show that the elasticities of both variables are not significantly different from zero at 95 percent confidence level (table 2.3). Therefore, it cannot be asserted that devaluation induces substantial increases in exports and significant reductions in imports for the countries considered in the sample. In most cases, the percentage change in exports and imports that is explained by variation in the exchange rate is low. Only exports during the same year of devaluation go beyond a value of 10 percent.

Regarding the trade and current account balances, the results of the test show that none of the elasticities is significantly different from zero, and that change in these balances attributed to variation in the exchange rate is not greater than one percent in any case (table 2.4). It cannot be stated that devaluation is a significant influence on the trade balance or the current account balance.

The effects of stabilization policy

To test the hypothesis on income effects of the IMF's adjustment program, we first estimated the least-squares regression coefficients whose general form is expressed in linear form:

$\Delta\%$ of GDP = constant + beta   ($\Delta\%$ of the exchange rate)

where:

$\Delta\%$ of GDP = percentage change in the gross domestic product; and

Beta = elasticity of GDP with respect to exchange rate.

In accordance with the results, we can state with 90 percent level of confidence that the percentage changes of GDP during the year of devaluation are negatively affected by a modification of the exchange rate, and the variance of GDP that can be explained by the variation in the exchange rate is 11 percent (table 2.5). Although it is not clear how the contractionary effect operates a year after devaluation (since the elasticity is not statistically significant), two years after devaluation, the slope is significant wth a negative sign at a confidence level of 95 percent. The variation in the exchange rate explains 40 percent of the decrease in the product's rate of growth.

Table 2.3.   Regression Equations for Cross-Section Study:
Exports and Imports
(1965-1975)

Item	Constant	Beta	Standardized Beta	R^2	F
Exports	16.17544	0.02400	0.15061	0.2268	0.74267
Exports (Lag = 1 year)	19.92961	0.01573	0.08200	0.00672	0.21665
Exports (Lag = 2 years)	26.20918	-0.03175	-0.17267	0.02982	0.98342
Imports	15.18656	0.01427	0.11752	0.01381	0.44816
Imports (Lag = 1 year)	14.53566	0.02109	0.16164	0.02613	0.85849
Imports (Lag = 2 years)	23.28714	-0.04019	-0.30062	0.09037	3.17913

Explanation:

Beta   Slope of the regression line: $\Delta\%$ of dependent variable = constant + Beta ($\Delta\%$ of exchange rate)

Standardized beta   Standardized value of the slope

R^2 Coefficient of determination

F   Estimated F value

Theoretical F is 4.15 at a significance level of 5 percent calculated with one degree of freedom for the regression and 34 for the residuals (in cases without lag).

Table 2.4.   Regression Equations for Cross-Section Study
(1965-1975)

Balance	Constant	Beta	Standardized Beta	R^2	F
<u>Trade Balance</u>	885.88160	-1.03908	-0.06098	0.00372	0.11943
Trade Balance (Lag = 1 year)	876.61186	-1.12707	-0.06625	0.00439	0.14108
Trade Balance (Lag = 2 years)	805.85882	-0.62794	-0.03689	0.00136	0.04361
<u>Current Account Balance</u>	75.97062	-0.10881	-0.09258	0.00857	0.27666
Current Account Balance (Lag = 1 year)	42.45673	-0.01476	-0.01220	0.00015	0.00476
Current Account Balance (Lag = 2 years)	-57.24597	0.01783	0.00880	0.00008	0.00248

Explanation:

Beta   Slope of the regression line: $\Delta\%$ of dependent variable = constant + Beta ($\Delta\%$ of exchange rate)

Standardized beta   Standardized value of the slope

R^2 Coefficient of determination

F   Estimated F value

Theoretical F is 4.15 at a significance level of 5 percent calculated with one degree of freedom for the regression and 34 for the residuals (in cases without lag).

Table 2.5. Regression Equations for Cross-Section Study: GDP
(1965-1975)

	Constant	Beta	Standardized Beta	R^2	F
GDP	3.18325	-0.00517	-0.33637	0.11314	4.08253
GDP (Lag = 1 year)	2.49835	-0.00234	-0.13094	0.01715	0.55824
GDP (Lag = 2 years)	3.84785	-0.01044	-0.63296	0.40064	21.39004

Explanation:

Beta   Slope of the regression line: $\Delta\%$ of dependent variable = constant + Beta ($\Delta\%$ of exchange rate)

Standardized beta   Standardized value of the slope

R^2 Coefficient of determination

F   Estimated F value

Theoretical F is 4.15 at a significance level of 5 percent calculated with one degree of freedom for the regression and 34 for the residuals (in cases without lag).

Given that this relationship can also come about by other variables due to introduction of other policies, a Kalecki-Keynes type of model developed by Krugman and Taylor was used to estimate the contractionary effect of devaluation on income.(18)   Devaluation itself causes negative income effects that can be explained by their direct impact on absorption such as:

Real money balances' effects.   When prices rise, the real money supply decreases.   By deciding to keep the stock of real money balances constant, the public spends less.

Redistribution of income effect.   Price increases in the tradable goods sectors and, indirectly, in those of nontradable goods redistribute income to those groups with high marginal propensity to save (capitalists and groups that live from their investments).   This is reflected in a decrease in expenditures, assuming that capital owners have a higher marginal propensity to save than salary earners.

Effect of an increase of the trade deficit in domestic currency.   This effect is due to an increase in the deficit measured in domestic currency as a results of a higher exchange rate.

Effect of an increase of the external debt in domestic currency.   Even when the debt and its service are the same in foreign currency, they increase considerably if they are calculated in domestic currency and, thus, reduce overall absorption in the economy.

These four effects come about simultaneously.   In the short run, it is not possible to observe them except as an aggregate effect of the real product (in addition to some effects which are reflected in direct reduction of expenditures), while others affect external expenditures through changes in stocks.   Nevertheless, it is possible to state that a contractionary policy shows up not only in the current product, but, with even greater impact, in the future ones due to decreases in the capital stock that stem from previous effects.

The Krugman and Taylor model only estimates the income effect that can be exclusively attributable to devaluation. Results of this estimate should be examined by taking into account that the real money balances and price effects (which we have shown are not considerable) partly neutralize the contractionary effect (table 2.6).   In columns A and B, it can be observed how in all cases in the sample, devaluations caused a contractionary effect in the real product and a percentage decrease in imports similar to that of real GDP, since it is assumed that the imported component of the product remains constant.

In columns C and D, where estimates of percentage changes in income corresponding to salary earners and to groups that live from their investments are shown, we can

Table 2.6. Estimate of the Contractionary Effects of Devaluation in Latin America During the 1965-1975 Period[1]

Income effect on the variables during the period covered between a change in the base rate up to the last exchange rate[2]

Country	Year of Devaluation	A Real GDP	B Imports	C Income of salary earners	D Income of groups that live from investments	E Trade balance (nat.cur.)	F Trade balance (dollars)
Argentina	1966	-4.840	-4.840	-4.780	-0.999	29.500	-4.950
Chile	1966	-0.053	-0.051	-0.051	-0.027	68.500	-0.054
Uruguay	1966	-0.504	-0.504	-0.493	-0.241	37.100	-0.509
Argentina	1967	-6.960	-6.960	-6.840	-0.245	30.800	-7.130
Chile	1967	-0.047	-0.047	-0.45	-0.024	40.700	-0.048
Jamaica	1967*	2.950	2.950	1.500	-37.400	-11.400	3.010
Peru	1967	-2.070	-2.070	-1.930	36.600	39.600	-2.120
Trinidad & Tobago	1967	-3.530	-3.530	-1.890	-0.268	12.700	-3.600
Uruguay	1967	-3.110	-3.110	-3.010	-1.450	142.000	-3.160
Chile	1968	-0.061	-0.061	-0.058	-0.030	36.400	-0.061
Uruguay	1968	-1.140	-1.140	-1.090	-0.509	23.0	-1.160
Chile	1969	-0.002	-0.002	-0.003	-0.001	0.812	-0.003
Jamaica	1969*	18.400	18.400	12.700	-41.700	-39.600	18.700
Argentina	1970	-3.060	-3.060	-3.020	-0.322	10.500	-3.120
Chile	1970	-0.083	-0.083	-0.080	-0.042	27.400	-0.085
Ecuador	1970	-3.11	-3.11	-2.620	30.300	32.200	-3.220
Argentina	1971	-5.320	-5.320	-5.240	1.580	17.500	-5.430
Jamaica	1971	-1.920	-1.920	-1.820	1.700	5.780	-1.920
Uruguay	1971*	-2.280	-2.280	-2.220	-0.899	42.200	-2.360
Venezuela	1971*	0.562	0.562	0.821	501.000	-1.480	0.632
Bolivia	1972	-5.610	-5.610	-4.870	50.300	57.300	-5.760
Chile	1972	-0.326	-0.326	-0.321	-0.154	99.300	-0.329
Jamaica	1972*	2.800	2.800	2.110	-4.600	-7.080	2.040
Trinidad & Tobago	1972	-0.390	-0.390	-0.274	1.460	1.300	-0.396
Uruguay	1972	-7.850	-7.850	-7.520	-2.750	82.800	-7.990
Chile	1973	-8.330	-8.330	-8.150	-3.700	793.000	-8.430
Jamaica	1973*	1.690	1.690	1.380	-1.560	-4.390	1.710
Trinidad & Tobago	1973	-0.357	-0.357	-0.250	1.220	1.05	-3.660
Uruguay	1973	-3.450	-3.450	-3.320	-0.961	22.100	-3.530
Venezuela	1973*	0.678	0.678	0.540	-1.280	-1.960	0.701
Chile	1974	-25.400	-25.400	-24.100	-2.830	237.00	-25.700
Costa Rica	1974	-2.150	-2.150	-1.380	29.100	25.500	-2.180
Trinidad & Tobago	1974*	0.340	0.344	0.174	0.594	-0.807	0.357
Uruguay	1974	-6.580	-6.580	-6.250	-0.565	28.600	-6.700

*In these cases the exchange rate was revalued

[1] Brazil and Colombia were excluded for having a minidevaluation system

[2] Changes over quantities in real terms

Source: Original work of the author based on Krugman-Taylor Model.

study the effect of income redistribution. In most cases, it is obvious that income of salary earners decreases in a greater proportion than that of groups that live from their investments, as a consequence of a parity change.

In columns E and F, the effect of an increase in the trade deficit in domestic and foreign currency is analyzed. It is clear that, for all those countries that devalued during this period, there is a contractionary effect on their economies. In spite of the fact that the deficit improved when measured in dollars, it deteriorated when measured in local currency. It is not possible to analyze the effect of the increase in foreign debt on domestic currency, since the debt to be paid is a stock, and this effect is reflected in an increase of this stock, which, in turn, causes an increase in the flow of debt service payments. In order to analyze an increase in service payments in local currency, the balance on current account must be included in the model.

Recurring effects

If we accept that adjustment mechanisms do not attack the causes of disequilibrium but simply affect economic variables by restricting growth of the economy and by contracting expenditures, it is natural that once supervision of stand-by or extended arrangements is over and normal expenditures are resumed, the imbalance will reappear. This recurrence in developing countries is due to the fact that resources are not reallocated to allow the industrialization process to continue and to make the economy less dependent on external flows of goods, services, and capital.

In this sense, the Latin American experience proves that one or two years after devaluation there still has not occurred significant resource reallocation. In the cases under study, approximately half of the countries showed an increase and the other half a decrease in the growth rate of exports, imports, GDP, consumption, and investment (table 2.7). The value of this percentage increase or decrease is important; but as a whole, it can be noted that the disequilbrium is recurring in the countries with the highest GDP, and they have to devalue again a few years later, as was the case in Argentina, Chile, and Uruguay. Adjustment is only temporary and, soon after, the balance of payments deteriorates again.

Conclusions

The main conclusion derived from this empirical analysis is that, according to the Latin American experience, adjustment mechanisms for external disequilibrium proposed by orthodox theory and the IMF's policies are not effective in permanently correcting the disequilibrium. This is attributable to the fact

Table 2.7. Variations in the Growth Rates of Macroeconomic Variables in the Sample of the Countries Under Analysis[1]

Item		Year of Devaluation		Year After Devaluation		Two Years After Devaluation		Three Years After Devaluation	
		# Countries	%	# Countries	%	# Countries	%	# Countries	%
1.	Exports								
	Increase	13	48	16	59	18	67	14	52
	Decrease	14	52	11	41	9	33	11	48
2.	Imports								
	Increase	15	55	14	52	13	48	17	68
	Decrease	12	45	13	48	14	52	8	32
3.	GDP								
	Increase	13	48	16	59	18	67	14	52
	Decrease	14	52	11	41	9	33	11	48
4.	Consumption								
	Increase	13	48	11	41	12	44	12	44
	Decrease	14	52	16	59	15	56	15	56
5.	Investment								
	Increase	15	56	14	52	11	41	14	52
	Decrease	12	44	13	48	16	59	11	48

1/ In some cases, there are less than 27 points because there were not enough data available for the corresponding lags. Of the 34 cases, seven were appreciations of the exchange rate and are not considered in this table.

that adjustment obtained by means of the policy package of stand-by or extended arrangements is only temporary. Instead of supporting resource reallocation toward the external sector, intensifying the export and import-substitution process, and stimulating a reduction in absorption through consumption, what is achieved is a decrease in imports as a result of the contractionary effect implied by the devaluation and stabilization policy implicit in these arrangements. This can be asserted because the empirical tests corroborate the three propositions upon which the main hypothesis of IMF's adjustment policy shortcomings is based: the effect on relative prices, on income, and on recurrence.

In the first place, it was shown that elasticity of current transactions with regard to the exchange rate is not significantly different from zero during the period under consideration. Thus, we can assert that the effectiveness of devaluation by itself in developing countries as an adjustment mechanism of disequilibrium is doubtful, since it does not bring about resource reallocation which will decrease the deficit on the trade or current account balance. On the other hand, the social and political effects of this measure are considerable inasmuch as the psychological effect of devaluation is reflected in the destabilization of economic variables which, in turn, leads to fear of another devaluation and contributes to a vicious circle of lack of confidence that limits the effectiveness of economic policy instruments.

In the second place, it was shown that a decrease in the exchange rate has a negative effect on the growth rate of gross domestic product, particularly in the year of devaluation and two years later. This conclusion was confirmed by studying the effects on real money balances, redistribution of income, increase of the trade balance deficit in domestic currency, and increase in the external debt in domestic currency, which represent direct effects on absorption with a negative incidence on income. If to this contractionary effect of demand we add those resulting from the package of stabilization policy on expenditures which includes monetary, fiscal, price, and salary measures of a deflationary nature (as the one which forms part of the IMF's adjustment program), it is obvious that the negative effect will be reinforced. Given the low elasticity of the variables in the external sector with respect to measures aimed at diverting demand (devaluation), it can be concluded that a temporary improvement in the disequilibrium is not due to a reallocation of resources toward the external sector nor to an intensification in the import substitution process, but, rather, to a decrease in imports as a result of a contraction in the real product and the absorption capacity of the economy.

In the third place, insofar as a reallocation of resources is not achieved, when attempts to reestablish growth are made,

the external restriction appears once again and it pressures
for a new devaluation of the exchange rate. In other words,
the phenomenon is recurring and adjustment has been only
temporary.

The final conclusion is that IMF's approach to the problem
of disequilibrium in developing countries is not the appropriate
one, since the origin and causes of the imbalance are due
mainly to structural factors. In order to correct this type of
disequilibrium, another approach should be used which takes
into account this particular situation, as well as the role of
the adjustment policy in the context of economic growth and
development.

THE NEED FOR CHANGE IN IMF'S APPROACH
AND POLICIES

Adjustment policies via relative costs and prices and level of
aggregate demand that the IMF uses are inadequate to correct
external disequilibrium in developing countries owing to the
special characteristics of their economics. In general, exports
are concentrated on one or two primary products, which have
a low price elasticity for both supply and demand in the short
run. In developing countries, in comparison to industrial
ones, the internal market participates in only a limited way in
total exports. Therefore, resources that are used for domestic
market producton can not be easily diverted to the export
sector in the short run. Consequently, varations in aggregate
demand and domestic income levels have less influence on the
developing countries' exports than those of developed countries, while variations in external demand have a substantial
impact on the level of internal economic activity.(19)

Developing countries' income elasticity of imports is high
when compared to a relatively low price elasticity of demand
for, even in semiindustrialized countries, the internal
production process is highly dependent on the import of capital
and intermediate goods.

Rigidity in trade balance is generally accompanied by
inflexibility in service payment for foreign capital. The
payment of dividends and royalties for foreign investment and
of interest on foreign loans lays an additional and fixed
burden on the deficit in the current account of developing
countries. Thus, foreign capital as a source of financing for
external disequilibrium is a "razor with two edges." While it
enables the deficit in current account to be financed "today,"
it lays the additional burden of a service charge on the
current account balance of "tomorrow." In addition to the
structural characteristics of the external sector of developing
countries, there are other inherent elements in an underde-

•

veloped economy: intersectional imbalances, inflexibility in supply, and factor immobility. Thus, the adjustment process of external disequilibrium necessarily demands structural changes in the context of economic growth.

To focus the problem of external imbalance and adjustment processes on only a short-run perspective, as the monetarist and the IMF approaches do, implies taking economic growth as given on the assumption of full employment. This approach does not take into account the very nature of the growth problem or of external disequilibrium in developing countries. Through trade and financial relations with other nations, developing countries import most of their capital goods and technology which, directly and indirectly, affects the process of capital accumulation, technological change, and factor productivity. External debt capacity and inflow of foreign investment will determine, to a great extent, not only the limits of the foreign exchange gap in current account, but also the supplement to domestic savings, which is fundamental to determine the economy's growth rate.

Developing countries' exchange and trade policies not only confront the problem of a balance of payments disequilibrium; but they are also a basic instrument in the development strategy, whether it be an "inward" growth strategy via import substitution or an "outward" strategy via export promotion. The governments of developing countries face a greater diversity of economic objectives, and a more limited range of policy options to achieve them than do developed countries. The problem of external imbalance is accompanied by problems of internal disequilibrium - low growth rates and inflation - and by structural unemployment, low standards of living for the majority of the people, and structural dependency on both technology and foreign capital. On the other hand, for this plurality of economic objectives, only a limited number of independent, effective, and efficient instruments is available. Tax structure rigidity nullifies tax policy as a means for regulating demand, and, at the same time, it limits possibilities for independent use of monetary policy and external debt policy for balance of payments purposes; these policies must be used to finance public expenditures. In economies undergoing industrialization, the exchange rate has the double objective of equalizing balance of payment and of providing sufficient protection for its new industry.

Developing economies have traditional and modern sectors. In traditional sectors, the market incentives of price and demand are not sufficient to reallocate resources and to increase production and investment. In modern sectors, such as the industrial, an external adjustment via reduction in imports not only requires an increase in the production of internal substitutes, but also demands the creation of productive capacity; that is, the generation of new investment

in the import-substitution industry. Because of this, to say
nothing of potential shortages in the agricultural and basic
sectors (energy, steel, etc.), it would be unrealistic to expect
price and demand mechanisms to be sufficient in themselves to
generate new investment plans in competitive import and export
industries.
     Because of the characteristics of developing countries
previously referred to, the adjustment process of their
external disequilibrium should be analyzed, not only within the
context of maladjustments in prices and demand in the short
run, but within the context of structural problems inherent to
their development stage at a given moment and within the
dynamic context of an economy undergoing growth and
structural changes.

Origin of External Disequilibrium
in Developing Countries

For the purpose of external disequilibrium analysis, three
types of nonoil-exporting developing countries may be
distinguished: primary economies; economies in the process of
industrialization that are at first stage of "easy" import
substitution; and economies that are at a more advanced
import-substitution stage (IS). The following analysis of the
origin of external disequilibrium and evaluation of this
phenomenon refers to an underdeveloped economy in the
process of industrialization. Primary economies face similar
but even more difficult circumstances than countries in the
"easy" state of IS. It is for this reason that characteristics of
the "easy" stage countries with respect to external imbalances
are generally applicable to primary-economy countries.

The structural origin of the external disequilibrium in the first stage of IS

When the economy begins the process of import substitution of
consumer goods with internal production (first stage of IS),
there is demand derived from the import of intermediate and
capital goods required by the industrialization process, which
the economy cannot produce precisely because it is at the first
stage of IS. This structural dependency on imports implies a
high income elasticity of import demand due to the high import
intensity of the substitution process. It also means a low and
insignificant relative price elasticity of import demand due to
the lack of domestic sustitutes of intermediate and capital
goods and some consumer goods. The consequences of this
phenomenon are the following:

- Income elasticity greater than one ($N_y > 1$) implies that imports grow more than proportional to income. The low and nonsignificant relative prices elasticity ($N_{\frac{pd}{Pm}} < 1$) means that, in spite of an overvaluation of costs and prices, the main determining factor of import growth will depend on income growth and not on growth of internal prices with respect to international ones. Thus, it is to be expected that, in the first stage of IS, there will be a rapid growth of imports at a higher rate than income, which will lead to disequilibrium in the current account balance.

- In the first stage of IS, exports will still be concentrated in few primary products and raw materials, and will not be able to grow fast enough to finance the imports required during this first stage. This can be explained as follows: 1) Internal growth and industrialization processes require some raw materials which are and can be exported. 2) The export of primary products depends greatly on the world market – on growth of demand and on development of substitutes – and not only on internal conditions. 3) Because it is in a period of maturation, infant industry is not efficient enough to compete in the international manufacturing market and can only do so under special conditions of world shortage.

- Rapid growth of imports and the relatively slow growth of exports causes a continous external disequilibrium – a deficit in the balance on current account – which gives rise to one of the main bottlenecks for growth, precisely the trade or foreign exchange gap.

- During the first stage of IS, the deficit is characterized as a structural external imbalance. Consequently, devaluation and/or other commercial and economic policies that attempt to affect relative prices as an adjustment mechanism cannot correct the trade gap and simultaneously foster economic growth. Devaluation cannot work as long as import demand is characterized by a high income elasticity and a low relative prices elasticity. Devaluation will not change the fact that imports will grow faster than income; and, even though some exports could be stimulated, they would not grow at a fast enough pace to close the trade gap.

- To foster growth during the first stage of IS, it is necessary to finance the continous and permanent external disequilibrium or trade gap which, at the same time,

implies a structural dependency on foreign capital: loans
from abroad and/or foreign investment.
• Another indirect implication of high income elasticity of
demand for imports is a high marginal propensity to
import and, therefore, a low investment multiplier. The
growth process could face another bottleneck in the sense
that an increase in investment cannot generate sufficient
effective demand to sustain the process. A low level of
effective demand could or could not become a possible
bottleneck, depending on the supply elasticity of the
economy. Nevertheless, the outcome will not change the
fact that the multiplier effect of investment will continue
to be low. (20)

The Semi-structural origin of external disequilibrium in the advanced stage of IS

When the economy reaches the advanced stage of IS -
substitution of intermediate and capital goods - the demand
function of imports undergoes a structural change: income
elasticity decreases ($N_y < 1$) and relative prices elasticity increases significantly with respect to the first stage ($N_{\frac{pd}{Pm}} > 1$).

The consequences of this phenomenon which characterize
the mode of operation of the IS model are the following:
• There is a semistructural dependency on imports.
The economy has practically attained the substitution
of consumer goods and has made progress in the
substitution of intermediate and capital goods.
Therefore, there are more internal substitutes that can
compete with imports which, in turn, explains the decrease in income elasticity and the increase in relative
prices elasticity. With regard to imports, disequilibrium
is semistructural in the sense that the hypothesis of
overvaluation of costs and prices is important in explaining the growth of imports ($N_{\frac{pd}{Pm}} > 1$), but income elasticity, while less than the unit, continues to be of considerable magnitude, and faces a more rigid structure of

- imports which is basically constituted by intermediate and capital goods.
- Although the economy has made progress in manufacturing and its export production capacity has increased, the prolonged IS model is characterized by an inefficient use of protectionist trade policy which generally restricts the exports of primary and manufactured goods. The export industry receives domestic inputs that have been substituted, but at higher prices than the international ones owing to excessively protected markets, which means an implicit export tax. The exchange rate, which is generally overvalued, also implies an implicit tax on exports and a subsidy for imports. A captive domestic market and a low subsidy level for exports do not make exportation of manufactured goods attractive or competitive.
- The trade balance continues to be in disequilibrium. Nevertheless, during the advanced state a "new" dependency on imports arises and accentuates the imbalance in current account, specifically the importation of services such as payments of rent on foreign capital - foreign investment and external loans - that were used during the first IS stage as an adjustment mechanism for disequilibrium.
- During the advanced stage of IS, the external disequilibrium is of a semistructural origin, even though it continues to depend on imports of intermediate and capital goods. The hypothesis of overvaluation of costs and prices explains, to a great degree, the prolongation of the external disequilibrium, for which an "adequate" trade policy (devaluation, tariffs, subsidies) and an adequate growth strategy can considerably reduce the trade gap and continue to promote the growth process.
- It is also important to observe that the low income elasticity of import demand implies a lower marginal propensity to import, which, in turn, means a greater investment multiplier with respect to the first period.

While in the first stage of IS, the structural nature of the external disequilibrium means that growth can only be promoted with a cost of dependency on foreign capital. In the advanced IS stage, the semistructural origin of the disequilibrium means that its permanence is attributable, in a great part, to an inadequate use of commerical and economic policies in general.

If we take a simple model where we can observe the structural change in import function with respect to the external disequilibrium and investment multiplier, we would see that exports (X) and investment (I) are given exogenously, and imports (M) and savings (S) are a function of income (Y). Therefore, we can represent the trade gap(X-M) and the savings gap (S-I) as in figure 2.1. The combined function (X-M) has a negative slope, because imports are subtracted from a constant export level, and imports are a function of income. The combined function (S-I) has a positive slope, because the constant level of investment is subtracted from savings, which is a function of income.

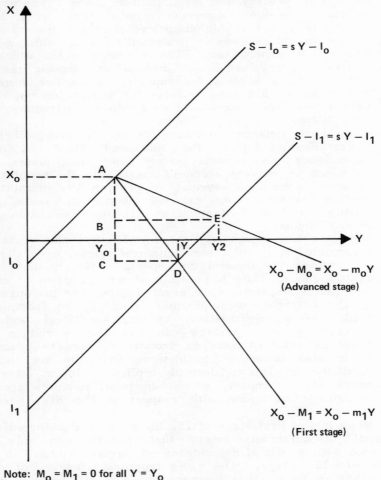

Note: $M_0 = M_1 = 0$ for all $Y = Y_0$

Fig. 2.1. External disequlibrium and growth during the IS stages.

Source: Rene Villarreal, El Desequilibrio Externo en la Industrializacion de Mexico (1929-1975): Un Enioque Estructuralista (Mexico: Fondo de Cultura Economica, 1976), p. 135.

In this case, two combined functions of the trade gap (X-M) are represented. Both contain the same initial level of exports (X_O), but the function $X_O - M_1$ implies a greater propensity to import than $X_O - M_O$. The function $X_O - m_1 Y$ represents the structural nature of external disequilibrium in the first stage of IS, and the semistructural nature of the disequilibrium is represented by the function $X_O - m_O Y$ in the advanced stage of the IS process, where $m_1 > m_O$. The intersection of the two functions $(X - M = S - I)$ at a point A shows equilibrium in national income and in the balance of payments or the trade gap position. At point A, income level is Y_O and the balance of payments registers a surplus, indicated by the distance AY_O.

Given these circumstances and our interest in the growth process, it leads us to ponder what the effect of an increase in investment (ΔI) on income (ΔY) and on the trade gap (X-M) would be according to the different stages of IS. The phenomenon that is of interest is the ex-post result and not the forces or mechanisms that lead the system to a point of equilibrium (ex-ante phenomenon). The idea is to show the effects of an increase in investment in situations where a key parameter (the marginal propensity to import) changes significantly according to the IS stage. If investment increases from I_O to I_1, the function $S-I_O$ shifts to $S-I_1$ and the economy would reach a point of equilibrium (D) if it were in the first stage of IS and a point of E if it were in the advanced stage. Given that $\Delta X=0$, the increase in the trade gap would be AC if the economy is at the first stage of IS (and the deficit of $Y_1 D = Y_0 C$), and only AB if it is at the advanced stage. Therefore, in the first case of a surplus (AY_0), the economy would show a deficit (Y_1D); while in the second case, the economy would still show a surplus (Y_2E). On the other hand, given the low investment multiplier during the first stage, an increase in income would only be $Y_1 - Y_0$, while during the advanced stage, the increase would be greater $(Y_2 - Y_1)$.

The important thing to observe is that, in the face of the same increase in investment, the magnitude of the trade gap is significant and substantially greater during the first stage of IS (the ABC distance is equivalent to a deficit of Y_0C or Y_1D, given the initial surplus of AY_0), since, in the advanced stage of the process, the gap is only AB (and the balance of payments continues with a surplus, though it is reduced from ABY_0 to BY_0). This holds true in spite of the fact that the income effect is greater during this stage, and the import intensity effect of the same IS process is substantially less, which is reflected by the low value of the marginal propensity to import.

In other words, we can say that an increase in investment (ceteris paribus) has, among others, two main effects: the income effect, and the trade or foreign exchange gap effect (increase in the deficit in the balance on current account or a decrease in the surplus). Thus, in the first IS stage, the income effect is significantly lower than in the advanced stage of the process and, paradoxically, the foreign exchange gap effect is greater. What explains this apparent paradox is that, during the first stage, the marginal propensity to import is very high (and larger than during the advanced stage), which determines the low income effect (low investment multiplier) and the high foreign exchange gap effect (high import intensity of the IS process).

Devaluation as an adjustment mechanism: the structuralist approach

The structuralist approach to the balance of payments establishes that devaluation as an adjustment mechanism can only work when the disequilibrium is of a semistructural nature, and when it is accompanied by a selective expansion policy of aggregate demand and by adequate resource reallocation. Then we would be in a position to speak of the following policy "package": the relative prices policy (devaluation) to divert aggregate expenditures or demand, the selective expansion policy of aggregate demand, and the supply policy to stimulate production and investment in the tradable goods sectors.

Relative costs and prices policy.   Devaluation of the exchange
rate causes an initial rise in the relative prices of tradable
goods with respect to nontradable ones and acts as a general
policy to divert demand to export and import substitutes.
However, devaluation generates an inflationary impact that
tends to cancel the improvement in relative prices and to deter
resources reallocation and increases in production and investment in the tradable goods sectors.   Thus, to temporarily
assure new production and investment, the use of trade
policy is required to selectively divert demand.

The stage of development a given country has reached
determines the type of trade policy it should follow.   If, for
example, the country is in the stage of industrialization during
which consumer goods are being substituted, trade policy
should provide sufficient protection to infant industry through
a policy of tariffs and import controls on consumer goods, if
necessary.   The structuralist approach establishes that
devaluation should be complemented with a protectionist trade
policy and a more liberal, but wise, use of tariffs and trade
controls adequate for the economy's particular stage of
economic growth.   This policy is, in essence, different from
the IMF's recommendation, which establishes a policy of foreign
trade "liberalization at all costs" as was the case during the
1970s in Chile and Sri Lanka.

Aggregate demand policy.   Contrary to what orthodox theory
of balance of payments and the IMF expound, devaluation in
developing countries causes a contractionary impact on demand
and income.   This effect is so great that fiscal and monetary
policies should be expansionary though selective.   The
diversion of demand toward export and import-substitution
sectors that devaluation causes should be complemented with a
managed expansionary policy of public expenditures and credit
that, in the end, will mean an increase in production and
productive capacity (investment) in these sectors.

Devaluation of the exchange rate in developing countries
significantly contracts aggregate demand due to the
combination of seven effects:
- The income redistribution effect.   A price rise is brought
  about in tradable goods and services and indirectly in
  nontradable ones.   There will be an increase in their
  demand as a result of the substitution effect.   This will
  cause a redistribution effect (ceteris paribus) in favor of
  high-income groups that own the capital.   If their
  marginal propensity to save is greater than in low-income
  groups, a reduction in expenditure is to be expected.
- The real money balances effect.   The value of the real
  money supply will be reduced by devaluation, since
  domestic prices of tradable goods and services will
  increase.   In order to reestablish the value of real money

balances and other financial assets, the public will reduce
its expenditures.

- The effect if an increase in domestic currency of the
external debt. Even though the service cost of external
debt (interests and amortizations) is fixed in foreign
currency, devaluation will increase the cost of these
services in domestic currency. Both the public and
private sectors – depending on their respective share in
the structure of external debt – will suffer an increase in
the cost in domestic currency of these services, which
could lead to a reduction in investment.

- The effect of an increase in the deficit of the balance on
current account in domestic currency. It is not unusual
to find that, even though the current account deficit
measured in foreign exchange decreases as a result of
devaluation, it increases in domestic currency during the
first year due to a new exchange rate. If this does
occur, there will be a sufficient reduction in absorption
to compensate for the increase in net expenditure abroad
in domestic currency.

- The fiscal effect. The inflationary impact of devaluation
allows for additional tax collection, particularly if the tax
structure is progressive. In general, export subsidies
are reduced and sometimes tariffs are levied on them.
With regard to imports, tax collection is significantly
increased through customs duties. All of these fiscal
effects reduce absorption or aggregate expenditures.

- The effect of investment contraction owing to an increase
in import costs of machinery, equipment, inputs, etc. In
developing countries, the imported content of investment
is quite high compared to industrialized countries.
Devaluation itself causes a direct increase in investment
costs, which tends to deter growth of productive capacity
in tradable goods sectors.

- The uncertainty effect. The orthodox approach to
devaluation has always adopted the assumption of all
things being constant (ceteris paribus) and, when devaluation occurs, a basic assumption is certainty. In
practice, devaluation by nature is a sign of "crisis and
uncertainty" and greatly affects expected results.

In developing countries, devaluation is accompanied by
stagflation, which brings about uncertainty in the economic
adjustment process. Furthermore, devaluation comes as a
surprise and does not immediately include a package of
complementary measures. In many cases, it means removal of
the public officials (Minister of Finance and Director of the
Central Bank) who implement the policy, but, at the same
time, this makes more acute the uncertainty with respect to
the guidelines and the path economic policy will take.

If devaluation is followed by expectations of yet another devaluation, importers will accelerate their purchases according to their liquidity possibilities and debt capacity, and savers and economic agents who maintain money balances in cash will demand more foreign exchange.

Diverse factors, such as uncertainty regarding the exchange and inflation rates, the increase in salaries and its impact on costs, in addition to price increases in imports of machinery, equipment and raw materials, will cause entrepreneurs to delay decisions to increase production and, even more so, to increase productive capacity.

These seven effects are so important that they are the source of considerable contractionary effects due to devaluation itself. It follows that if adoption of the "prescription" proposed by the orthodox and IMF approaches to the balance of payments which advocate use of contractionary monetary and fiscal policies means an additional reduction in the level of production and employment, it not only represents an unnecessary cost but also hinders the process of resource reallocation due to the low level of aggregate demand.

The structuralist approach establishes that in developing countries, unlike industrialized ones, devaluation of the exchange rate is itself contractionary and should be accompanied by a selectively expansionary fiscal and monetary policy that will aid resource reallocation to export and import-substitution sectors.

The supply policy.   For a development policy to be feasible, it is basic to make the growth process compatible with equilibrium in the balance of payments. In such an imperfect market system as the one that prevails in developing countries, it cannot be expected that the incentive of relative prices and aggregate demand will be sufficient to assure resource reallocation and to increase production and investment in export and import-substitution sectors.

These systems require a policy of direct promotion of domestic supply that establishes and stimulates investment and production programs in tradable goods sectors and in areas where there are bottlenecks. Incentives' policies of domestic production generally require a strengthening of, or a change in, trade and industralization policies. In general terms, the import-substitution policy presents a well-defined anti-exporting bias which, in spite of devaluation, does not stimulate increases in production in this sector. In addition, according to the stage of industrialization, resource realloca-tion will occur depending on the type of policies available to support it. For example, in the case of Mexico's devaluation in 1976, the decrease in imports meant the Mexico should enter the stage of capital goods substitution. Price and demand incentives already existed but were not sufficient, because

production of machinery and equipment requires special
programs to protect industry, for long-range financing, for
transfer of technology, and so forth.

PROPOSALS FOR A NEW IMF APPROACH

The definition of a NIEO implies the establishment of a
monetary system that will solve the problems of adjustment,
liquidity, and confidence. Empirical evidence for Latin
America shows that, quite contrary to established orthodox
theory, price elasticity of variables in the external sector with
respect to the exchange rate is not significant. Devaluation
on its own brings about significant contractionary effects
which, when taken together with those induced by the
stabilization program's contraction of aggregate demand,
manage to reduce the disequilibrium, but only temporarily.
This phenomenon is not due to a diversion of resources toward
the export sector nor to more intensive import substitution
but, rather, to a reduction in imports caused by contraction in
investment and the real product.
     It is evident that the orthodox approach and the IMF's
adjustment policy are not adequate for developing countries,
since the origin and causes of the disequilibrium are more
attributable to structural maladjustment than to price-cost
maladjustment and/or excess demand which generally are
symptoms of disequilibrium. Based on the preceding
statements, the need for a new approach and adjustment
policies in the IMF is evident. The way to correct this type
of disequilibrium is to adopt another approach that takes into
account structural malajustments of an economy undergoing a
growth process and, within this framework, propose adjustment
policies for external disequilibrium. This is the structuralist
approach to the balance of payments on which the new IMF
approach and adjustment policies for developing countries
should be based.
     The "new IMF approach to the balance of payments" should
analyze the problem of external disequilibrium and the
adjustment process, not as short-term phenomena, but in a
growth perspective. For developing countries, the problem is
how to promote and guarantee sustained economic growth
without falling into external maladjustments. In this sense,
adjustment policies should resolve the problem of how to
correct an external imbalance, so that, once sustained growth
is reached again, the economy does not regress to a state of
disequilibrium.
     With respect to diagnosis of the origin of external
imbalance, the new IMF approach should distinguish between
symptoms and causes of the phenomenon before establishing an

agreement of conditional financial assistance. In a growing economy, disequilibria due to overvaluation of price costs and overspending are generally symptoms that can make the phenomena appear to be worse; the causes are to be found in structural maladjustments intrinsic to a particular stage of the country's development, whether it be at the primary products exporting stage, at that of easy substitution of imports, or at the semi-industrialized stage.

The new IMF policy with respect to adjustment measures for external disequilibrium should reorient relative prices-costs and demand policies in accordance with the characteristics of the adjustment process in an economy undergoing growth and with structural problems. In addition, it will be necessary to include a policy of direct incentives for supply and productive investment, absent at present in agreements that cover conditional assistance.

Policy of Relative Prices-Costs

Devaluation of the exchange rate

As a general diversion policy of aggregate demand toward the export and import substitution sectors, devaluation of the exchange rate shall be used in cases of overvaluation of prices-costs and when these sectors have a significant elasticity response. In the primary-exporting and incipient-industrialization economies, price elasticities of demand for exports and imports are generally small; therefore, this measure would only be adequate in semistructural disequilibria.

Trade policy

Devaluation as a general diversion policy of demand should be complemented by a selective diversion policy. This trade policy should consist of assuring, on a medium- and long-run basis, a favorable real and effective exchange rate for the export and import-substitution sectors. This implies a more flexible use of tariffs, controls, and incentives for foreign trade than the IMF has traditionally established. The Fund generally requires an "at all costs" liberalization policy, with regard to both the exchange rate and trade. This not only slows down the import substitution process, but also eliminates industries that, even under the comparative but dynamic advantage criterion, could be efficient. In this sense, we are dealing with a stage program for gradual liberalization and for reduction of excessive protectionism, as well as for the establishment and stimulation of adequate protection for new import substitution industries.

Price and salary policy

IMF policies on price liberalization and rigid salary control should be more flexible in the case of basic consumer goods (salary goods). Salary regulation should be parallel in its growth rate to those of the country's main trading partners. However, the inflationary impact of devaluation is of such importance that the increase in the cost of living will be greater than the increase in salaries of their main trading partners, so that, in order to avoid the adjustment burden falling unfairly on the working class, there must be a direct support program for the supply of basic consumer goods (salary goods) and their price regulation. The importance of this policy goes even further than strictly economic considerations, since, quite often, pressure from worker strikes has led several countries to introduce a more authoritarian and repressive political system during the adjustment period, a development which is not necessarily reversible.(21)

Sometimes, insufficient internal production of basic consumer goods (salary goods) with a low capacity to respond on the short run makes necessary the importation of greater quantities of these goods, which could require special financial assistance from the IMF, under a facility that could be set up for such cases. This would allow the IMF to comply with the objective established in its Articles of Agreement, Article I, (v):

> To give confidence to members by making the general resources of the Fund temporarily available to them under adequate safeguards, thus providing them with the opportunity to correct maladjustment in their balance of payments without resorting to measures destructive of national or international prosperity.

Policy of Selective Demand Expansion

Given the special characteristics of developing countries, devaluation of the exchange rate produces a contractionary effect in aggregate demand to such a degree that this measure should be complemented with a selectively expansionist policy of aggregate demand in both fiscal and monetary terms. The monetary policy should divert and increase credit at an adequate interest rate for the export, import-substitution and basic industries sectors that face bottlenecks. Fiscal policy should reorient investment expenditures to these sectors, and temporarily lower the ratio of current expenditures in the overall budget. The IMF has established a contractionary demand policy in both monetary and fiscal terms as the main instrument for adjustment.

Policy of Direct Incentives for Productive
Supply and Investment

The imperfect market and structural characteristics of a growing economy necessarily mean that the adjustment process
through price and aggregate demand mechanisms is insufficient
to bring about resource reallocation to the tradable goods
sectors and to continue encouraging growth. Thus, according
to the stage of development of each particular country, the
IMF's program of conditional financial assistance should
include a program to stimulate production and investment in
the areas of export and import substitution. This program
would require a broader support in financial aspects and
during the adjustment period.

Recently, the IMF has established the "Extended Facility
Agreement," which is a step in the right direction, but,
unfortunately, it focuses on the traditional devaluation
(liberalization) demand contraction conditions. In other words,
only price and demand mechanisms are required. In this
sense, the new IMF policy does not require an "at all costs"
liberalization and contraction program, but, rather, a program
to expand and to selectively divert demand as well as to
stimulate production and investment in the productive sectors
of tradable goods.

Undoubtedly, the IMF's financial resources will be
insufficient for a support policy of this nature, and it will be
necessary to count on special additional financial support for
the adjustment process from the World Bank (IBRD) and
regional banks, such as the Inter-American Development Bank
in the case of Latin America. In terms of a policy to stimulate
internal supply, the role of the development bank is of great
importance, given that the incentive to produce can only be
obtained by financing an increased productive capacity and by
eliminating bottlenecks that hinder the efficient use of the
present installed capacity.

Traditionally the IMF and IBRD have established their
policies for developing countries by focusing on apparently
different problems. The IMF has channeled its efforts toward
"circumstantial" problems of the balance of payments, and the
IBRD on "structural" problems of development. Nevertheless,
balance of payments disequilibrium and their adjustment
policies and mechanisms are intrinsic problems of the growth
process and of structural changes in developing countries that
require common and integrated approaches and policies.

CONCLUSIONS

A NIEO for the 1980s requires an international monetary system capable of providing an adequate adjustment mechanism for the problem of balance of payments disequilibria. The IMF approach and adjustment policies for developing countries, from Bretton Woods to date, have been based on orthodox theory's approach to and policies on the balance of payments, especially the monetarist approach which claims that the origin of the disequilibrium is due to prices-costs maladjustments, and to excess demand attributable to an ex-ante excess flow of the money supply. This approach has led the Fund to establish, in its agreements of conditional financial assistance, requirements for a package of measures which include the following policies: devaluation, liberalization, contraction of demand, and economic activity.

Historic proof of balance of payments adjustments processes in Latin America shows that IMF's policies do not correct external disequilibrium and, when they do, adjustment is only of a temporary nature and is achieved at high social and economic costs, thereby violating the basic objectives established in Article I of its Articles of Agreement. It is, therefore, necessary to consider a new IMF approach and adjustment policies with respect to developing countries' external disequilibria. The new approach and adjustment policies should be based on the structuralist approach to the balance of payments which differentiates between disequilibrium symptoms - such as malajustment in prices-costs and in demand - and causes due to intrinsic maladjustment of the developing economy's growth stage. This approach proposes that the new IMF adjustment policies should include a package of measures with the following characteristics: devaluation, adequate protection, selective expansion of aggregate demand, and a program of direct incentives for production and investment in the tradable goods sectors.

APPENDIX

Financial Facilities of the Fund and Their Conditionality

Tranche policies
        Reserve tranche
        Condition-balance of payments need.

        First credit tranche
        Program representing reasonable efforts to overcome balance of payments difficulties; performance criteria and installments not used.

Higher credit tranches
Program giving substantial justification of member's efforts to overcome balance of payments difficulties; resources normally provided in the form of stand-by arrangements which include performance criteria and drawings in installments.

Extended facility
Medium-term program for up to three years to overcome structural balance of payments maladjustments; detailed statement of policies and measures for first and subsequent 12-month periods; resources provided in the form of extended arrangements which include performance criteria and drawings in installments.

Compensatory financing facility
Existence of temporary export shortfall for reasons beyond the member's control; member cooperates with Fund in an effort to find appropriate solution for any balance of payments difficulties.

Buffer stock financing facility
Existence of an international buffer stock accepted as suitable by Fund; member expected to cooperate with Fund as in the case of compensatory financing.

Supplementary financing facility
To be used in support of programs under stand-by arrangements reaching into the upper credit tranche or beyond, or under extended arrangements, subject to relevant policies on conditionality, phasing, and performance criteria.

SOURCE: IMF Survey, September 18, 1978 (The Fund Under the Second Amendment: a Supplement). p. 295.

NOTES

(1) It is sufficient to examine the "classics" on the topic of international finance, such as Richard Cooper or Carl Kindleberger, in which, without questioning the origin of the balance of payments disequilibrium, the subject dealt directly with is the adjustment mechanisms.
(2) Richard Cooper, International Finance; Selected Readings (Harmondsworth, England: Penguin Books, 1969), p. 8.
(3) Cooper, "An Analysis of Currency Devaluation in Developing Countries," in International Trade and Money, ed. Connolly and Swoboda, pp. 167-96; Blackwell, "Monetary Approach to Balance of Payments Needs Blend-

ing with Other Lines of Analysis," and "Eclectic Approach to Balance of Payments Adjustment Policies and Programs."

(4) Polak, "Depreciation to Meet a Situation of Overinvestment"; Bernstein, "Strategic Factors in Balance of Payments," Review of Economics and Statistics.

(5) "Desequilibrio Fundamental y Fomento Economico"; Noyola, El Desequilibrio Externo en el Desarrollo Economico Latinoamericano, LaPaz: CEPAL, May 1957; Rene Villarreal, "External Disequilibrium and Growth without Development: The Important Substitution Model. The Mexican Experience 1929-1975." (Ph.D. diss., Yale University, 1976); Villarreal, El Desequilibrio Externo en la Industrializacion de Mexico (1929-1975): Un Enfoque Estructuralista.

(6) United Nations, Report on the Balance of Payments Adjustment Process in Developing Countries.

(7) Alexander, "Effects of a Devaluation on a Trade Balance."

(8) Ibid., pp. 362-63.

(9) Ibid., p. 369.

(10) Frenkel and Johnson, "The Monetary Approach to the Balance of Payments: Essential Concepts and Historical Origins," pp. 20-26.

(11) The most modern version of representing the quantity theory is to use the same equation of exchange described before (MV = PQ), but in terms of percentage growth for each one of the variables ($m = \triangle M/M$, $v = \triangle V/V$), etc.; that is $m + v = p + q$, which indicates that the growth rate of the supply of money (m), plus the growth rate of income velocity (v) is equal to or is alloted between the growth rate of prices (inflation, p) plus the growth of real production (q).

(12) In strict terms, the monetarists are assuming that V is constant, and, therefore, $V = \triangle V/V$ is equal to zero. Thus, the deficit in the reserve balance would only originate when $m > p + q$.

(13) Johnson, "Monetary Approach to Balance of Payments: A Nontechnical Guide," p. 260.

(14) Rudolph R. Rhomberg and H. Robert Heller, "Introductory Survey," in The Monetary Approach to the Balance of Payments (Washington: IMF, 1977), pp. 6-7.

(15) Frenkel and Johnson, "The Monetary Approach," p. 24.

(16) Harry Johnson, "The Monetary Approach to Balance of Payments Theory and Policy: Explanation and Policy Implications," Economica 44 (1977): 227.

(17) Rhomberg and Heller, "Introductory Survey," p. 12.

(18) Paul Krugman and Lance Taylor, "Contractionary Effects of Devaluation," Journal of International Economics, October 1976.

(19) United Nations, "The Adjustment Process in Developing
      Countries" (UNCTAD/FIN/L), Money, Finance and De-
      velopment: Papers on International Monetary Reform, New
      York, 1974, p. 28.
(20) Rao, "La Inversion, la Renta y el Multiplicador en una
      Economia Subdesarrollada."
(21) John Sheahan, "Market-Oriented Economic Policies and
      Political Repression in Latin America."

SELECTED BIBLIOGRAPHY

Alexander, Sidney A. "Effects of a Devaluation on a Trade
    Balance" IMF Staff Papers, Vol. 2, April, 1955, pp. 263-278.

Bernstein, Edward M. "Strategic Factors in Balance of Pay-
    ments," Review of Economics and Statistics, February, 1958,
    pp. 133-142.

Blackwell, Carl. "Monetary Approach to Balance of Payments
    Needs Blending with Other Lines of Analysis," and "Eclectic
    Approach to Balance of Payments Adjustment Policies and
    Programs," IMF Survey, February 20, 1978, pp. 52-55 and
    March 6, 1978, pp. 71-73.

CEPAL.   El Desequilibrio Externo en el Desarrollo Economico
    Latinoamericano (External Disequilibrium in Latin America's
    Economic Development). Bolivia, May 1957.

Cooper, R. N. "An Analysis of Currency Devaluation in
    Developing Countries," in M.B. Connolly and A. K.
    Swoboda, eds. International Trade and Money. George
    Allen and Unwin, London 1973.

____. "Currency Devaluation in Developing Countries."
    Princeton Essays in International Finance, No. 86. Prince-
    ton, N.J.: International Finance Section, 1971.

____. Financiacion Internacional: Textos Escogidos (Inter-
    national Financing: Selected Texts). Madrid: Editorial
    Tecnos, 1974, pp. 7-21.

Frenkel, Jacob and Johnson, Harry G., eds. The Monetary
    Approach to the Balance of Payments. Toronto: University
    of Toronto Press, 1976.

International Monetary Fund (IMF). Articles of Agreement.
    Washington: IMF, 1978.

Johnson, Harry G. "The Monetary Approach to the Balance of
    Payments: A Nontechnical Guide," Journal of International
    Economics, August, 1977, pp. 251-268.

___. "The Monetary Approach to Balance of Payments Theory and Policy: Explanation and Policy Implications," Economica, August, 1977, pp. 217-229.

Kindleberger, C.P. International Economics. Homewood, Illinois: Richard D. Irwin, 1973.

Krugman, Paul and Taylor, Lance. "Contractionary Effects of Devaluation." Journal of International Economics, August 1978, pp. 445-456.

Noyola, Jean F. Desequilibrio Fundamental y Fomento Economico (Fundamental Disequilibrium and Economic Development). Thesis, UNAM, Mexico, 1949.

Polak, J.J. "Depreciation to Meet a Situation of Overinvestment," IMF Memorandum, September 19, 1948.

Rao, V.K.R.V. "La Inversion, la Renta y el Multiplicador en una Economia Subdesarrollada" (Investment, Rent and the Multiplier in an Underdeveloped Economy), in Agarwala-Singh. La Economia del Subdesarrollo (Economics of Underdevelopment). Madrid. Editorial Tecnos, 1963, pp. 175-185.

Sheahan, Joan. "Market-Oriented Economic Policies and Political Repression in Latin America." The Center for Development Economics, RM-70. Williams College, Massachusetts, June 1978.

United Nations. Report on the Balance of Payments Adjustment Process in Developing Countries. UNDP/UNCTAD project INT/75/015, New York, January 1979.

United Nations Conference on Trade and Development. Money, Finance and Development: Papers on International Monetary Reform. United Nations, New York, 1974.

Villarreal, R. El Desequilibrio Externo en la Industrializacion de Mexico (1929-1975): Un Enfoque Estructuralista (External Disequilibrium in Mexico's Industrialization (1929-1975): A Structuralist Approach). Mexico. Fondo de Cultura Economica, 1976. Ph.D. dissertation at Yale University entitled, External Disequilibrium and Growth without Development. The Import Substitution Model. The Mexican Experience 1929-1975.

3 Liquidity and International Finance
Pedro Paz

INTERNATIONAL MONETARY LIQUIDITY

The term 'international liquidity' expresses the availability and characteristics of the means of payment within the international community, and also the quantity and types of means of payment which a country has at its disposal to meet its financial and commercial commitments in the outside world. In both cases, the analysis must take into account sources of liquidity, and the facts which explain the need for it.

Monetary Liquidity at an International Level

The current functioning of the capitalist economy and its objective trends are causing a continuous and increasing excess in liquidity, in relation to the international monetary needs of trade and the flow of capital. This is a result of a variety of factors of which the most important are as follows:
* internationalization and exclusiveness of capital in its various cycles;
* a worsening of the crisis which, in turn, aggravates the problem of sale and reduces accumulation levels, thus increasing surpluses that are transferred into the financial sphere in order to reproduce and fix a price on capital;
* a consolidation and greater autonomy of financial capital in relation to the capital of production and trade;
* a reduction in power and capacity on the part of the national and supranational monetary authorities to control the level of liquidity, to establish accepted or imposed

mechanisms, to regulate international monetary and financial relations, and to introduce instruments to balance the dissymmetries and disequilibria in world trade.

When one goes beyond a static observation of the workings of the economy, and attempts to understand the long-term transformation in economies and societies, one discovers certain general and all-embracing trends that can explain this transformation process. In this context, one has to admit that, as a general trend, the capitalist system tends to produce a monetary surplus greater than that needed for the accumulation process, a differential which increases in times of crisis. Keynes himself suggested that a general long-term tendency of the capitalist system is an excess in savings over investment opportunities. Analytically, this can be explained by a decreasing propensity in the long term to consume. Therefore, within the framework of this system, economic policy must try to expand investment opportunities until they reach the level of full employment of income. In order to reach this goal, in times of recession, monetary policies must aim at a lowering of the rate of interest, so that those investments which are planned with low marginal efficiency of capital can become real investments. In turn, fiscal policy, faced with a deficit in real demand (a general trend), must try to increase the level of income of full employment.

In the financial area, an excess in savings in relation to investment implies that there will be a growing mass of liquidity with no outlet. In Marxist thought, also, there is concern that, under capitalism, the crisis of realization (expressed as a crisis of underconsumption and disproportion) when combined with a fall in the profit rate of the organic composition of capital will slow down accumulation and, in this way, increase the mass of money which is removed from the production process, causing further concentration and centralization of capital, and a need to export capital. In the long term, crises would tend to become more acute and deepen the contradictions in a production method, which, like capitalism, is of an antagonistic nature.

These processes do not follow the same lines, since the system itself generates mechanisms to overcome the crisis and enters into an expansive phase at a new level. This expansive phase, in turn, has its own contradictions which lead to new crises. The evident simplification with which Keynes and Marxist theorists presented certain trends in the workings of capitalism only made the point that excess liquidity tends to be a general and inherent phenomenon in capitalism in the long run.

From a wider perspective, it must be specified that the concept of international liquidity includes not only those elements which are considered to be the constituents of international reserves, but also all payment methods which are used in international transactions and which are created by or in the power of the private sector. Normally the total reserves of particular countries are taken as indicators of international liquidity. One includes in these international reserves official holdings of foreign currency, monetary gold, special drawing rights, and the position of reserves in the IMF. From a conventional point of view, Carlos Massad suggests that private holdings of reserve assets be taken into account when analyzing the needs and availability of international liquidity. To this effect, he suggests the introduction of "total liquidity" as a concept.(1) Only with this more comprehensive outlook can one analyze the great changes which have taken place in recent years in the composition and levels of international liquidity. One will also be able to identify more clearly the very different sources of liquidity in the two periods 1950-69 and 1970 onwards, which we shall be examining, and find that international liquidity has increased considerably since 1950. This expansion is one of the factors that explains the current "maladjustments" in the international monetary and exchange systems.

From Bretton Woods to the 1960s

From the Bretton Woods Agreements until well into the 1960s, sources of liquidity increased only moderately, and there was even talk, in various international forums and meetings held by experts, of international "illiquidity" and the need to implement new mechanisms in order to create liquidity within the framework of the existing international monetary system. One must note that those countries with a significant balance of payments surplus (mainly countries in the EEC and Japan) nearly always took a different view of the plans to increase international liquidity.

Sources of liquidity in that period

From Bretton Woods to the 1960s, sources of liquidity were monetary gold holdings (the production of gold minus its nonmonetary use), holdings of reserve center currencies, the position of reserves in the IMF, and certain mechanisms between the monetary authorities which could be classed as "indirect sources" of international liquidity.

Increases in holdings of monetary gold were limited by a slower growth in the production of gold, which increased at an average accumulative rate of one percent annually, compared to

the 9-10 percent growth rate of world trade. As a result, a
serious gap appeared between world trends in monetary gold
and its capacity to satisfy the liquidity requirements of a
dynamic international trade, and of the growth in capital
movements brought about by the increasing internationalization
of capital, which marked the period. Thus, during the 1950s
and 1960s, the gap between monetary gold holdings and the
growing monetary needs of the great expansion in trade and
capital flows was filled by balance of payments deficits in the
main reserve currency, the US dollar.

As will be explained later, the balance of payments deficit
of the United States, while satisfying the liquidity
requirements of the international economy, was at the root of
the instability in the international monetary system.

Other sources of liquidity were found in the position of
reserves in the IMF (resources of depositing countries, of
which short-term use could be made without being subject to
conditions). Quantitatively, this source of liquidity was not
very significant, given the conservative nature of the IMF,
particularly with regard to underdeveloped countries. It has
been only since 1958 that funds available in the IMF are
accepted as international reserves.

In the 1950-69 period, a whole new set of mechanisms was
created and strengthened which can be regarded as an indirect
source of international liquidity, inasmuch as it diminished the
need for liquidity in the international monetary system. By
this we refer to certain monetary and financial agreements in
some economic areas, for example, the European Payments
Union or the Compensation Chamber of the LAFTA (Latin
American Free Trade Association). SWAP agreements for
currency interchange between central banks fulfill the same
goal. These are used to grant certain facilities to countries
with a balance of payments deficit. They operate in the
following manner: the central bank of the nation in deficit
requests the central bank of another country to advance a
certain amount of its currency to help reinforce its own
currency. This advance is carried out by an official
exchange, with the central bank of the country requesting the
advance putting up the equivalent sum in its own currency as
a guarantee. This mechanism is, on the whole, of a transitory
nature; that is to say, it operates as long as the requesting
country has the means to attenuate or eliminate the balance of
payments deficit. Certain other financial and administrative
agreements between the central banks, through which they
establish special financial transfer mechanisms (such as
opening special accounts in the central banks, in order to
facilitate financial transactions with the outside, agreements on
correspondents, etc.). also serve this purpose. These
mechanisms have contributed to a lessening in the need to
maintain large stocks of international reserves and,
consequently, in reducing the need for international liquidity.

During this same period, the Sterling Area was a significant factor in the lessening of the need for international liquidity. This area was made up of the Commonwealth countries (excluding Canada, South Africa, Burma, Ireland, Bahrein and Kuwait). Commonwealth countries deposited their reserves in London, under whose umbrella they operated. This lowered the pressure for greater liquidity in relation to other currencies - dollars, in particular - and monetary gold; at the same time, commercial operations and financial conveyancing between them were simplified. At the end of the period, and in the face of the collapse of sterling as a unit of international reserve, the mechanism became virtually nonexistent.

The elements shown as sources of international liquidity had varying importance during the period, and this can be seen in the changes which occurred in the composition of international reserves. Briefly, it can be said that the role of monetary gold was still significant in the international monetary reserve stock, but its increase was four times slower that of the availability of foreign currencies. Monetary gold made up 72 percent of all international reserves in 1952 and only 52 percent in 1969. The reserves available from the IMF were of limited importance. The balance of payments deficits of the reserve centers, in particular the United States, remained at a reasonable level during most of the period, but from the mid-1960s onward the situation worsened. In turn, expansion in liquidity was uneven, as the increases in gold and currency reserves tended to be concentrated in the developed capitalist countries, with the exception of the United States where reserves started to fall after 1958(2) These changes reflect the importance of the different sources in the evolution of international liquidity in the period.

International reserves in foreign currency underwent changes: dollar holdings increased significantly, payments in sterling diminished, the yen, and the German mark and other European currencies started to consolidate their position as reserve currencies. This was reflected in how far these different currencies, which served as international reserves, were accepted as means of payment. Even though gold was the preferred means of payment (though not as a means of exchange), the dollar replaced gold as a source of liquidity. Immediately after World War II, the dollar fulfilled all the functions of gold; but from 1958 on and especially after 1961, continuous pressure on the dollar and growing fears of its devaluation increasingly lowered confidence in the dollar as a reserve asset. The reasons for this loss of confidence will be examined later. As the dollar weakened, other currencies grew stronger, since they had the support of quite dynamic economies with fast and sustained growth, and favorable balances of payments. With all this, it was not possible to

reconcile the power of the dollar with the power and magnitude
of the United States economy.

The expected devaluation of the dollar, together with the
persistent balance of payments deficits of the United States,
created a climate of mistrust in the dollar as a reserve asset.
On the other hand, the currencies which were strengthening
managed to fulfill the role of a reserve asset only in a very
small way. In fact, this meant that a lack of confidence began
to spread throughout the international monetary system,
despite repeated and prompt measures taken by the
international monetary authorities and the responsible
organizations of the countries with the greatest financial and
economic importance. Furthermore, some European countries
wished to convert their dollar holdings into gold, thus
worsening the growing instability in the international
monetary system, which still marks the situation today.

International liquidity and the instability of the international
monetary system

Since 1958, international liquidity has tended to move within
the framework of a highly unstable international monetary
system. In that year, as a reaction to the possible imminent
devaluation of sterling, financial pressures and speculation on
gold increased. Sterling was devalued by a small percentage
only, but even this was enough for agreements to be made
between the international financial authorities and the
authorities of the central banks of the main industrial
countries in order to neutralize imbalances and speculative
pressures. In 1961, heavy pressure was put on the dollar
once again as a result of a group of countries (mainly
European) converting much of their dollar holdings into gold.
This led to the creation of a "pool" of gold in order to
counteract gold speculation trends. This involved commitment
by the main industrial countries to bring their gold into any
market where pressure of the demand for gold could increase
its price in the free market in relation to its parity in the
United States (35 dollars per ounce). There followed a period
of relative stability which lasted until November 1967, when
Great Britain devalued the pound by 14.3 percent in order to
solve its balance of payments deficit problems. This resulted
in a new run on gold and an increase in the market price over
its international monetary vlaue of 35 dollars an ounce.

During the first few months of 1968, the United States,
partly as a result of its persistent balance of payments deficit,
committed itself to adopting a series of measures in order to
alleviate the deficit and create a relatively calm climate in the
international monetary system. Added to this there was a
compromise in the gold pool in order to split the gold market
into two parts: a strictly monetary market to be managed

through agreements between the central banks of the stronger
countries; and a system which would allow the value of gold to
float on the nonmonetary markets.

In August 1968, immediately after the social and political
tensions of May, France was forced to devalue the franc and it
fell from 4.93 to 5.53 francs to the dollar. In October 1969,
faced with a continuous balance of payments surplus, West
Germany agreed to revalue the mark by 9.29 percent. This
had been preceded by a significant run on the mark, which
had created great instability in the international monetary
system and, once again, new pressures on the price of gold.

The continuous tensions in the international monetary
system, which we have briefly outlined, were nothing but an
outward manifestation of a basic problem in its organization.
The established monetary system had had its raison d'etre and
full economic justification in 1944, when it was structured in
terms of the undisputed predominance of the United States
economy: the great quantity of gold deposits held in Fort Knox
and its consequent support for the dollar; the ease of its
trade balance and balance of payments at that time; and the
political and military strength which the United States held
immediately after the war.

However, from a theoretical viewpoint, the system was
intrinsically irrational. It resulted in increasing needs for
liquidity in the face of increases in trade flows; and, given
the relative stagnation in the production of gold, these needs
had to be satisfied by dollars. But if these dollars were to
remain as reserves at the disposal of central banks, for the
servicing of ever growing trade, a balance of payments deficit
in the United States economy was inevitable.

The continuing deficit in the United States balance of
payments resulted, in the long run, in an increasing lack of
confidence in the dollar since devaluation was the only means
of solving the balance of payments problems. Two
suppositions would have had to be made for this not to
happen: the amount of gold reserves in the United States must
be so great that the possibility of them running out would be
remote; and the rest of the world economies must be willing to
give credit to the American economy ad infinitum, and,
consequently, transfer real resources to this economy.
Doubtless the events of the last years have not supported
these suppositions.

This mechanism linked the international monetary system
to the chance variations in the economy of just one country.
This was nonsense, since that country had an overpowering
importance in the world economy. This link, therefore, turned
into one of the basic elements in the instability. In other
words, given the relative stagnation in the production of gold
and the growing needs for liquidity, it was necessary for
those countries whose currencies were reserve assets to have

balance of payments deficits. Now this same deficit, when it
becomes persistent, impels these countries to find measures to
correct it; and the devaluation of currency or the
implementation of economic policies which have a similar effect
play an important role in such measures, but immediately cause
lack of confidence in these currencies. In this way, the very
operation of the system is intrinsically unstable.

On the other hand, insofar as countries must keep dollars
in their central banks for their international liquidity needs,
de facto, this mechanism turns into a transfer of real
resources from these economies to the United States economy.
For example, suppose that the dollars held by some countries
in the vaults of their central banks come from a surplus in
their trade balance (which in real terms means that they
export more than they import), the difference which
results from an exchange of goods ultimately becomes a
transfer of real resources, from the countries which are
accumulating dollars, to the United States economy.

Suppose further, for argument's sake, that the dollars
accumulated in the central bank of a particular country X are
a result of American investment. In order for these dollars to
reach the central bank of this country X, they have had to be
exchanged for the use of real resources within that economy
(the payment of salaries or wages, contracting the construction
of buildings or factories, acquiring equipment or raw materials, etc.). If these dollars are kept as reserves, or not used
to acquire real resources from the United States by way of
imports, the result will be an indirect form of the transfer of
real resources. All this and more can happen if these dollars,
accumulated in the central bank, come from the acquisition by
American companies of shares in existing companies in country
X. In this case, this could lead to a transfer of patrimony
which, in some cases, could result in the transfer of decision
making from the country receiving dollars to the American
economy. In the case of loans given by the United States
which are used for the importation of goods from the United
States, an inverse situation occurs. The American economy
lends real resources which it can then retrieve by using the
financial resources which it receives when the debt and
interest are paid off. However, if loans are used for imports,
dollars do not serve as international reserves inasmuch as
their significance is reduced in the context of the situation
being analyzed.

We must stress that the kind of analysis we have been
pursuing is a formal oversimplification, since dollar stocks held
as international reserves by the monetary and exchange
authorities are, at any one time, the final result of a great
number of very complex financial and commercial transactions
in the outside world. We are only using this simplification to
describe some of the mechanisms involved in the transfer of

real resources by a country while it holds increasing stocks of
dollars as international reserves. The dollar commitments of
the United States abroad are enormous. Insofar as these
dollars do not revert to the United States economy in the form
of imports such as equipment, raw materials, or consumer
goods, and are unlikely to do so in the short or medium term,
it is reasonable to assume that all these financial and monetary
movements have resulted in a transfer of real resources from
the rest of the world to the economy of the United States.
Such a transfer has operated as a flow of "credits" made by
various countries to the Untied States economy. These credits
involve a lower "endorsement" or "guarantee," due to the loss
of dynamism of the United States economy, its replacement in
many markets by some European countries and Japan, and the
great reduction in its gold reserves. The backing and
economic might which the dollar had when the system was first
evolved is no longer there. Recently, a balancing effect has
begun with the purchase of real assets in the United States
by European and Japanese dollar holdings, an activity engaged
in especially by countries with an oil surplus.

At the end of the period being analyzed (1950-69), a
growing part of trade was being financed by mobile,
short-term loans and credit from the suppliers. This was yet
another element of instability in the international monetary
system. Already at that time the changes in the composition
of international reserves and the instability in the international
monetary system were pointing to the worsening of monetary
and exchange disturbances, which actually came about in the
1970s. One can see the changes in economic power relations
between the main developed countries and the limitations that
were put on the hegemony the United States had held after the
end of World War II. This crisis of hegemony is an essential
factor in the analysis of the prospects, possibilities, and
characteristics of a New International Economic Order. Just as
an example, it is interesting to note that in all the proposals
of the Trilateral Commission, the need is stated for the EEC
and Japan to "share responsibilities" in the contemporary
economy and society.

International Liquidity in the 1970s

In the 1970s, the creation of international liquidity has greatly
changed. Its expansion was significant, sources of liquidity
became diversified, and the official regulatory mechanisms were
undermined. Moreover, this has taken place within the
context of world inflation and a crisis in the international
monetary system.

The inherently unstable nature of the international
monetary system has shown itself in all its crudity during this

decade. In August 1971, the dollar broke its links with its
gold backing. Immediately, the main currencies were faced
with maladjustments in the exchange rate, giving rise to
increasingly generalized adoption of the "floating" system.
Proposals for the reform of the international monetary system
collapsed at the institutional level. On top of this came the
so-called energy crisis and the great surpluses in the oil
exporting countries. Inflation and recessions have occurred
together, thus destroying the old and well-established myths
of the traditional monetary theories. And it is in the areas of
the international economy and the monetary system that the
specific historical background of these changes is to be found.

Sources of liquidity

One must remember that the concept of international reserves
is only a partial indicator of the level of international
liquidity. During this period, the composition of international
reserves changed. Special Drawing Rights (SDRs) have
appeared with allocations being given to countries in relation
to their share holdings in the IMF. The bulk of allocation of
SDRs took place in 1970, 1971, and 1972 and there have been
hardly any more since then, thus frustrating the hopes which
had been built around them. Holdings in monetary gold have
increased only slightly (1.9 percent annually). Reserves in
the IMF also deteriorated between 1970 and 1973; but since
1974, these have increased in defense of the new forms of
unconditional credits which the IMF temporarily established.
Foreign currency holdings (which in 1970 made up 48 percent
of total reserves) reached 70 percent by 1975; from 1970 to
1975 the accumulative annual increase was 21.1 percent.
Tables 3.1 and 3.2 show the changes in composition of
international reserves between 1970 and 1975, as well as the
sources and beneficiaries of the creation of international
reserves.
        The widening of international reserves can be explained
basically by the increase in foreign currency holdings, which
was the main characteristic of the decade. With international
inflation and the popularity of the floating system, the
instability in the value of international reserves has taken
second place.
        The international monetary system is no longer a
generally accepted means of payment, and the system of fixing
the value of SDRs is only a sad attempt to rely on a basic
unit. These facts are the concrete manifestations of the crisis
in the international monetary system. The crisis, in turn, is
the result of a breakdown of the political and economic power
structure which had established the Bretton Woods monetary
system. Neither the EEC nor Japan have been able to impose
a new power and hegemony plan on the United States; nor has

Table 3.1. Structure of International Reserves*
(Millions of Dollars)

	1970	1971	1972	1973	1974	1975	Annual Growth Rate % 1970-1975
World Holdings**	41,095	44,520	44,745	49,670	50,355	48,090	2.6
International Financial Institutions	4,100	5,535	6,095	6,175	6,839	6,525	7.7
Country Holdings	36,995	38,985	38,650	42,955	43,525	41,565	1.9
International Reserves**	93,250	133,795	159,075	183,655	220,470	227,470	14.8
Gold	36,955	38,990	38,655	42,955	43,530	41,565	1.9
SDRs	3,124	6,378	9,431	10,624	10,845	10,259	19.8
Position in IMF	7,697	6,896	6,867	7,441	10,829	14,778	10.8
Foreign Exchange	45,434	81,534	104,125	122,633	155,266	160,867	21.1

*Includes gold holdings + SDRs reserve position in IMF + foreign exchange.
**Except socialist countries.

Source: United Nations Statistical Yearbook 1976.

Table 3.2. SOURCE AND BENEFICIARIES OF INTERNATIONAL RESERVE CREATION
1970–1974
(billion SDRs)

	World	Industrial Countries USA	Industrial Countries Other Countries	Total	Developing Countries Total	Developing Countries OPEC Countries	Developing Countries Other Countries
I. Surplus or deficit in the balance of payments (III-II)	0.3	- 66.2	22.5	- 43.7	44.0	33.6	10.4
II. Beneficiaries of credit reserve creation	99.6	62.4	34.0	96.4	3.2	0.2	2.9
A. Concerted reserve creation	7.3	1.2	2.8	4.2	3.2	0.2	2.9
1. SDR allocation	9.3	2.3	4.7	7.0	2.3	0.4	2.0
2. Net IMF lending	1.4	- 1.0	- 1.2	- 2.2	0.9	- 0.1	1.0
3. Net BIS-EF lending	- 0.6	---	- 0.6	- 0.6	---	---	---
B. Acceptance of national currencies as international reserves.	92.3	61.1	31.2	92.3	---	---	---
III. Gross reserves (I + II) at the end of 1969	99.9	- 3.9	56.5	52.7	47.2	33.9	13.3
1970	78.1	17.0	45.7	62.6	15.5	4.2	11.3
1971	92.4	14.5	60.0	74.5	18.0	5.0	13.0
1972	120.0	12.1	86.8	98.9	21.1	7.7	13.4
1973	145.6	12.1	104.7	116.8	28.8	10.0	18.8
1974	150.7	11.9	103.5	115.5	35.3	12.0	23.3
	178.0	13.1	102.2	115.3	62.7	38.1	24.6

Source: Jan Tinbergen, RIO. Reshaping the International Order (New York: Dutton, 1976), p. 201.

the United States been able to recapture the power it had at Bretton Woods. Until this problem is resolved, more international monetary problems will follow. In such an impasse, the underdeveloped countries, which have always stood by when monetary and financial decisions were taken, will be seriously affected.

The crisis in the international monetary system is a clear obstacle to the establishment of a NIEO; yet, to confront these obstacles from a Third World position, demands a drastic change of orientation in the thinking that pervades discussions in international forums. The breaking down of these obstacles to a NIEO is a question of power, and the Third World must find strategies based on alliances where power will play a part. The developed world and dominant countries should note that, at least on a theoretical level, underdeveloped and dependent countries have moved from simple awareness to critical awareness in identifying problems and their causes.

On the other hand, the crisis in the international monetary system has accentuated the asymmetrical character of international economic relations, and placed a particular seal on the expansion of international liquidity. On an international monetary and financial level, this asymmetry is shown by the fact that the main beneficiaries of the creation of new international reserves have been the industrial countries, inasmuch as underdeveloped countries can only attain the international liquidity needs (currency) at the cost of an enormous foreign debt, which increases their dependence and puts their future international monetary surpluses in jeopardy.(3)

The monetary crisis created specific conditions for the expansion of international monetary liquidity on the sidelines of the rules of international monetary and financial institutionalism. International liquidity outside the official circles (national and international) is ever increasing, and the sources of growth mechanisms of international liquidity originating from the private sector have diversified. This leads to a pattern of excess in international liquidity over which official control is very restricted. New unconventional sources of international liquidity, which have appeared and developed during this phase in the world economy, are being added to traditional sources. We will try to describe this process below.

Diversification of sources

The 1970s, thought of as a transition period toward a new type of accumulation or toward a new international division of labor, have shown special manifestations in the international monetary and financial sphere. Greater internationalization and privatization of capital have resulted in a transfer of surpluses

to the financial sphere for revaluation, a process that has
tended to be accentuated as the crisis continues. This has
generated marked expansion in liquidity through continued
growth and diversification of unconventional sources of
international liquidity. The crisis in the monetary system,
world inflation, and the hegemony crisis at an international
level have created favorable conditions for marked expansion
and a greater importance for financial capital of private origin.
We will analyze these mechanisms in brief, in order to identify
the different expansion channels of international liquidity.

The euro-currency market. Since the middle of the 1960s,
and particularly in the 1970s, the inflationary participation of
private banks in international financial trends has attained new
heights. They operate through the euro-currency market, a
market that has remained outside the control of the monetary
authorities of the EEC, Japan, the United States, and the IMF
itself. The marked expansion of this market can be seen in
its evolution: in 1965 its operating level reached 15 billion
dollars; by 1969 this had risen to 44 billion; by 1973 to 132
billion; and estimates for 1976 are around 250 billion.
        The figures speak for themselves. This expansion of
international liquidity through the operations of the
euro-currency has led to a greater economic and patrimonial
concentration, with a more decisive role being played by the
most important banks in the United States. It has also led to
the Third World becoming the largest user of these resources.
At present, more than half of the external loans to
underdeveloped countries are of private origin. It becomes
clear that private international banks take the initiative in the
distribution of the aforementioned credits. Robert Derlin
wrote: "foreign bankers would want to give us money even
before we ask for it. The Italians have Liras for our dam;
the French have Francs for our steel factory."(4) In 1970, 75
percent of profit originated in activities undertaken abroad.
"Privatization" and "internationalization" are, thus, prere-
quisities for a widening in the operating level of the market.
This magnitude of loans is only possible with a very high
banking multiplier not under the control of the monetary
authorities; and this entails an accelerated creation of international money; that is to say, a significant increase in the
level of international liquidity.
        The national and international monetary authorities, faced
with the inability to effectively control limitations in the expansion of the euro-currency market, have attempted to impose
tighter controls on the underdeveloped countries that are the
main users of this market. To this end, a strengthening of
the IMF and other official multilateral financial organizations
has been suggested, and one of the ways of achieving it is to
increase sharply their operational capital in order to raise the

level of credits that may be offered to underdeveloped countries. This, again, implies an increase in international
liquidity originating from official sources.

Increase in the level of operations of the multilateral financial
organizations. The IMF has never been able to operate
exactly like the World Bank, with functions and powers to
impose rules upon all the participants in the monetary and
financial relations. Initially, it was an instrument of
domination (first for the United States and then for the
"Group of Ten,"(5)), over the rest of the world's economies.
It was incapable of neutralizing the financial expansion of
private international banks and of balancing the sharp asym-
metries in the international economy. It was not able, nor is
it now, to force upon the United States its classic policies of
adjustment for countries with a balance of payments deficit.
Neither has it put pressure on the developed capitalistic countries with surpluses, in order to force them to reduce the
asymmetry in trade and capital flows.

It has exercised power over those who are not their own
masters - the underdeveloped countries. It has become a good
watchdog in forcing these countries to adopt a financial
discipline which entitles them to credits as responsible debtors
in their international financial obligations. Its praises and
condemnations, the "congratulations" or "damnations" through
its publications, are key aspects of the different treatment
accorded the underdeveloped countries by the international
financial community.

The inability of the IMF to limit international monetary
expansion of private origin, and the direction this takes
toward underdeveloped countries, has led to an increase in
loanable resources. In fact, agreement has been reached to
increase its quota by 33 percent (which amounts to a little
over ten billion dollars). This increase in quotas will enable
the IMF to raise its level of operations, yet, at the same time,
it implies an increase in international liquidity. The paradox
is that, in seeking to stop monetary expansion and the
increase in international liquidity, the IMF is unable to control
the private sources of this monetary expansion; the increase in
its own loanable resources is, thus, creating more international
liquidity.

The World Bank and the regional banks have also
increased their loan resources, generating additional sources of
international liquidity. In Latin America, near the end of
1978, a meeting of the governors of the Interamerican
Development Bank (IDB) recommended an increase of around
ten billion dollars in their resources. This will bring the
resources of the IDB up to thirty billion dollars. All in all, in
the last few years, the international financial institutions have
turned into sources of expansion in international monetary
liquidity.

The recycling of petrodollars.   From the large increase in oil
prices   at   the   end   of   1973   to   1976,   the   OPEC   countries
accumulated   a   surplus   in   their   current   account   reaching
approximately   145   billion   dollars.   These   surpluses
(petrodollars)   were   deposited   in   private   banks   in   the   United
States and Europe, thus placing these banks in a key position
to control their recycling.
      The large proportion of oil surpluses being deposited in
private   banks   to   a   great   extent   explains   the   vast   expansion   of
the euro-currency market.   This expansion has been, in turn,
one   of   the   sources   of   increased   international   liquidity   of
private origin.
      It   can   be   seen   that   the   channeling   of   petrodollars   into
private   banks   and   the   resulting   excess   in   liquidity   are   the
products of a monetary system in crisis, multilateral financial
institutions which are controlled by only a few countries, and
the   process   of   privatization   and   internationalization   of   the
capital circulation cycles.   This point of view is different from
the   approach   that   blames   the   OPEC   countries   for   the   general
economic   crisis   and   the   international   monetary   and   exchange
disorders.   In any case, the euro-currency market had already
vastly increased its level of operations between 1965 and 1973,
before   the   rise   in   the   price   of   oil.   The   depositing   of   oil
surpluses may have speeded up this process, but it did not
create it.   The   same   can   be   said   about   the   international
monetary and economic crises.
      It has been estimated that the current account surpluses
of the OPEC countries have reached an annual average of 45
billion   dollars   since   1974,   and   it   is   generally   estimated   that
this   annual   average   will   remain   around   40   billion   dollars   for
some   years   to   come.(6)   It   is   also   estimated   that   the
recirculation   process   of   these   surpluses   will   continue   to   be
handled   by   private   banks,   and   that   the   prospects   for   the
euro-currency   market   are   rather   good.   This   implies   that
excess   liquidity   is   certain   to   continue,   thus   perpetuating
instability in the international monetary and exchange systems.

The European monetary system.   The   crisis   of   hegemony
which is seen in the crisis of the international monetary system
led   to   a   decision   taken   by   the   EEC   (with   Great   Britain
abstaining)   to   establish,   from   the   beginning   of   1979,   a
European Monetary System.   This system will be based on a
common   adjustment   mechanism   in   order   to   ensure   a   certain
stability in the parities among European currencies, sheltered
from the fluctuations of the dollar.
      At   this   point   in   time,   it   is   difficult   to   foresee   the
economic and monetary repercussions the joint action will have.
One can say, however, that the implementation and perfecting
of its operation mechanisms will tend to channel some financial
and   monetary   operations   into   the   system   and,   in   this   way,

decrease the need of its participants for other sources of monetary liquidity. If this does happen, the new system will become, indirectly, a new source of excess international monetary liquidity.

Special drawing rights. The allocation of Special Drawing Rights (SDRs) is a source of international liquidity; countries consider SDRs as part of their international reserves. The hopes which heralded the introduction of SDRs were dashed. The bulk of them were issued between 1970 and 1972 and prospects for new allocation of SDRs is fairly remote.

The United States failed in its attempt to transfer the dollar holdings of other countries into SDRs. It is likely that this was due to the fact that, whereas SDRs were paraded as being the seeds of a future world currency, their way of operating left all decisions in the hands of the IMF authorities regarding which countries were to receive SDRs and those who should reconstitute their holdings. Matters such as the voting system for the election of officials and, in fact, the whole power structure within the Fund do not reflect properly the power relations in the world economy; and it is likely that the more generalized use of a mechanism such as the SDRs as a source of international liquidity will encounter strong resistance. The prospect of their being used in the financing of development, as suggested by the NIEO, are even more remote.

Nonetheless, the future development of SDRs will have to be carefully watched as the Trilateral Commission maintains that a new international monetary system would have to give preference to SDRs over other reserve assets.(7)

Other possible sources. The continuing surplus in the current accounts of some European countries and Japan in their trade relations with the Third World has led to an increase in the mass of international reserves held by these countries. If the world economy cannot recover from its recession, part of the currency surpluses will tend to be channeled into the financial circuit, so that they do not remain idle. As financial trends are becoming increasingly private and international, and as the trade surplus of these countries implies a deficit in others (particularly in the Third World), which will have to be financed, the process described can be seen as another source of international liquidity.

We must also refer to the fluctuations in the gold market. The Gold Standard is already a chapter in monetary history. Gold is continually losing its place in the composition of international reserves; many important decisions taken by the monetary authorities have tended to demonetize gold (sales by the IMF, the creation of SDRs, the break of gold's link with the dollar and the SDRs, the floating of the dollar, etc.). If

instability in the exchange system and the monetary crisis
persist, gold will become a more "noble" reserve asset than the
other currencies which, at present, fulfill the function. This
position will be reinforced, if gold maintains or increases its
present price. If so, and despite the efforts being made by
the monetary authorities, gold could well regain its position as
an international currency. This, again, would be a further
new source of international liquidity.

Conclusions

Traditional sources of international liquidity, together with the
new ones, make up a pattern of excess liquidity which is likely
to continue. One must question the capacity of the IMF and
the monetary authorities of the main industrial countries to
arrest or at least regulate this large creation of liquidity.
The financial community will continue to give loans to the
Third World, which will become increasingly risky, given the
levels reached by foreign debt, the services of direct foreign
investment, and the trade deficit. This great availability of
credit will be accompanied by pressures for the imposition of
stricter conditions for countries receiving loans, these being,
of course, the underdeveloped and dependent countries. It is
not only the multilateral financial organizations, but also the
private banks who operate as creditors for these countries,
who are, on the one hand, interested in lending and, on the
other, pushing for stricter borrowing conditions. These
conditions refer to "suggestions" that borrowing countries
should adopt "adequate" policies to control their balance of
payments deficits in order to meet the currency commitments of
a large part of their debts.
        The organization responsible for imposing such conditions
is the IMF. Its presence, experience, and importance in
underdeveloped countries has given it a relevant role in seeing
that the recognized policies of "financial discipline" are
adopted. It is logical to expect that both the Group of Ten
and the private international banks will see fit to give the IMF
greater disciplinary powers in order to impose stricter control.
This would accentuate what is euphemistically called "the
asymmetric behavior of the IMF." It would tend to lose control
over industrial countries and their private banks, at the time
when its role of "watchdog" of the policies of underdeveloped
countries will become more evident, since the fund will take
action on behalf of the interests of the Group of Ten, the
international private banks, and some "donating" countries of
OPEC. In this context, the developing countries would have
to devise a new strategy vis-a-vis external financing.

International Liquidity for Developing Countries

Sources of liquidity

Despite efforts to demonetize it, gold is actually becoming one of the most acceptable forms of payment. Among foreign currencies, there will be those which, depending on the economic power and financial position of the countries supporting them, will be more or less acceptable in the commercial and financial international markets. The same thing happens with regard to a country's right to credit or loans, which can be considered as part of international reserves. Some credit, be it commercial or the loan rights from the IMF, provide rapid liquidity. In order to know the level of liquidity of each of these financial assets, one will have to examine their characterisitics and the conditions under which they are granted. The use of SDRs depends on the level of holdings in relation to the amount assigned to a country, and its balance of payments situation. Although SDRs are included in the reserves of some countries, their use is conditioned, and they are not reserve assets of rapid liquidity.

Liquidity needs

It is difficult to determine with any precision the actual amount of liquidity required by a country to finance its trade and currency needs. In many specialized analyses, the problem of international liquidity for a single country is presented only in relation to the level of trade and its fluctuations; or else, the reserve requirements of a country are defined in terms of pragmatic criteria of an arbitrary nature, for example, when it is established that a country must have a minimum level of reserves sufficient to finance three months of imports. The issue should be reexamined in relation to the acute financial problems which underdeveloped countries are facing at the present time. Persistent trade deficits, unusual growth in foreign debt, and the increasing weight of direct foreign investment all increase the need for liquidity in these countries.

Liquidity requirements, types of foreign trade, and the characteristics of the foreign exchange system.

A part of a country's liquidity requirements will depend on the volume of trade and its fluctuations. The greater the fluctuations, the greater the need for liquidity. Some of the characteristics and types of exchange (for example, medium and long-term trade agreements, with detailed programs regarding dates, prices, volume, and payment methods in the settlement of exchange) could allow for greater security and precision in currency estimates and, consequently, reduce liquidity requirements.

However, one must appreciate the repercussions of the
different exchange systems on liquidity requirements. To
understand this, one must analyze the links between
commercial, exchange, and financial policies. A fixed
exchange rate with different tariffs and subsidies for certain
types of imports and exports is a sort of multiple exchange.
In the same way, a free exchange rate (to which the monetary
authorities would allow certain narrow variations) will be able
to demand a considerable mass of currency liquidity so that
this exchange rate does not go beyond these margins,
depending on the economic and financial situation of the
country. Moreover, in the case of a country of limited
importance in the international market, the analysis becomes
more complex, in that any changes in the financial and
currency situation of other countries may significantly
influence its reserve and exchange rate, making the country's
liquidity requirements react quickly to external factors. If
one adds to this the great mass of speculative capital which is
moved from one country to another as a result of the
privatization and internationalization of capital, the analysis
becomes even more complex as it is difficult to predict the
actions and behavior of the financial power centers.

Theoretical estimates, based on many simplified
assumptions, become increasingly removed from reality and
cannot shed any light on the problem or serve as a reasonable
guide for practical action. For example, according to the
neoclassical theory on international trade, the operation of a
totally free fluctuating exchange rate system would slightly
reduce liquidity requirements; a contrario sensu, a multiple
exchange rate system would result in an increase in liquidity
requirements. Before the general adoption of the floatation
system, neither fluctuating nor multiple exchange rate systems
existed in most countries. On the contrary, exchange rates
were fixed, a certain tolerance existed for variation, and
exchange rates adjusted themselves in time. In such
circumstances, an additional quantity of reserves was needed
in order to maintain exchange rates at a level, and within
margins, with economic policies in general, and exchange
policies in particular. Now, when the exchange rate is
unstable or when devaluation is likely, greater quantitites of
currency are needed to maintain the exchange rate and vice
versa. If we wish to examine the relationship between
international liquidity and the rate of exchange, we must
analyze the economic and financial situation of the country.
Consequently, it is a difficult task to adjust liquidity
requirements in terms of modifications in the exchange
situation.

The structural features of commercial exchange of Third
World countries are well defined. This results in what
ECLA calls a trend toward external disequilibrium, a result of

dependent countries being inserted into the system of the
international division of labor. This phenomenon can be seen
in the exchange of raw materials and manufactured food
produce, in the deterioration of terms of trade, and in the
ever decreasing participation of the Third World in the
expansion of world trade. If one adds the fact that these
countries do not have adequate commercial infrastructures or
services to go hand in hand with commercial trade (merchant
navy, insurance companies for foreign trade financing of
exports, etc.), and the multinational corporations' practice of
overcharging on imports and undercharging on exports, it is
possible to perceive all the various factors that contribute to
trade deficits in these countries. Since the deficits must be
financed, higher reserve levels are needed.

Liquidity requirements and foreign capital services. The
need to depend on a set level of international reserves arises
not only from foreign trade of underdeveloped countries, it
also derives from the characteristics of the movement of
foreign capital. The greater the financial commitments with
the outside world, the greater the liquidity requirements.
However, one must not confuse the volume of foreign financial
commitments in one period with the average stocks of
currencies which must be held in reserve (liquidity) to meet
these commitments. In this respect, we suggest as a
hypothesis that, given the dependent nature of the Latin
American economies, a growing financial burden will emerge as
a result of the various services of foreign capital
(amortization, interest and other financial costs of the loans,
remittance of profits, interests and royalties which are the
financial counterpart of direct foreign investment and the sale
of patents, licenses and trade marks). To this burden must
be added the debts which arise from growing foreign financing
of many activities in the public sector. All these elements
increase the currency demands and put the balance of
payments under acute pressure, which, in turn, leads to
growing foreign debt. The total of foreign financial
commitments which generate debt, the trade deficit, and the
growing presence of foreign capital in these economies create
new needs for foreign credit, which, in turn, increase
financial commitments, leading to what is known as a spiral or
vicious circle of foreign debt. This process generates growing
currency needs, which will also lead to increased international
liquidity. Therefore, the characteristics and trends of the
movement of noncompensatory capital play a significant role in
the international liquidity requirements of underdeveloped
countries.

INTERNATIONAL FINANCING OF DEVELOPMENT

The Concept of IFD

We will understand by International Financing of Development (IFD) a flow of surpluses or foreign saving, directed toward giving financial support to investment programs which sustain a policy of development, and foreign resourses which are channeled toward increasing social programs necessary to such development policies. This implies the adoption of restrictive criteria in defining of the concept of IFD. Consequently, short-term loans, credit from suppliers and other similar credits (of the EXIM-BANK type), and direct private foreign investment are excluded from this concept. Short-term balance of payments loans and credit from suppliers are not taken into consideration because they are not directly linked to the development policies, and are generally used to replenish reserves or to finance commercially certain imports. These headings are registered in the balance of payments as compensatory financing. It is short-term foreign financing whose net effect is hardly significant in the medium term.

The exclusion of direct private investment as an element of IFD is a prerequisite for demystification and honesty. The perception of the role of foreign investment in underdeveloped countries has suffered irreversible changes. Once a first phase of clear apologetic spirit (in which foreign investment was considered to be foreign aid) was over, a second phase began in which foreign investment (hoped for and often begged for) was seen as a necessary support for development policies.

Today, Latin American economic thinking, which is becoming increasingly clear and is supported by a whole range of empirical studies, is seriously questioning the different economic and financial repercussions of unrestricted access for foreign investment. This access implied putting a particular stamp on the accumulation pattern in our countries; or, in other words, influencing decisively a new "style" or model of development which aggravated the dependent and excluding nature of Latin American economies. In the financial area, it resulted in growth in external services, which is one of the elements that explain the increasing size of foreign debt. This new view of foreign investment, which implies a move from primitive to critical and objective awareness, must not be lumped together with rigid nationalism nor seen as a systematic objection and opposition to foreign investment. It should only be a means of objectively assessing reality in order to evolve policies on foreign investment capable of defining and negotiating adequately its aims and limitations.

The difference between the net contribution in direct investment from the United States and the remittance of profits to that country by Latin America was negative to the tune of 6.7 billion dollars in the 1960-68 period.(8) The gap tended to widen in the 1970s. In fact, from 1970 to 1975, foreign companies in Latin America repatriated profits at an average annual rate of 3.3 billion dollars, while in the same period, the flow of net direct foreign investment reached an annual average of 1.1 billion dollars.(9) Consequently, the difference between capital flows in that period was a negative balance of 12.8 billion dollars. This is because a great part of profits transferred abroad does not correspond to the results in activities of capital brought in from the outside, but rather to the surpluses generated in the Latin American countries themselves (reinvestment of profit) to which other local capital was added, mobilized, or channeled by foreign companies.(10)

These figures show that, if we were to consider foreign investment as an important element in IFD, we would have a contradiction in terms. One could maintain that, given the trends in Latin America, foreign investment would be an international "definancing" element of development, maybe necessary at times, but ultimately negative.

Alternative Approaches

Once we have defined the factors included or excluded from IFD, it is necessary to single out the analytical perspectives about IFD.

The attitude of credit giving countries and, to some extent, the view of the main multilateral financial organizations is to consider all export of capital to be aid or a contribution to the development of Third World countries.

Discussions in certain specialized UN agencies, (UNCTAD, UNIDO, ECLA, etc.) and in other international forums have forced the industrial and the underdeveloped countries to confront each other. In these meetings it is often proposed to enlarge IFD, searching for agreements between debtors and creditors. The limited success, at a speculative level, of these efforts has depended on a minimal consensus on certain abstract objectives of a moral nature (equity, freedom, democracy and participation, solidarity, the eradication of poverty, etc.), or on abstract common interests. Many proposals about IFD in the context of the New International Economic Order share this approach, hence their intrinsic weakness.

"Styles" of Development and Financing Schemes

IFD must be conceived as a part of the global plan to finance the new development strategies which Third World countries need. Different "styles" or models of development lead to or lean upon different external financing. In the last two decades, a good number of Latin American countries have strengthened a pattern of dependent accumulation, which tends to be supported more and more by various sources of international finance. Results have not been very positive: a widening of the trade gap, disequilibria in the balance of payments, growing external debt of both private and official origin, increases in the charge on debts, deficits in the public sector, which once again have to be paid for with external credit, and so on.

At least in its financial aspects, such a process reached its limits in some countries in the region leaving two alternatives: either change the "style" or model of development, or adjust the said model with traditional stabilizing policies. The deficit in the balance of payments being the worst pitfall, a change in the model would imply very different schemes from those prevailing in matters of external financing. But in contrast to these needs, the international financial system (both private and public) has continued to adopt old criteria for readjustment by means of stabilizing policies. One must ask oneself whether these well known stabilization policies are an inescapable necessity for all processes of adjustment, or whether they are inherent to the style or model of dependent development which had been adopted by many of our countries. In this chapter, the latter thesis is maintained. From this stems the need to find new roads in development policies, and readapt the policies of international external financing.

PRELIMINARY BASIS FOR IFD STRATEGY
FOR THIRD WORLD COUNTRIES

When thinking of a new, just economic and social order, one concludes there is a need for new development strategies. Underlying this is the idea that the new development policies would have to have different aims from the exisitng ones and, consequently, fresh means of achieving them. In other words, the strategies would imply changing the model or style of development; in the economic area, this would mean a change in the capital accumulation pattern.

As Latin America is one of the Third World regions which is most advanced in its interpretation of the development process, it is well placed to indicate which would be the basic ingredients of a new development strategy. Within this, it could put forward its own views on strategies for the International Financing of Development (IFD).

Latin American economic thinking has made significant advances in the understanding of its own reality. Independent from the analytical, conceptual, and ideological differences of the two main theories (the structuralist approach and the "dependency" viewpoint), the dependent and excluding nature of the workings of the region's economies are at the base of any interpretation. This is what explains underdevelopment. If this appraisal is correct, development strategies or policies will have to be based on objectives of liberation and participation. If these are the objectives, and without them secondary aims could not be reached, we must conclude that such aims should also be the nucleus of the IFD strategies. In this context, a two pronged action is required in order to attain these goals: a foreign policy leading to coherent positions in international relations, and internal policies that clearly define the role of external financing.

Foreign Policies On International Financing

The Third World has become conscious that international monetary and financial relations have adverse effects on it, and that it is, therefore, necessary to move into a direction where the system would take into account the interests and needs of the Third World. The understanding is not quite so good, however, regarding concrete proposals backed up by united action and studies of the power relations which define the structure and workings of the international monetary and financial system. In terms of results, so far there has been little success and adverse conditions persist.

In the complex international financial relations the Third World has played a passive role. The governments and monetary authorities of the main industrial countries (the Group of Ten) establish the policies, reach agreements, and take decisions, while the Third World countries are mere observers. On the other hand, the multinational corporations establish their own strategies for the accumulation of capital, in which the Thrid World is seen as a provider of natural resources, with a surplus of cheap labor and an internal market for the expansion of production. This causes serious economic and financial repercussions in that the responsibility of the Third World is virtually nil, even though it must suffer the consequences.

The complexities of the balance of power at an international level and the dependent nature of Third World participation is such that it requires great imagination and conviction to define general outlines and concrete proposals for the shaping of foreign policies regarding external financing.

Internal Policies Regarding IFD

Internal policies on foreign financing should adjust themselves to the aims of development policies. This means that,
as a first step towards the formulation of an IFD policy compatible with development policies, an interpretation and
diagnosis of underdevelopment must find an explanation to why
developing countries fall into spiraling foreign debt.

When explaining the external debt of underdeveloped
countries, the main reasons to be taken into account are: a
tendency to foreign trade disequilibrium, the recent pattern of
industrialization where multinational corporations are the main
actors, the financial behavior of the public sector in the
current "style" or model of development, and the absence of
any strategy for external financing.

In the light of a more precise explanation of the causes of
foreign debt, we can understand the difficulties involved in
the formulation of a strategy for external financing in keeping
with development strategies aimed at changing the exisitng
pattern of accumulation; that is to say, a policy of liberation
and participation for those sectors so far excluded from the
development model.

A part of the exisitng foreign debt in developing countries cannot be justified either economically or financially. In
fact, not all credit or increase in foreign debt has a positive
or expansive effect on Third World economies. Higher levels
of debt and direct foreign investment can only be justified in
very specific areas and in the context of increased exports
income and improvement in the terms and conditions of foreign
debt. Only in this way will it be possible to meet the financial
obligations of foreign debt, without depressing the need for
large scale development imports and without falling into
recession measures as the only way of adjusting the disequilibrium in the balance of payments.

NOTES

(1)   Carlos Massad, "Liquidez Internacional Total: Evaluacion
      Economica y Consecuencias de Politica," mimeographed,
      August 1972.
(2)   International Financial Statistics, 1953 to 1969.
(3)   See Pedro Paz, "Causas del endeudamiento de los paises
      del Tercer Mundo," Investigacion Economica 37, no. 143:
      205-30.
(4)   Robert Derlin, "Financiamiento externo y los bancos
      comerciales," Revista de la CEPAL 1 (1978): 88.
(5)   The "Group of Ten" includes Belgium, Canada, France,
      The Federal Republic of Germany, Great Britain, Italy,
      Japan, the Netherlands, Sweden, and the United States.

(6)   David Dollock and Carlos Massad, "El fondo monetario
      internacional en una nueva constelacion financiera inter-
      nacional: comentario interpretativo," Revista de la CEPAL
      1 (1978): 238.
(7)   "Towards a Renewed International Monetary System,"
      Report by the Trilateral Monetary Group in CIDE,
      Cuadernos Semestrales, no. 2-3 (1978), pp. 321-28.
(8)   CEPAL, Estudio Economico de America Latina, 1970.
(9)   Ibid., 1975.
(10) Anibal Pinto maintains that the participation of indige-
      nous funds and other local funds in total investment of
      American subsidiaries rose from 67 percent in 1957-59 to
      91 percent in 1963-65 (Inflacion: raices estructurales,
      Mexico: Fondo de Cultura Economica, 1973).

4 Special Drawing Rights and Development Assistance
V.K.R.V. Rao

Special Drawing Rights (SDRs) were first conceived during the early 1960s when countries were finding it difficult to add to their gold reserves. At the same time, increasing dependence on US dollars as a major reserve asset was also causing concern. This was how the problem of liquidity came to the front in international monetary circles during the early 1960s, when it mainly concerned the industrial countries that accounted for nearly 75 percent of the world trade. The capacity of these nations to protect their domestic economy against the impact of temporary payments imbalances could not be assured by drawing on the IMF, partly because of the magnitude of their imbalances and partly because they did not like the attached inquisitions and conditions that offended their dignity as major industrial powers. A search was then made to find some way of increasing liquidity for the developed countries outside the existing framework of conditionality.

It was natural at that time, that this quest was confined to the industrially developed members of the IMF and that the developing countries were not brought into the picture. The international agreement on SDRs was the result of discussions and negotiations mainly in the Group of Ten and in the Fund. As mentioned by Joseph Gold, "at one stage, four joint sessions were held of Executive Directors of the Fund and the Deputies of the Ministers and Central Bank Governors of the Group of Ten. Drafting of the outline and later the amendment of the Articles which was based on the outline was undertaken in the Fund."(1) Switzerland was also involved in the discussions through its Central Bank, namely, Svereiges Riksbank. Gold points out that

> the debates on the international monetary system in
> the 1960s led to the conviction that, sooner or later,

it would be necessary for a variety of reasons, to have the means to augment the liquidity that would be unconditionally and automatically available to members of the Fund. Members could not rely on the traditional reserve assets of gold and reserve currencies, and they should not rely on the reserve currencies to provide sufficient liquidity of this kind to ensure a satisfactory expansion of international economic activity.(2)

It was felt that additional liquidity of this kind should be provided by or through the IMF but without the conditionality attached to regular drawings. This could have been done by a special increase in quotas financed by national or convertible currencies contributed by the members and operated by special drawings that did not have to be subject to conditions applicable to normal drawings from the reserve tranches. But the discussion showed some preference for a type of international liquidity that would be based on national guarantees of acceptance rather than on a mobilization of real resources (thus returning to some of the ideas recurrent at Bretton Woods and subsequently in the proposals of some monetary economists), but retain the concept of international regulation. This was how, eventually, the concept of Special Drawing Rights emerged and they have become an international unit in which all reserves – both national and IMF – as well as monetary transactions are now expressed.

Eventually, it was decided to extend the facility to all members of the Fund including the developing countries. This decision was based not so much on securing the acceptance by all members of the Fund of the necessary amendment to its Articles of Association, but on the fact that the bulk of the benefits arising from the proposed new facility would accrue to the major industrial countries because of the principle accepted for the distribution of SDRs, namely pro rata with their IMF quotas. Their volumes, additions, and cancellations were also to be determined by voting based on IMF quotas. Thus, both the volume and distribution of SDRs were under the firm control of the major industrial countries, a fact that could not be upset by the developing countries, even if they acted as a collective group. As a further safeguard against possible pressures by industrial countries with recurring balance of payments problems to increase the volume of SDRs, the amendment included the provision that allocations or cancellations would be based only on long-term global needs for supplementing existing reserve assets, and that they would not give rise to either excess demand and inflation, or deflation and world economic stagnation. Global liquidity was, thus, made the cornerstone of this new supplement to existing reserve assets, the initiative for proposing new

allocations (or, cancellations) being left to the Managing
Director, after prior consultations with members to establish
that there was broad support among them for the proposal,
and with the concurrence of the Executive Board.

SDRs were to be operated by an ad hoc department in the
Fund. All allocations were to be credited to participating
members and withdrawals or receipts debited or credited to
their individual accounts. All participants undertook the
obligation to give convertible (later called freely usable)
currencies in exchange for SDRs received from other members
in an amount double their allocations when requested to do so
by the Fund. Participants had a right to ask the Fund to
designate a transferee, and the Fund had a duty to do so to
enable the participant to use its Special Drawing Rights.
Interest was paid to the participants whose holdings exceeded
their allocation and paid by the participants whose holdings
fell below their allocations. While there was a ceiling on the
SDR holdings that designated participants were required to
honor, there was also a floor on the SDRs that participants
could use since they had to reconstitute their holdings by 30
percent in case their actual drawings took their holdings below
the floor.

Thus, while SDRs in some way represented an international currency that could be freely used for settling balance
of payments commitments without being subject to consultations
with and conditions imposed by the Fund, and for getting
allocation which did not require any parting of real resources,
the rules governing their creation and use provided ample
safeguards against both global inflation (or deflation) and
individual extravagances or hardships.

Unlike money which earns no interest for its holders,
SDRs give interest when an individual participant's holdings
exceed its allocations, while a premium has to be paid when it
falls below allocations. Again unlike money, there is a ceiling
on its acceptance as legal tender by the designated participant
who is to receive it, and it cannot be used to get convertible
currency from participants other than the ones designated by
the Fund. At the same time, though subject to payment and
receipt of interest, it is not a credit facility; the participant
who receives SDRs and gives convertible currency in return
does not select his partner in this exchange, nor does he lay
down any conditions regarding the admissibility of the
exchange or the purpose for which it will be used. Thus,
SDRs constitute a unique instrument for settling balance of
payments commitments. It is neither international money nor
a credit facility in the accepted sense. It differs from credit
tranche drawings from the IMF insofar as there is no
conditionality attached and no real resources that have to be
surrendered to the Fund in order to get the right for
drawings, and no repayment is to be made except to the

limited extent of reconstitution of individual holdings to a prescribed minimum.

As already pointed out, the developing countries came into the picture only on grounds of universality, and not with a view to giving them the right to receive real resources for their developmental requirements. There was, thus, no question of SDRs being treated as a form of development assistance in the initial thinking of those who brought this facility into existence. There was, however, one essential feature of the SDR which was bound to raise questions about the nature of the assistance it gave in meeting the problem of liquidity and balance of payments adjustment which differed fundamentally from the adjustment assistance previously given by the Fund (apart from the adjustment facilities by way of reserve assets built by individual countries from their own resources). This was the absence of conditionality about the use of drawing rights on IMF resources. Drawing rights on the IMF were based on quotas which corresponded to a transfer of real resources to the Fund by its members (25 percent in gold and the rest in its own currency usable by the Fund for its operations); in the case of Special Drawing Rights, there were no such transfers of real resources to the Fund. Special Drawing Rights were, thus, not only unconditional and automatic as distinguished from credit tranche drawing rights; they were also free to the drawer, as they did not involve any transfer of real resources to the Fund. SDRs represented a fiduciary element in adjustment payments and constituted, therefore, a kind of assistance more akin to ODA than temporary and repayable credit facilities. But they were alloted to members not on equity considerations in global development, but on the basis of their IMF quotas (related to importance in world trade) and represented a system of global development. They are under growing attack on the grounds that they endorse and perpetuate an inequitable international economic order.

To suggest, as some distinguished Western economists have done, that allocation of SDRs on the basis of IMF quotas permits a neutral distribution of SDR seigniorage assumes that the initial distribution of world income among different countries at the time the quotas were determined was optimal. Not only is this far from true, in fact, the distributional pattern among developed and developing nations has since become worse. Once the nature of the assistance given by the SDRs to IMF members became clearer and as world concern at the extent of inequity and injustice in international economic relations became greater and more articulate and pressure for ODA increased, it was only to be expected that a demand should arise for reconsidering the accepted basis for the allocation of SDRs among IMF members.

The amendment of the Articles of Agreement of the IMF took effect on July 28, 1969, and SDRs came into being on August 6, 1969. The Board of Governors decided at their October meeting of that year that a total of SDRs equivalent to approximately 9.5 billion US dollars would be allocated during the period of three years beginning on January 1, 1970. Allocations were made on January 1, 1970, 1971, and 1972 for 3.414 billion, 2.949 billion, and 2.952 billion units respectively. The bulk of the SDR allocations went to the industrial countries and not to the Third World, as they were distributed pro rata according to the member countries' original quota of the IMF.

When the SDR scheme was first formulated and brought into operation, the basic idea behind it was that it would serve only as an additional resource asset for increasing global liquidity, though it offered the special advantage of unconditionality and did not require surrender of real resources. But the situation changed dramatically when the dollar was delinked from gold in August 1971. The global currency crisis that ensued brought together the Group of Ten, and the Smithsonian Agreement reached in Washington at the close of the year attempted some retrieval of international monetary stability. But this did not last; the dollar was again devalued, currencies started floating, the old Bretton Woods IMF seemed to be on the verge of collapse, and wide public and governmental discussions ensued on the need for reform and the creation of a new international monetary order.

The developing countries made it clear that they were as much interested in the subject as the industrial countries, and would like the discussion to be under the auspices of the Fund in which they were also represented. On July 26, 1972, the Board of Governors of IMF established a Committee to advise and report to the Board with respect to all aspects of reform of the international monetary system. This committee, popularly known as the Committee of Twenty, consisted of representatives of all the countries which were members of the Board of Governors. Thus, it included not only a number of representatives of the Third World, but was chaired by Ali Wardhana of Indonesia.

The Committee of Twenty appointed a Committee of Deputies who were to do the spade work and formulate proposals for the Committee's consideration.

In their meeting of March 26-27, 1973, the Deputies agreed that "aid flows should not be restricted as an adjustment device by deficit countries, and surplus countries should be encouraged to increase aid,"(3) After stating that "an important objective of the reformed system is to give positive encouragement to economic development and to promote the flow of resources from developed to developing countries,"(4) they added that "proposals for a link between

SDRs and aid have still to be discussed by the Deputies."(5)
At their May 1973 meeting, a number of Deputies from
developing countries favored the principle of a link between
aid and SDRs, subject to the understanding that the total of
SDR allocations should continue to be decided on the basis of
the global need for liquidity. However, the committee as a
whole did not conclude its discussion on the topic.

The draft Outline of Reform submitted by the Committee
of Deputies to the third meeting of the committee of Twenty
(July 30-31, 1973) reaffirmed their view that the main features
of international monetary reform should include arrangements
for "the promotion of the flow of real resources to developing
countries."(6)   It then listed six issues on which they made a
number of recommendations, some of which were of an
alternative character.   The sixth issue concerned the link and
credit facilities in favor of developing countries:

> A link will be established between SDR and
> development finance.   This link will take the form of
> the direct distribution to developing countries of a
> larger proportion of SDR allocations than they would
> receive on the basis of their share in Fund
> quotas.(7)

In the finalized version of the first Outline of Reform
presented to the Committee of Twenty which was prepared by
the Chairman and the Vice Chairman of the Committee of
Deputies, the position regarding the link underwent a change
and was now formulated as follows:

> In the light of the agreed objective promote economic
> development, the reformed monetary system will
> contain arrangements to promote an increasing flow
> of real resources from the developed to developing
> countries.   If these arrangements were to include a
> link between development assistance and SDR
> allocation, this could take one of the following forms:
> a)   A link would be established between
> development finance and SDR allocation, the
> total volume of which will be determined
> exclusively on the basis of global liquidity
> needs.   This link would take the form of the
> direct distribution to developing countries of a
> larger proportion of SDR allocations than they
> would receive on the basis of their share in
> Fund quotas.   Link resources so allocated would
> be distributed to all developing countries in
> such a way as to be relatively favourable to the
> least developed countries.

b)   A   link   would   be   established   between
development finance and SDR allocation, the
total   volume   of   which   will   be   determined
exclusively   on   the   basis   of   global   liquidity
needs.   This link would take the form of direct
allocation   to   international   and   regional
development   finance   institutions   of   a
predetermined share of SDR allocations.   Link
resources distributed to development finance
institutions would be disbursed to developing
countries on the basis of development needs and
in such a way as to be relatively favourable to
the least developed countries.   The use of link
funds   by   development   finance   institutions,
including their distribution and terms, would
reflect   the   nature   and   purpose   of   these
resources.(8)

This outline was presented by the Committee of Twenty to the
Board of Governors of the IMF at their annual meeting in
Nairobi, September 1973.   The Board took note of the report,
the significant progress the committee had made on some
important issues, its intention to continue its efforts on final
recommendations for a reform of the international monetary
system, and urged it to complete its task.
     Meanwhile came the oil crisis which directly affected the
industrial countries even more than the developing countries, a
fact that produced immediate concern about its indirect effects
upon the long term interests of the developing countries.   The
Committee of Twenty, meeting in January 1974, discussed the
large rise in oil prices and the implications for the world
economy.   At the same time, it expressed determination to
complete its work on the main features of a reformed
international monetary system in the coming months, and
discussed the valuation and yield of the SDRs, but not their
link with development assistance.   The Committee concluded its
work at a sixth and final meeting on June 12-13, 1974, and
submitted the final report, containing an outline of reform
based on such agreement as had been reached in their
deliberations.   There were, however, a number of unsettled
issues, which they suggested should be looked into by a new
committee of the Board of Governors that would be established
as an interim committee with an advisory role, pending final
establishment by an amendment of the Articles of Agreement.
Among the unsettled issues was the link proposal.   Referring
to it, the committee stated:

     The Committee is not unanimous on the question of
     establishing a link between development assistance
     and SDR allocation.   The committee is agreed that

the Interim Committee should reconsider, simultaneously with the preparation by the Executive Board
of draft amendments of the Articles of Agreement,
which it is envisaged would be presented for the
approval of the Board of Governors by February
1975, the possibility and modalities of establishing
such a link.(9)

The Committee asked the Executive Board to prepare draft
amendments to the Articles of Agreement to give effect to Part
II of the outline for further examination by the interim
committee and possible recommendation to the Board at an
appropriate time. It then added that, in particular, draft
amendments should be prepared on seven proposals of which
the sixth was "to authorize the Fund to implement a link
between development assistance and SDR allocations."(10)
    In the annexes dealing more fully with the areas on which
agreement had not yet been reached, annex 10 referred to the
link:

The establishment of a link has not been agreed. It
is, however, generally agreed that if a link were to
be established the amount of SDR allocations and the
principal characteristics of SDRs should continue to
be determined solely on the basis of global monetary
requirements and that these characteristics should be
the same for all SDRs whether distributed through
normal allocations or through a link.(11)

The Board of Governors noted the lack of unanimity on the
link and invited the interim committee to consider the
possibility and modalities of establishing such a link.(12)
    The developing countries had, meanwhile, set up a
Group of 24 to formulate their views on international monetary
reform in order to influence the deliberations of the Committee
of Twenty. On the conclusion of their meeting, they issued a
communique on March 24, 1973, which stated, inter alia, that
the new international monetary order should provide for a
well-functioning adjustment mechanism, and the collective
management of international liquidity, through strengthening
the role of SDRs, and should ensure adequate transfers of real
resources to developing countries. This would enable them to
finance balance of payment deficits incurred for developmental
expenditure beyond their own resources and, thus, provide
for a transfer of real resources from the developed to the
developing countries.
    The communique further stated that "in this connection,
Ministers reaffirmed their support, previously expressed, for
the creation of a link between SDRs and additional development
finance."(13) In their communique of June 9-10, 1974, the

Ministers referred to the Outline of Reform presented by the
Committee of Twenty. They affirmed their position that the
immediate reform package should reflect, in a balanced manner,
items of interest to both the developed and the developing
countries. They suggested, therefore, that such a package of
immediate steps should include, inter alia, establishment of a
link between development finance and SDR allocation. They
emphasized that "this political acceptance of the link is
overdue and a final decision to establish it should be taken
without further delay, and its provision included in the draft
composite resolution to be considered by the Committee of
Twenty."(14)   They were emphatic that any solution to the
problem of gold should not jeopardize the effective
implementation of the link, SDRs becoming the prinicpal
reserve asset, or accentuate the already inequitable
distribution of world liquidity. They also recommended that,
if necessary, an amendment to the Articles of Agreement
should be adopted to ensure that any rate of interest charged
on the use of SDRs would not place an additional burden on
developing countries.
     In May 1974, the UN Declaration and Programme of Action
on the adoption of a New International Economic Order
recommended that there should be "early establishment of a
link between SDRs and additional development financing in the
interests of developing countries."(15)   The UN General
Assembly Resolution of September 1975 on Development and
International Economic Cooperation contained a specific request
to the IMF to consider the establishment of a link between the
SDR and additional development finance for the benefit of all
developing countries.(16)
     Since the adoption of the program of action on the
establishment of the N.I.E.O., there have been many
statements reaffirming the desirability of an SDR/aid link.
Thus, the Latin American conference on Industrialization held
in December 1974 called for the use of SDRs to finance
industrial development in the developing countries.(17)   At the
same time, the General Assembly Resolution 3347 (XXXIX) of
December 1974 emphasized that "a political decision on the link
between development finance and SDRs allocation will have to
be reached without delay."(18)   The Committee for
Development Planning referred to the haphazard fashion in
which international liquidity had been created with traditional
assets and other strong currencies, and affirmed the
continuing importance of reserve creation under international
auspices.   This meant that SDRs should be kept on the agenda
along with the issue of their link with development
finance.(19)
     The final communique of the meeting of Commonwealth
Heads of Government (May 1975) took the position that
"developing countries should have a priority call on SDRs

through some form of link mechanism.(20)   A report by the
Economic Commission for Africa (April 18, 1976) endorsed this
view and stated that "it is necessary to see to it that the role
of the SDR in the International Monetary System is
strengthened and that provision is made in the IMF.   Articles
of Agreement for the link between SDRs and development
financing, which has long been sought by the Association of
African and Central Banks."(21)   In May 1977, the Guatemala
Appraisal supported the introduction of a new international
monetary system based on SDRs that "would be linked to
development financing."(22)   Also, during the same month, the
Ministers of the Group of 24 (finance minsters from the Group
of 77 countries) indicated their support for the NIEO objective
and, after referring to the need for a second allocation of
SDRs and moving toward making the SDR the principal reserve
asset of the international monetary system, stated that "serious
consideration should be given to the establishment of a link
between SDR allocation and the provision of financial resources
to developing countries."(23)

In spite of all this, when the issue was finally taken up
by the interim committee, the decision went against the
establishment of any link between SDRs and development
assistance.   In the Second Amendment to the Articles of
Agreement adopted by the Board of Governors at their
Washington meeting in September 1978, which gave a much
enhanced treatment to SDRs in the international monetary
system, the link did not find a place either.   An explanation
for this has perhaps been given by Joseph Gold when he wrote
in an article in the March 1978 issue of Finance and
Development:

> Topics such as these were included in the list of
> possible amendments not because there was
> widespread sentiment in favour of them in the
> Committee of Twenty, but because there were
> opposing and strongly held views about them.   The
> inclusion of them in the list was a compromise that
> bought time, but, as it turned out, not agreement.
> Draft amendments on these topics were prepared and
> discussed, some eagerly and others fitfully, but the
> proposals were abandoned when it became apparent
> the agreement was still impossible even after
> consideration of them at the ministerial level in the
> Interim Committee.(24)

Thus, while the proposed link with development assistance for
SDRs was dropped from the Second Amendment, the reformed
IMF gives SDRs a far more important place than in the past.
SDRs are now given the role of principal reserve asset of the
international monetary system, replacing gold.   For purposes

of the Fund, members are no longer to define the exchange value of their currency in terms of gold. The official price of gold (SDR 35 per fine ounce) has been abolished, and members are free to trade and account for gold at any price consistent with their domestic legislation. Nor are they required to pay in gold to the Fund in connection with any transaction or operation, its place now having been given to SDRs or other currencies prescribed by the Fund. While what the Fund originally termed "convertible" and now calls "freely usable" currencies (American dollar, English pound, French franc, German mark and Japanese yen) will continue to be used as national reserve assets and can be used by members in connection with their transactions or operations with the Fund, SDRs are expected to increase their share in both situations. The process is expected to be accelerated if and when SDR allocations are linked with the reduction in national outstanding holdings of reserve currencies through a substitution account administered by the Fund. Eventually, SDRs will become the principal reserve asset, and global liquidity supplies will be determined by the Fund in accordance with its assessment of global liquidity requirements. This, at any rate, is the ideal picture that emerges from the attempted international reform, and to complete it further action is contemplated.

The link, however, has been left out. One can understand this, if the IMF is to function purely as an organization intended for adjustment assistance of a temporary repayable character for balance of payment difficulties. But the IMF has the objective not only of regulating exchange rates policies so that national restrictions are not imposed on foreign trade, and world trade is allowed to expand, but also of promoting employment and economic development throughout the world. Moreover, an important and accepted objective of the proposed international monetary reform is to promote the flow of real resources from the developed to the developing countries. This is not identical with adjustment assistance which is available to all countries and is, in fact, of much greater quantitative significance to the industrial powers.

As long as the IMF was only concerned with exchange stability, and the assistance it gave had to be both temporary and repayable (since the resources it used for this purpose were drawn from member countries who had to part with real resources for this purpose by way of their quota payments of loans to the Fund), it was understandable that the magnitude of the assistance developing countries could look for from the Fund should be regulated with respect to the relative magnitude of their quotas. The Fund was able to operate with larger funds than represented by its quota subscriptions only by borrowing from members whose reserve positions enabled them to lend, and from other national and international financial institutions.

Today, things have undergone a radical change with the issue of SDRs and the setting up of a Special Drawing Rights Department in the Fund for administering them. Allocation of SDRs to member countries who participate in the scheme does not call for any surrender of real resources on their part to the Fund, while the SDRs they get are as good as gold or convertible currencies, which they can use for their balance of payment adjustments. This real resource is a free good to them unlike IMF credits of their national reserve assets. Unlike IMF credits, use of SDRs is permitted to be both automatic and unconditional. It, therefore, became possible for the IMF to transfer real resources from the developed to the developing countries and, thus, implement new objectives. This, in fact, is the logic behind the link of development assistance to SDRs.

A fresh allocation of 12 billion SDRs has been made, spread over the three year period 1979 to 1981, their distribution as before linked to IMF quotas. This new allocation is not for the purpose of meeting a liquidity need, as was the case with the first one, but is really for the purpose of increasing the IMF role in global exchange rate policies, and meeting the threat of the unhealthy and unstable increase that has taken place in global liquidity by the operations of the Eurodollar market and the credit policies of transnational banks operating accounts in reserve currencies. While one can understand the linking up of these fresh allocations with IMF quotas, and with the substantial increase that has been simultaneously effected in the quota amounts themselves, one simply cannot comprehend why they should continue to be given freely on the basis of the IMF quotas. It is even more difficult to justify this action when the intention is to make the SDR the principal reserve asset and not just a supplement as was contemplated earlier. In an unequal world, and with the acceptance of the objective of promoting a new international economic order, it would have been more logical to have linked SDRs with development assistance if they were to continue being given without any return in real resources to their allotees. An internationally costless asset, thus, has been used to give more to those who have more and less to those who have less. This is a veritable negation of the new international economic order accepted by the United Nations General Assembly, and of the flow of real resources from the developed to the developing countries, defined as one of the major objectives of the reformed international monetary system.

The new position given to the SDR in the international monetary system is a testimony to its popularity and the position of confidence it has now acquired in the world of international monetary transactions. Both developing and industrialized members have been using SDRs. In fact, a larger net use of SDRs has been made by the industrial

countries which, of course, is accounted for by their larger
allocations. At the same time, the bulk of SDR holdings in
excess of net allocations has also been by the countries
belonging to this combined group. This has been enhanced in
recent years by the growing volume of SDR transactions by
agreement (as distinguished from those by designation) by
countries belonging to this category. Thus, as of August 31,
1978, four industrial countries showed a net use of 881.8
million SDRs, six nonindustrial countries of Europe showed a
net use of 198.9 million SDRs, and the three countries of
Australia, New Zealand, and South Africa showed a net use
of 186.6 million SDRs, making a total of 1,267.3 million SDRs.
        As against this, ten industrial countries had a surplus
holding of 782.7 million SDRs, and two nonindustrial countries
of Europe had a surplus holding of 9.6 million SDRs, making a
total of 792.3 million SDRs. Of the seven oil exporting
countries who are participants, one showed a net use of 56.8
million SDRs, and six had a surplus of 112.2 million SDRs; 67
less developed countries accounted for a net use of 861.6
million SDRs, while eight had a surplus or a deficit over their
net cumulative allocations.(25)
        Regarding holdings in excess of net cumulative
allocations, 12 developed countries showed a figure of 792.3
million SDRs, as opposed to only 35.8 million SDRs shown by
eight less developed countries (excluding six oil exporting
countries which had a surplus of 112.2 million SDRs). It is
clear, therefore, that the less developed countries had a much
greater need for the use of SDRs as contrasted with their net
accumulations, whereas the reserve was the case with the
developed countries. In contrast, the industrialized countries
had a much larger surplus of holdings above their net
cumulative allocations; less developed countries, excluding the
oil exporting countries, had practically no such surplus.
Thus, even without taking into account their developmental
requirements, developing countries had a larger demand for
adjustment assistance in the context of their SDR allocations
than the industrialized powers. This fact alone raises the
question of revising SDR allocations in favor of the less
developed countries, even without going into the question of
an SDR/ODA link.
        Two main objections have been advanced to the link. One
is that the creation of liquidity and the transfer of real
resources are two separate subjects that should not be mixed.
This would be true as long as the liquidity made available is
based on a surrender of real resources by the allottees, as
was the case with regular IMF drawings. However, SDRs fall
in a separate category, as their allocation does not require a
prior surrender of real resources on the part of allottees. In
fact, they constitute some kind of an international fist money
and not just a credit facility. Even in the case of credit, a

transfer of real resources from one sector to another is involved without any loss of confidence in the stability of the banking system. In the case of national reserve assets, when selected currencies are used as reserve currencies and held as reserve assets, there is a transfer of real resources to the countries whose currencies are held as reserve currencies, though it is subject to recall and earns a return. Such transfer of real resources has not destroyed confidence in the reserve currencies, even though they are mixed up with the liquidity requirements of the countries that hold them. There should, therefore, be no question of confidence being destroyed by SDRs being linked with a transfer of real resources to the developing countries. This is more so because the creation of SDRs was an international decision and its volume is to be determined by considerations of global liquidity and not of development assistance.

The question of establishing a link between SDRs and development assistance arises only because of its 'fist' character and it is only fair that the seigniorage it carries should accrue to the poor and less developed countries rather than to the rich and industrialized ones.

The second negative argument advanced rests on even more flimsy foundations. It is argued that establishing such a link would lead to inflationary consequences through the pressures it would generate for an excessive creation of SDRs. This is an imaginary fear, as all the developing countries have unanimously agreed that the total volume of SDRs should be determined on the basis of global liquidity needs and this is stated in the Amendment bringing SDRs into existence. Moreover, no change in the total volume of SDRs or fresh allocations of SDRs can be made except with approval of 85 percent of participant quotas, which gives complete veto power to the industrial countries. In fact, all that has been asked for is that, given the volume of SDRs, a link should be established between SDRs and development assistance. No one has demanded that there should be a special issue of SDRs based on development assistance.

It must also be pointed out that SDRs do not constitute a major part of international liquidity. When SDRs were first created, they were conceived of as a supplement to national reserve assets which then consisted of gold and reserve currencies, with the hope that they would gradually grow in their importance to the total volume of national reserve assets. In actual fact, though gold has declined in importance and many someday be phased out altogether, reserve currency assets have increased enormously in their volume and importance during the last six years. Much of this increase has taken place, not by surrender of real resources by their holders, but by an increase in liabilities and indebtedness thanks to the growth of the Eurodollar market, and nonspend-

ability of a large portion of the receipts from oil exports.
When liabilities became reserve assets this led to a multiplier
effect that added to the volume of liquidity. It is this
large increase in reserve currency assets that has added
so much to global liquidity and resulted in inflationary
consequences, and not the creation of SDRs. Thus, from the
end of 1972 to the end of 1978, global reserves increased from
147 billion to 279.5 billion SDRs; SDRs remained more or less
constant, 8-8.5 billion; gold at about 35 billion; and the
foreign exchange component increased from about 96 billion to
about 205 billion SDRs.(26) These figures are based on the
official price of gold at 35 SDRs per ounce.

In fact, even the fresh allocation of 12 billion SDRs
decided upon in 1978 in the Special Drawing Rights Department
has not been based upon considerations of being needed for
global liquidity.

It is evident that this fresh allocation of SDRs has been
made in the interests of the industrial countries in order to
wean them away from their present tendency to increase their
liquidity through foreign exchange reserves, acquired partly
by surrender of real resources and partly by increasing their
liabilities to the private sector in international banking.
Another major purpose of this allocation is to strengthen the
role of the IMF in its surveillance operations and regulation of
national exchange rate policies. The argument formerly used
against the link, that SDRs could be created only for meeting
a felt need for additional lquidity, was now abandoned by this
fresh allocation in the face of the current excess in global
liquidity. This was only because it was now in the interests
of the developed world to do so, and it clearly shows that
political rather than technical considerations have stood in the
way of establishing an SDR/ODA link.

The time has now come to take a fresh look at the whole
question of an SDR/ODA link in the light of the recent
decision to make a new allocation of SDRs and gradually use
them to replace the foreign exchange component in national
reserves. It appears that the international monetary order is
now steadily moving toward an international fist money for
settlement of international transactions and adjustment
payments. As fist money, no surrender of real resources is
involved on the part of those to whom the SDRs are allotted.

The crucial question that needs reviewing is not so much
that of establishing a formal link between SDRs and
development assistance, as that of the basis on which SDR
allocations are being made among individual members of the
Fund. The initial allocation of nine billion SDRs was made on
the basis of members' IMF quotas; and the same basis has been
continued in the distribution of the fresh allocation of 12
billion SDRs. It is this basis of using IMF quotas of member
countries as the determinant of their share of allocations that
needs reexamination.

Quotas were originally fixed at the time of the establishment of the IMF and were primarily determined on the basis of the magnitude of a country's foreign trade and its general economic development and level of national income, which were taken to be indicative of its balance of payments requirements. These quotas determined the relative magnitudes of adjustment assistance that members could expect from the Fund. But quotas also involved subscriptions which meant surrender of real resources by member countries. Thus, the inequality in their right to receive adjustment assistance from the Fund was also determined by a corresponding inequality in their surrender of real resources by way of subscriptions to the Fund. Voting power and, therefore, control of the Fund was based also on the quotas. Thus, the IMF was dominated by the developed countries, who were entitled to the larger portions of IMF assistance and who also made the largest surrender of real resources to the Fund. The IMF was, thus, an international institution that reflected the unequal international economic order.

Since then, there have been some changes in the quota distribution due to the inclusion of new members and the changed status of the oil exporting countries. But the industrial countries continue to hold the majority share of the total quota. Thus, at the end of August 1978, they held a quota of 58.75 percent of the total, while the less developed countries of the Western hemisphere, the Middle East, Asia, and Africa (excluding the oil exporting countries) had 22.2 percent of the total. An examination of the total drawings made on the Fund up to the end of August 1978 shows that, against a quota of 58.75 percent, 53.1 percent of the drawings were made by the industrial countries. If we excluded from this figure the Reserve Trade drawings which are unconditional in nature, their share comes only to 42.9 percent. Even of this figure, the main share was that of only three industrial countries - the United Kingdom, Italy, and France - the rest of the industrial countries, accounting for only 0.4 percent.(27)

If we take the figure of net drawings (that is, after allowing for repayment) only two countries - the United Kingdom and Italy, with a total quota of 10.68 percent - accounted for 34.9 percent of this figure; the remaining industrial countries with a quota of 48.07 percent showed a nil figure under net drawings. If we take the figure of the net Fund sales of currency, which shows the net use made of member currencies by the Fund for its transactions, industrial countries (other than the United Kingdom and Italy) accounted for 43.2 percent of the total, while the oil exporting countries accounted for practically the entire balance with 55.2 percent. If we take the reserve position in the Fund of the industrial countries (again discounting Italy and the United Kingdom), these countries accounted for 60.7 percent of the total reserve

position of all members, while the oil exporting countries
accounted for 31.3 percent. The less developed areas, with
their quota of 22.2 percent, accounted for only 5 percent of
the total reserve position.

What is clear from an examination of these figures is that
the main net users of the Fund's credit facilities have been the
United Kindom and Italy from the industrial countries; together
with most of the less industrialized countries of Europe; the
group of three countries of Australia, New Zealand, and South
Africa; and practically all the Third World, excepting the oil
exporting countries. Thus, the industrial countries, excluding
Great Britain and Italy and now the oil exporting countries,
have either made no net use of the Fund's credit facilities or
have built up surpluses with the Fund (for which they receive
remuneration) unlike the other members. In effect, a majority
of the industrial countries have really been functioning as
creditors who do not make a net use of the credit facilities
available with the IMF, while a few of the industrial countries
(notably the U.K. and Italy) have been functioning as
debtors, making net use of their IMF drawings. The same is
the case with the oil exporting countries. The IMF has been
borrowing from the industrial countries and the oil exporting
countries to supplement its resources for lending to its other
members. The question, therefore, arises whether the time
has not come to review the whole basis on which quotas are
determined, as there seems to be no symmetry between the
quotas of suppliers of resources to the IMF and of actually
operated claims on IMF drawings.(28)

Apart from this larger question, there can be no doubt
that there is something radically wrong with a system that
allocates a costless asset like the SDRs to countries that do
not require them. Even the industrial countries which use
them do not need this free asset, as they are in a position to
acquire foreign exchange resources for meeting their
requirements either by surrender of real resources or by
incurring liabilities to the Eurodollar market and the
transnational banking institutions in the private sector. It is
the less developed countries that are most in need of funds
even for meeting their normal balance of payment
requirements. If they go in for developmental programs to
accelerate their economic growth and reduce their disparity
with the developed countries, they do not get any assistance
from the Fund in spite of its newly accepted objective of
facilitiating a flow of real resources from the developed powers
to the developing countries. Now that, by the creation of
SDRs, the Fund is in a position to generate costless resources
that can be used for meeting international payments,
considerations of both equity and facilitating the desired
movement to a new international order require that allocation of
SDRs should be used to enable the less developed countries to
speed up their economic development.

It must be pointed out that SDRs are not expected to meet the entire volume of the developmental requirements of those countries in terms of foreign resources. There are already in existence various forms of international and bilateral aid for development. The snag is that not only is their volume much below the accepted percentage of the GNP of the developed countries, but also that they are conditional, and do not facilitate long range planning as their annual volume has to be constantly negotiated. What the developing countries need is a stable and unconditional volume of assistance that can be used in the manner and for purposes which they think are most suitable in their national developmental interests. A linkage of SDRs with ODA would be an ideal instrument for this purpose. And such SDRs need be no more than a part of the required developmental assistance.

There is no intention of departing from the current national responsibility attached to the allocation of SDRs, namely, that allottees not only have the right to receive convertible foreign exchange in return for SDRs, but also to give such foreign exchange if they are designated to do so. The expectation is that as the less developed countries succeed in speeding up their development and increasing their export capacity along with their national standards of living, they will be in a position to be designated to receive SDRs and, thus, help the developed countries, also, to meet their adjustment problems. In the last analysis, therefore, while SDRs for development assistance would draw real resources from the developed countries in the immediate future, eventually, the countries so aided would be in a position to render balance of payment assistance to the developed countries themselves, as well as to provide them with a larger market. SDRs for development assistance would be like the quality of mercy, that blesses both those who give and those who receive, and thus would fulfill the original function of the IMF for the promotion of world trade and world employment.

It must be pointed out that while the SDRs do not require repayment (except for the limited obligation of reconstitution which is likely to disappear in the future), they do involve the payment of interest on their net use. This would apply to all SDRs, including those employed in development assistance. There would be no difference in this respect between SDRs, regardless of the use they are put to, whether for developmental assistance or for meeting normal balance of payment adjustments.

Finally, the total volume of SDR issues would be determined not by the interested wishes of the developing countries, but by the IMF, where the developed countries have a majority vote, and where the majority needed for a fresh allocation of SDRs gives them a complete veto on increase in the volume of SDRs.

Therefore, what is contemplated under an SDR/ODA link is not an increase in their total volume unrelated to the basic principle of the need for global liquidity on which their creation was initially based. It has been seen, however, that, in the explanation given by the Managing Director of the Fund on the fresh issue of 12 billion SDRs for the period 1979–81, the principle of the need for global liquidity has been reinterpreted, and that considerations of giving SDRs a more important place in national reserve assets and increasing the influence of the Fund on exchange rate policies of members have been brought into the picture. This can continue to regulate the volume of SDRs, even after the establishment of the link. What the SDR/ODA link contemplates is a change in the pattern of distribution of SDRs to the member countries, by taking into account development assistance and not just the IMF quotas which determine subscriptions and drawing rights on the Fund.

If considerations of development assistance are to be taken into account in the allocation of SDRs, the question arises as to how this is to be done with references to the SDRs which have already been issued and allotted, and those which are still to be issued in persuance of the decision taken in 1978, as well as further allocations that may be decided on in the future.

With regard to the SDRs already issued and allotted – namely, 13.3 billion dollars, nine industrial countries (the United States, Germany, Japan, Canada, the Netherlands, Belgium, Denmark, Austria, and Norway) have made no net use of them. These countries have, in fact, met additions to the volume of SDRs allotted to them, and have a much stronger reserve position in the Fund than other members. In addition, the net use by these members of their regular IMF drawing rights outside the reserve tranches is negligible. Under the circumstances, there is no reason why the allocation of 5,952 million SDRs made to the nine countries should be continued on the 'free' basis, and not subject to a surrender of real resources. The suggestion the author would make is that they should surrender their own currencies of an equivalent value to the Fund in return for the SDRs they were allotted; and, against this receipt, the Fund should make a supplementary issue of SDRs which would be allotted only to the developing countries in proportions determined on some acceptable criteria by the Fund. The developing countries, in turn, should deposit in the Fund the SDR allocations made to them to be credited to their reserve assets on which they can draw unconditionally. The Fund would be able to honor these drawings with the currencies it has obtained from the members concerned as payment for the allocation of SDRs already made to them. This would, in effect, mean a transfer of real resources from countries with strong position in the Fund to

LDCs for aid in their development. This would be a
once-for-all operation.

As regards future allocations, including the 4 billion
SDRs envisaged for 1980 and 1981, the author suggests that 50
percent be allocated to all members on the basis of current IMF
quotas and the remaining 50 percent only to the developing
countries in proportions determined on some criteria acceptable
to the Fund. The acceptable criteria should be the same
for both these allocations and the allocations referred to in
the preceding paragraph. In this way, the objective of
transferring real resources from the developed to the
developing countries by the Fund would have been achieved.
A link would have been established between SDRs and development assistance, and allocation of SDRs would still be on a
'free' basis to all members. The total volume and timing of
fresh issues of SDRs would continue to be determined by the
IMF by a majority vote which would give an effective veto to
LDCs on cancellations of SDRs. As SDRs will still form a
minor proportion of national reserve assets, confidence in them
will continue unimpaired. As net acquistions will continue to
earn interest, this will enhance the attractiveness of holding
them. Net use will continue to be charged interest, thus
strengthening their utilization for really worthwhile purposes.
In turn, both these factors will help to promote the increasing
use of SDRs in the new international monetary order.

There is a fear that distribution, even of a part of
SDRs, on the basis of development assistance needs would lead
to inflationary consequences in the countries which are not
transferees of SDRs, as their supply management could take
into account the unknown and unpredictable increase in the
demands made on their economies by an SDR/ODA link. This
is most unlikely to happen, as the volume of SDRs to be linked
to development assistance would constitute a neglibible
proportion of the exports of these countries, which are not
only large in absolute terms but also tending steadily to
increase over time. In fact, the volume of SDRs linked with
development assistance will be a small fraction of the normal
increase in the exports of these countries. Secondly, even
today, all development assistance is not of a bilateral character
which could presumably be taken care of in supply
management. World Bank loans and IDA are untied and their
relevance to supply management will be no different from
linked SDRs which would also not be tied to supplies from any
specified country. If international aid can be handled by the
countries contributing to it, there is no reason why this
should not also work in the case of development linked SDRs
by the countries accumulating the SDRs.

Development linked SDRs would not be different from
other SDRs in respect to the obligation to give convertible
currencies in exchange when designated to do so by the Fund.

In the case of LDCs, it would take some years before they will
be in a position to discharge this obligation; but there would
be a sufficient increase in their exports to enable them to be
designated to receive SDRs from the developed or other
countries.   Along with the institution of an SDR/ODA link,
there could be an evaluation of the use of such SDRs and
their effect on development, exports, and world trade at the
end of ten years, at which time a review of the entire scheme
may take place.

The only objection the author can see to the link is that
it would increase development assistance, thereby contributing
to world inflation, and that this would be done through the
Fund.   This objection is not valid as the current level of
development assistance is far below the figure already accepted
by the developed countries.   In view of all this, it is the
author's contention that the question of establishing an
SDR/ODA link should be reviewed and early action taken
thereon by the Fund.

NOTES

(1)   Joseph Gold, Finance and Development (IMF Pamphlet
      series, March 1978).
(2)   Ibid.
(3)   Report by the Chairman of Deputies submitted to the
      Second Meeting of the Committee of Twenty held on March
      26-27, 1973, at Washington, D.C., Par. 40.
(4)   Ibid., Par. 5.
(5)   Ibid., Par. 5.
(6)   Draft Outline of Reform submitted to the Third Meeting
      of the Committee of Twenty held on July 30-31, 1973, in
      Washington, D.C., Par. 1.
(7)   Ibid., Par. 32.
(8)   Outline of Reform presented at the Annual Fund/Bank
      meeting held in September 1973 at Nairobi, Par. 34.
(9)   Communique of the Committee of Twenty issued on June
      13, 1974, at the conclusion of its Sixth & Final Meeting in
      Washington, D.C., Par. 8.
(10) Ibid., Par. 11, clause (b).
(11) Outline of Reform, June 1974, Annex 10, Par. 5.
(12) Resolutions adopted by the Board of Governors of the
      IMF on the work of the Ad hoc Committee on Reform of
      the International Monetary System and Related Issues and
      on a Programme of Immediate Action, Par. 7 of the Fourth
      Resolution.
(13) Communique of the Group of 24 issued on the conclusion
      of its deliberations on March 24, 1973 in Washington,
      D.C., Par. 6

(14)   Communique of the Group of 24 issued at the conclusion
       of its deliberations on June 9-10, 1974, in Washington,
       D.C., Par. 1 on "The Link and International Liquidity."
(15)   Ervin Laszlo, Robert Baker, Elliot Eisenberg, Venkata
       Raman, eds., The Objectives of the New International
       Economic Order, UNITAR (New York: Pergamon Press,
       1978) pp. 104 ff.
(16)   Ibid., p. 104.
(17)   Ibid., p. 106.
(18)   Ibid., p. 106.
(19)   Ibid., p. 107.
(20)   Ibid., p. 110.
(21)   Ibid., p. 107.
(22)   Ibid., p. 107.
(23)   Ibid., p. 108.
(24)   Joseph Gold, Finance and Development.
(25)   Ibid.
(26)   Compiled from International Financial Statistics, October,
       1978.
(27)   IMF Survey, October 2, 1978.
(28)   The statistical review and analysis contained in this and
       the previous two pages is based on data compiled from
       International Financial Statistics, October 1978.

II

External Debt

5 Trends of Public External Debt of Developing Countries
Rosario Green

In the field of international finance, there are many obstacles to the implementation of a New International Economic Order:

- the failure to comply with the official assistance goals of the United Nations Second Decade for Development;
- the overwhelming increase in the external public debt of the Third World countries and its financial and political consequences;
- the increasing privatization of that debt;(1)
- the formation of surplus international liquidity as a result, initially, of the crisis of the capitalist centers mainly in the United States, and later of the revaluation of energy prices and its impact on the internationaliza-tion of capital and world inflation;
- the dysfunctional effects of the emergence of a number of international financial centers in developing countries, centers that avoid any possibility of being regulated; and
- the inability to link Special Drawing Rights with official development assistance.

Implicit in this margination and in the impossibility of regulating the transnational performance of the international banks is the recognized irrelevance of the International Monetary Fund and the need not only to reform it, but also to make it more democratic.

The question of the transfer of financial resources from the industrialized powers to the developing countries has always been one of the central points in the North-South Dialogue. The origin of this debate stems from the insertion of the principle on international cooperation in the United Nations Charter signed in 1945; but the systematization of this effort has been evident in UNCTAD since the 1960s. In this effort, the developing countries have insistently outlined

questions related to the insufficient amount of financial
resources for development that come from industrial countries,
as well as to the elimination of all ties on these resources; the
preference for credits for programs over loans for projects;
and the preference for multilateral flows instead of bilateral
ones.   Other questions have also arisen related to specific
aspects of these countries' foreign public debt: the onerous
financial conditions of a part of that debt; the relief from the
weight of the debt service; and the need to favorably
renegotiate both components, private as well as official.   These
and other similar demands have ended in an agreement on a
Third World strategy and even an "ideology" with respect to
the transfer of financial resources for development and foreign
debt.

The clearest elements of this conception are articulated in
important documents on the position of the Group of 77, which
includes most of the developing countries.   It should be
remembered that in UNCTAD I (Geneva, 1964) the setting out
of this concern was begun by indicating that finance channeled
by the industrialized countries to the developing ones ought to
be at least equivalent to one percent of the national income of
each one of the donor countries, and granted under
concessional conditions (annual interest rates of no more than
three percent, and partially reimbursable amounts in national
currency).

Years later, in the document known as the Charter of
Algiers, and which preceded UNCTAD II (New Delhi, 1968)
with respect to foreign development financing, it was pointed
out that the industrialized countries should recognize their
responsibility in international financial cooperation by
complementing the domestic savings of developing countries.
This would allow them to accelerate the process of capital
formation.   It was also indicated that there was a need for the
industrialized countries to participate in that effort with an
adequate and just percentage of their national income and that,
whenever possible, the assistance should be multilateral and
granted under favorable conditions to programs and projects
without undermining the paying capacity of the debtor
countries.

Based on these outlines, the International Strategy for
Development, in the context of the United Nations Second
Decade for Development (1970-1980), specified goals when it
pointed out that by 1975 the industrialized countries ought to
channel 0.7 percent of their GNP for Official Assistance for
Development to Third World countries, under highly
concessional terms.   Nevertheless, this goal remained on
paper.   It was not carried out.

In 1975, DAC members as a whole (Australia, Austria, Belgium, Canada, Denmark, the United States, Finland,
Portugal, the German Federal Republic, the United Kingdom,

Sweden, and Switzerland) gave a meager 0.36 percent of their GNP in the form of ODA to Third World countries. If it is true that within the DAC there were countries such as Sweden which exceeded the goal and channeled 0.82 percent of their GNP in ODC, others, such as the United States, allotted a mere 0.26 percent. At that time, the foreign public debt of the Third World countries had become a serious problem for various reasons:

1. It size, although, as we shall see, this is not the main difficulty. From 1965, when the total sum of that debt was 34.3 billion dollars, to 1977, when it reached around 244 billion dollars, a nominal increase of more than 700 percent was noted, resulting from a constant annual increase since 1970 of more than 20 percent.

2. Its degree of concentration. In 1977, ten developing countries accumulated around 80 percent of the Third World's total foreign debt: Brazil, Mexico, Argentina, and Chile in Latin America; India, Indonesia, and South Korea in Asia; Iran in the Middle East; and Algeria and Egypt in Africa. A strange mixture of interests and specific situations prevailed which included countries with low, middle, and high incomes, as well as oil producing countries.

3. For a large number of Third World countries, the foreign public debt took on a private character as a result of the inflexibility of the volume of foreign financial assistance, bilateral and multilateral, as well as the generation of a surplus supply of capital in loans in private international markets. This is a reflection of recession in the main industrialized countries and the recycling of so-called oil dollars (or petrodollars). While, in 1967, the private component amounted to only 28 percent of the Third World's total foreign debt, in 1977, it was 48 percent, with cases such as Brazil and Mexico where the private component was more than half the total. As we have already pointed out, the trend toward privatization is not seen in every case. There are some countries, like India and Pakistan, for example, where the official component represents a very high percentage - more than 90 percent - it having been contracted, for the most part under concessional terms.(2) For countries suffering from such a tendency, privatization of the debt has resulted in making financial terms tougher. This necessarily has repercussions on the burden of their debt servicing. It is paradoxical that due to the presence of variables such as foreign exchange earnings through exports, levels of national and individual incomes, etc., the situation is less distressing for these countries than for those with low incomes and without access to the private market for capital.(3)

4. Due to the growing private "banking component" of the
    Third World's foreign debt, credits from the big financial
    entities have displaced other important credit providers.
    Thus, while in 1969, these represented 49.6 per cent of
    the private total, in 1977 they hardly made up a third, at
    a time when the credits coming from private banking and
    financial institutions meant more than half of the total
    flow of private resources to the Third World.

5. The persistence of the trend toward bilateralization of the
    debt   of   an   official   origin,   in   spite   of   the   slight
    modifications noted in recent years and the fact that many
    Third World countries requested an increase in their
    multilateral credits to balance and, eventually, revert
    such   a   trend.   In   1969,   bilateral   credits   made   up   76.6
    percent   of   the   official   total.   For   1977,   although   the
    figure had slightly changed, those credits continued to be
    predominant   in   the   total,   thus   reflecting   the   slowness
    with which resources from institutions such as the World
    Bank are increased, and the power of national government
    agencies granting loans to developing countries.   Many of
    these agencies tie their credits to highly political terms
    and important trade advantages.

6. The concern caused by the perspectives of the developing
    world's foreign debt, in the short and middle term, in a
    period of world recession accompanied by inflation, the
    deterioration in the trade terms of the developing coun-
    tries without oil, and the growing needs of resources
    to pay accumulated debts and finance projects that will
    confront social demands of a difficult political solution.

7. The growing concern about the paying capacity of the
    Third World countries, where the demands that arise from
    the debt's servicing have multiplied.   That debt servicing
    represented 37 billion dollars in 1977 is a cause for alarm.
    If we take into consideration the fact that between 1976
    and 1977 the total debt increased by 15 percent and in
    1977 the debt service represented 15 percent of that
    debt's   total,   we   can   understand   the   nature   of   the
    so-called "vicious circle of the debt."   According to this
    phenomenon, debtor countries continue incurring further
    debts to meet the payment of the accumulated ones.   We
    can,   thus,   question   the   extent   to   which   this   debt
    contributes to the growth of a large number of countries
    for years immersed in such a vicious circle.   For these
    countries,   dangers   include   bankruptcy   and   the
    undertaking of measures that are received with great
    hostility by the creditors, measures such as massive
    renegotiations,   suspensions,   moratoria,   and   unilateral
    suspensions.   With respect to the Third World's paying
    capacity, the intensity of the response has to do with the
    intensity of the problem.   If it is true that countries with

high income levels face the complications of a growing privatization of their foreign debt, it is also a fact that the dynamics of their economic process makes the burden of debt servicing relatively less serious than for countries with low incomes, which are frequently characterized by the existence of a nondynamic and excessively dependent sector. This latter group of countries, in spite of being debtors mainly to official agencies and beneficiaries, to a large extent, of concessionary terms, has seen the relationship between servicing and foreign exchange earnings from exports evolve unfavorably between 1967, when the figure was 12.5 percent, and 1976, when it was 23.3 percent. This not only indicates an expansion of the foreign debt, but also the deterioration of the paying capacity.

For oil exporting countries, the situation is very different. On the one hand, they observed an increase in the relationship between servicing and foreign exchange earnings, rising from 2.6 percent in 1967 to 6.7 percent in 1976; on the other hand, the increase was less serious for them in the context of their economies. The countries with middle incomes experienced a decline in the ratio between servicing and foreign exchange earnings from 10.4 percent in 1967 to 9.7 percent in 1976, having registered moments of temporary relief in 1974 and 1975 when the ratio was only 8.5 percent.

Nevertheless, the situation for the developing countries is so serious that in UNCTAD IV (Nairobi, 1976), the Group of 77 succeeded in outlining questions as delicate and as pressing as the improvement of multilateral financing mecanisms, and, in renegotiations, the advantage of including the debt from official sources, seeking concessional terms. Another item raised was the need to foresee with greater clarity the so-called debt crisis, so as to avoid the adoption of measures that are not always constructive and which are provoked by emergency situations. As we shall see, the representatives of the developing countries in the North-South Dialogue used this reference framework as a point of departure to outline specific propositions which were very alarming for the industrial powers on account of their high degree of consensus and coherence.

For their part, the industrialized countries have proceeded to strengthen their defensive position in the face of Third World demands, especially in recent years when these demands have been put forward as resolutions in world meetings - e.g., the United Nations Assembly - and have been passed by overwhelming majorities. This has been interpreted by the industrial countries as an act of confrontation and an example of the "tyranny of the majority."

In summary, and barring the exceptions already pointed out, the position of the industrial countries goes so far as to deny the validity of Third World perceptions of their own problems. They maintain that if an accelerated growth in the developing world's foreign debt has taken place, the real problem is not the insufficient transfer of resources from rich to poor countries or the terms under which this transfer is carried out; but is due to balance of payments problems, poor administration, and corruption.

Nor is it possible, the developed countries also maintain, to talk of a general problem of foreign debt, not only because the world debt is highly concentrated in ten developing countries, but also because each one of these cases has its own peculiarities. They affirm that it is not the same when the debt is largely contracted with private institutions as when it is contracted with official agencies. In this sense, many developing countries agree with the industrialized countries. It is clear that in those cases where the private component is the predominant one (Brazil and Mexico, for example), the adoption of global policies (massive renegotiations, moratoria, etc.) is not convenient, since that can eventually impair access to the international financial markets. These countries are convinced that their negotiation capacity and credit prestige allow them to solve, on an individual basis, any problem related to their external debt. The industrialized countries have reinforced this position by arguing that the eventual application of general relief measures to the Third world's external debt would give the impression of a general loss of credit solvency and could even reduce the amount of available official resources (and, of course, discourage private resources) or, finally, could be interpreted as a premium for bad management and corruption.

Perhaps the Conference on International Economic Cooperation (Paris, 1976-77) was the gathering in which the contrast between these two approaches to the Third World's foreign debt became most evident. The developing countries placed the problem within the context of middle-term economic development and in the framework of international financial cooperation. They underlined the insufficiency of available financial resources, the inflexibility of the terms they are subjected to, and emphasized the establishment of a world economic order that is just and equitable as a sine qua non for the solution of this and other very important questions. The industrialized countries, on the other hand, maintained that the problem of the foreign debt does not necessarily constitute an indication of economic weakness, and nonfulfillment of the principle of international cooperation established in the United Nations Charter. According to this, the debt should not be considered as a consequence of the present international economic order which, in their opinion, is not just.

The Paris Conference took place under the impact of oil. This was to become one of the Conference's main limitations, in spite of initial enthusiasm. Even though it was first seen as a meeting of oil exporters and importers to deal with questions related to energy, it ended by incorporating other developing countries. France, for everyone's benefit, sought to avoid confrontation between both groups of countries by widening the agenda to include questions on primary products, the real transfer of resources, and the external debt, mainstays of the New International Economic Order.

The 19 countries that represented the developing world in the Paris negotiations(4) were conscious of the fact that, as recent experiences had shown, their strength was in their unity. They revealed signs of great solidarity in spite of the diversity with which the themes set out had a bearing on their economies. The eight countries representing the industrialized capitalist world(5) were somewhat convinced that the diversity of situations would result in the projection of differing interests and the emergence of potential allies, as well as in the ensuring of triumph in the questions that most interested them, i.e., reduction in oil prices and security of supply. A relevant fact was the socialist countries' refusal to attend the dialogue.

Two different viewpoints obvious from the beginning, according to which the South would seek to introduce structural changes in the international economic system while the North had decided not to alter the world's political and economic equilibrium, were to be projected throughout the negotiations.

With respect to the questions of the Third World's debt and external assistance for development, the lack of understanding was total. In spite of the fact that the developing countries swore solidarity and pledged the defense of the cause of the relatively less developed nations, it was evident that basically they had different objective positions. The countries with access to the international capital markets and with highly important private components within the total of their foreign debt did not wish to be strongly associated with proposals such as rescheduling and moratoria which could affect their access to such markets. The countries with weak economies and difficult situations with respect to their debt insisted on the adoption of general measures so as to strengthen their negotiating position.

In order to safeguard the group's solidarity, the representatives of the developing world agreed on a formula which can be summed up in four points:

1. consolidation of the trade debts of the "interested" developing countries and rescheduling of the payments on a 25 year basis at least;

2. transformation of the official debts into grants, especially in the case of low income countries;
3. establishment of a facility under the sponsorship of the IBRD or the IMF to refinance short-term loans; and
4. expansion of the resources of multilateral financing institutions.

In addition, the Group of 19 insisted on the need to adopt international measures to face the future problems of the foreign debt that have a bearing on all the possible aspects of the question: financial and other conditions with respect to credits and reorganization of the debt's structure.

The industrialized countries refused to accept a solution of global application to a problem that did not appear general to them. They announced their readiness to outline partial aid mechanisms, such as the proposed "program of special action," adopted at the end, to which one billion dollars were given to be directed to low-income, developing countries in order to alleviate their balance of payments problems. They, thus, put forward a somewhat isolated and partial solution to the enormous problems of underdevelopment, but took into consideration only some of the world's developing countries. Moreover, it was insufficient in comparison with two important matters: the Third World's total debt of more than 194 billion dollars, and the deficit in current account of the developing countries which, according to estimates made by UNCTAD in 1976, would exceed 100 billion dollars in 1980.

The Conference's final declaration listed the theme of the developing countries debt among those for which it was not possible to come to mutually agreed recommendations or conclusions, thus revealing that, basically, the dialogue had been one of no communication. In the context of the need to establish a New International Economic Order, fundamentally defined in terms of the aspirations, ambitions, and needs of the Third World countries, the agreements of the Paris Conference are practically of no importance. The main explanation of this failure probably stems from the fact that it was a mistake to conceive the Paris Conference as a serious attempt by the industrialized countries to find formulas negotiated through consensus to put into operation the principles of the NIEO. It is, perhaps, also a mistake to think that consensus can be reached when it is a question of modifying a world order which, being highly unjust, has served the aims and interests of a few. The relations between the weak and the powerful are relations of might where consensus is superfluous.

The recognition of the previous fact and the forwarding of the questions discussed in Paris to world gatherings such as UNCTAD and the United Nations General Assembly for further negotiation suggested the return to old practices.

These and other questions will continue to be discussed in the same terms in which they have been presented before: confrontation and majority triumph of decisions whose practical implementation will continue to be a goal that is practically impossible to reach on account of the industrialized nations' veto powers. When all is said and done, it is these nations that have recovered the political power to conserve their positions as real leaders of the system.

The mistake of the developing countries in Paris consisted in outlining - and sticking to it throughout the discussions - a package of proposals which involved an inherent weakness. It included a problem of great importance, i.e., the foreign debt, with respect to which they could not fix a firm and uniform negotiating position. This was due to the fact that the situations which gave rise to the problem were not of equal magnitude, nor were the possible repercussions the same.

The consideration of these and other problems related to the Third World's foreign debt is of concern to the debtor countries as well as to the credit institutions and governments; it is even an issue on the plane of international public opinion that has expressed its uneasiness in recent years in the form of a specific question: if the situation is so serious, why do the debtor countries continue to incur debt, and the creditors grant loans?

It is important to point out that, traditionally, the foreign debt incurred by the developing countries has been explained, if not justified, in terms of the demand for funds, that is, of financial needs stemming from two kinds of fundamental imbalances within the debtor countries. In the first place, the imbalance is to be found in the foreign sector, and more specifically in the current account of their balance of payments. This is the result not only of the greater value of import commodities over export commodities, due to different reasons, among them the deterioration in trade terms, but also of service payments - fundamentally the payments on capital - which are a source of important foreign exchange expenditures. Secondly, the imbalance at the level of public finance, due to high government expenditure which seeks to confront the growing social demands outlined by a constantly expanding population without having to greatly change the local political and economic power structures. A result of such a nature would be implicit, for example, in the case of the implementation of an authentic fiscal reform which, besides being redistributive of the national income, would increase the state's resources and allow it to reduce its dependence on foreign capital.

It would be necessary to incorporate additional elements to this traditional explanation of the debt incurred through imbalances in the debtor countries: the absence in the Third World of a long range strategy with respect to the (internal and external) financing of their development. In replying to the question of why creditors continue to loan, considerations would have to be introduced on the supply of funds.

The existence of greater availability of savings in the private international capital markets is due to the creation of the market of Eurocurrencies and the transnationalization of banks. This can be seen as an incentive of an exogenous nature for the debtor countries.

The synthesis of the arguments outlined with respect to the Third World's growing debt would lead us to two conclusions. It is true that, for the debtor countries, the matter has become a way of alleviating or solving some of the problems resulting from their internal and external imbalances without introducing far-reaching reforms in the political, economic, and social set up; however, it is also true for the debtor countries that the export of capital - be it in the form of direct foreign investment or loans - constitutes a fundamental factor in ensuring the maximization of profits as well as the reproduction of capital.

The present transnationalization of capital finds one of its explanations in the uncontainable foreign expansion of American private banks. During the initial stage, the main function of the American banks' expansion abroad was to serve their clients, the big transnational corporations. This expansion was inspired by the establishment, in 1965, of a Voluntary Program of Credit Restriction Abroad, one of President Lyndon Johnson's measures to control the export of U.S. capital and to reduce the deficit in the American balance of payments. The Voluntary Program sought to halt the exit of U.S. dollars, restricting the increase of foreign loans from American banks in that first year of the program to no more than 5 percent of the December 1960 operation levels. The continuous deterioration in the American balance of payments decreased the limit to 3 percent in 1968, yet broadened the base to the 1964 figure. This situation was maintained until 1971 when the Voluntary Program exempted from the 3 percent limit all export loans abroad.

Nevertheless, the impact of these controls did not diminish in any real way loan activities abroad of American private banks. The only change occurred in the structure of their liabilities. The funds obtained abroad to be converted again in loans on the domestic market were registered, as before, in the liabilities of the central offices or the national offices of the American banks. The funds obtained from abroad to be given in loans in the foreign market were registered in the books of the subsidiaries abroad, thus avoiding the Program's restrictions. This explains the fact that, from 1965, American banks began to open subsidiary and affiliated branches abroad. As an example, it is enough to point out that, while in 1960 only eight American banks had

subsidiaries abroad, with assets in the range of 3.5 billion
dollars, by June 1976, more than a hundred banks had
subsidiary branches outside the country, with assets in the
region of 181 billion dollars. It is in this way that the big
financial centers or fiscal paradises appeared in industrialized
areas - London, New York, Paris, Berlin, - as well as in the
underdeveloped regions: The Bahamas, Grand Cayman,
Panama, Beirut, Bahrain, Abu-Dhabi, Singapore, and Hong
Kong.

It is necessary to point out that the advantages which the
international financial centers theoretically bring to the
developing countries in which they settle, in particular the
possibility of obtaining resources and channeling them abroad
by "sterilizing them" - that is, by invalidating their possible
inflationary effect - have been almost always eliminated by
their disadvantages. Among these disadvantages, we find that
because of the absence of an efficient economic framework, a
characteristic of the developing countries, the international
financial centers set up there tend to insert, absorb, and
administer the greater part of the monetary liquidity created in
those countries, directing it away from other uses. Thus, the
centers serve the expansion of the transnational corporations
and banks of the system's periphery and the maximization of
their global profits, a substantial and growing part of which is
precisely acquired in that periphery. Furthermore, they act
as capital refuge for industrial and developing countries, and
as a base for international speculation with currencies,
especially in periods of exchange instability. Finally, they
create a double financial market with less regulation than that
of the industrial countries, one that serves as a strategic base
for international operations.

In a second stage, a new form of external expansion of
the American banks became indispensable in the light of the
stagnation of the U.S. economy and the decrease in the needs
of their transnational clients, who reinvested an increasing
part of their profits and complemented their financial needs by
having recourse to the local capital markets. In these
circumstances, only international loans allowed the maintenance
of the sustained growth of profits of the main American banks.
It is a fact that for a dozen of those banks controlling two
thirds of the American banks' foreign dealings, the source for
half of their profits (on average, for some banks it is more) is
to be found abroad. Such dependence on foreign operations
has given rise to a totally new phenomenon which was very
evident in the 1970s: the search for clients among the
developing countries.

Due to the large amount of liquidity on the market and
fierce competition among banks on account of this liquidity,
the American private banks began to grant big loans under
more liberal terms to certain developing countries. Their

apparently "neutral" character (due to the assumption that the only goal was profit with abstention from any political judgment or pressure) soon turned them into big favorites of governments with financial problems, and with difficult - or costly, in political terms - access to official financial sources. Thus, the American private banks ended up playing a very important role in the accelerated growth of the external public debt of many developing countries.

The process of internationalization of capital reflected in the extraordinary expansion of the foreign dealings of the American private banks and the accelerated growth of the market for Eurocurrencies, to which the recycling of petrodollars contributed in an important way, has had considerable repercussions on different aspects of the international economy. In effect it has added to world inflation in a significant way and has put off the consideration of important options that sought to favor the access of the poor countries to international liquidity.

In concrete terms, it has made the struggle to link Special Drawing Rights with official development assistance irrelevant. Furthermore, it revealed the inability of the governments of the central countries to control the external activity of their banks, and that of the IMF to regulate the expansion of international liquidity, supposedly one of its basic functions. Finally, it contributed to the accelerated growth of the external public debt of the developing world. For many of the countries that make up this world, it is preferable to use external resources which are available sometimes under good terms - there have been years in which world inflation annuls and even renders negative the real interest rates - than to introduce internal reforms which would alter the status quo and imply a high political cost. Nevertheless, what is often forgotten is that an excess of external debt without adequate criteria can equally imply a political cost, revealed in the loss of bargaining power of the country in question and the alienation of a part of national sovereignty, particularly of some national decision making centers.

In spite of everything, it is expected that the Third World's external public debt will continue to increase as a result of the financial needs of debtor countries as well as the fact that most of the required transfers of resources will come in the form of loans - not grants - carrying with them a financial burden which, in one way or another, has a bearing on the growth of the debt.

Insofar as the private component of the total debt increases more rapidly than the official component, that is, in that the trends toward a private banking system with respect to the debt are established with greater firmness, the panorama of the developing world's external debt will tend to deteriorate, unless radical measures (meaning new and efficient measures) are taken to avoid it.

If political commitment and good will were to become a norm, we could recognize the problem of the Third World's debt as one which transcends the mere financial sphere or that of the transfer of resources so as to involve the debtors as well as the creditors, and demand that the search for solutions be based on the adoption of measures and adjustments on both sides. The debtor countries must increase collaboration between themselves and, at the same time, find a way of increasing their internal savings through reforms which would include those of a fiscal and administrative nature. They must also increase their foreign exchange earnings by seeking to augment their exports. Fundamentally, in times of difficult access to the world markets, they must rationalize their imports. For their part, the creditor countries must increase their flows of financial assistance, concentrating on the relatively less-developed countries, aiding countries with middle and high incomes through better trade policies, improving the terms in which they transfer technology to these developing countries, opening their markets of capital and making sure that the private flows received by these countries are subject to less burdensome conditions, at least by extending the paying period.

Only the combination of these and other actions which involve both debtors and creditors can help to solve some, if not all, of the problems to which the Third World's foreign debt gives rise. In this way, the cases of insolvency and the measures it provokes (renegotiation, moratoria, etc.) will be notably reduced and could be attributed more to phenomena such as poor administration or corruption than to the existence of disproportionate and unjust relations between creditors and debtors.

NOTES

(1) By "privatization" the author understands the ever-increasing participation of private banks in the structure of the public external debt of developing countries.

(2) By financing of a concessional kind we mean financing provided under more favorable conditions than those existing in the international markets, with respect to interest rates, grace periods, and amortization terms.

(3) The classification of countries according to their income level - including the category of oil exporting countries - is that used by the World Bank. The countries with low incomes show annual levels below 200 million dollars; those with middle incomes fluctuate between 200 and 499 million, and those with high incomes obtain levels higher than 500 million dollars.

(4)   The 19 developing countries designated to the dialogue were: Algeria, Argentina, Brazil, Cameroon, Egypt, India, Indonesia, Iraq, Iran, Jamaica, Mexico, Nigeria, Pakistan, Peru, Saudi Arabia, Venezuela, Yugoslavia, Zaire, and Zambia.

(5)   The eight industrialized countries designated to the dialogue were: Australia, Canada, the EEC, Japan, Spain, Sweden, Switzerland, and the United States. In this case, the EEC represented all of its nine member countries.

6 Renegotiation of Third World Debt and Appropriate Adjustments in International Trade

Amit Bhaduri

It has been recognized that persistent tendencies toward accumulation of financial liabilities by some countries and corresponding accumulation of financial claims by others is only a surface phenomenon, reflecting more fundamental tendencies in the international payments mechanism. Therefore, the general issue of international debt cannot be treated in an isolated manner. It has to be viewed in the context of the present pattern of international trade and financial flows, because the question of debt management is throughly interlinked with the working of the international monetary system and the pattern of international trade. Reorganization in any one of these fields must result in corresponding reactions and adjustments in all related fields. The main purpose here is to attempt a comprehensive view, by setting the entire question of debt renegotiation in the perspective of international trade flows and monetary management.

The question of renegotiation of Third World debts has assumed special significance since 1973, following the sharp rise in the price of oil. This phenomenon brought about drastic changes in the international payments flows affecting almost all the trading partners. Broadly, all the non-oil producing countries were immediately affected, although the extent of this unfavorable impact varied considerably between developed and developing countries, as well as between individual countries within each group. It is useful to start with some idea of how much the international payment magnitudes changed in the course of a few months, taking 1973 as the 'base year' position. Table 6.1 presents the global current account payment flows during the years 1973 to 1976 by broad country groups.

Two rather important features emerge from Table 6.1, crucial for an understanding of the international debt

Table 6.1.   Global Current Account 1973-1976
(in US $ billion)

	1973	1974	1975	1976
Non-oil developing countries	- 8.6	-29.7	-38.3	-28.1
Major oil-exporting countries	6.2	67.2	35.3	44.0
OECD countries (excluding Turkey)	11.6	-20.1	8.8	- 6.9
Others[a]	- 4.3	-10.1	-17.7	-16.1
Total[b]	4.9	7.3	-11.9	- 7.1

[a]Includes centrally planned economics as well as Israel, Malta, and South Africa.

[b]Total of the four above specified regions, i.e., world total whose algebraic sum should be zero.   This item thus reflects inconsistencies in the recording of balance of payments.

Source: Figures are based upon IMF data compiled in Table IV.1, The External Debt of Developing Countries, Report No. 1595, The World Bank, May 1977.   The figures for 1977 are still not fully processed, and even 1976 data are subject to serious revision. Thus, according to the Annual Report of the Executive Director for the Fiscal Year Ended April 30, 1977, IMF, p. 15, the current account surplus of oil-exporters (last item of row 2) was 41 billion in 1976.

negotiation problem.   First, the magnitude of current account deficit of the Third World as a whole has gone up most sharply from somewhere around 9 billion to around 30 billion dollars. Secondly, this sharp deficit has been more than compensated by the current account surplus of OPEC (except in 1975), so that, in effect, OPEC countries have become the net lenders to the rest of the Third World.   It is exceedingly important to grasp this point because OECD countries have ceased to have an unambiguous current account surplus over a number of years and, in the final analysis, they are no longer net lenders to developing countries.   Thus, a fundamental change has come about in the international payments flows insofar as one group, the oil-producing countries, is now the ultimate lender to the rest of the Third World.

The fact that the total import bill of OPEC countries has systematically been well below their export proceeds, a tendency most likely to continue in the near future, necessarily means a corresponding deficit on the part of the rest of the world, particularly the non-oil developing countries. (NODCs). While this deficit has continued to be covered primarily through the creation of international debt, it is possible to conceive of at least three other major avenues. First, the surplus countries could acquire direct ownership rights or equities in the deficit countries. Secondly, the countries in surplus could make direct grants to countries in deficit. Lastly, the IMF could issue special drawing rights on a scale large enough to cover deficit by countries that would exhaust their reserves if they did not borrow. It has, by now, become evident that international debt is the main way in which imbalances are being financed. International debt, thus, reflects imbalances in international payments, and, for the most part, only one among several possible methods is being used to cover such imbalances. As a result, two questions can be distinguished in relation to debt: Why do systematic imbalances in international payments continue? Why is it that these imbalances have to be covered through debt creation alone?

Any attempt to understand these two issues must involve an analysis of the external economic problems of the countries where debts are accumulating sharply, and an analysis of the workings of the international monetary system. But first it is helpful to make a quantitative assessment of the overall debt problem facing the Third World.

As revealed by available data, one of the most striking features of the developing countries' debt is the changing role of public and private creditors in the international capital market. Private creditors have increasingly come to dominate as lenders to the Third World. This tendency has consistently been evident at least since 1967, and there was no dramatic break in the "trend-line" around 1973. Thus, it seems valid to argue that the increasing dominance of private creditors in the international capital market is almost an inherent tendency of that market, rather than the outcome of some "special event" like the rise in oil price.

One of the most unfavorable consequences of this change in the source of credit from public to private lenders has been the worsening burden of debt falling on NODCs. This can partly be seen by looking at an index called the time-profile of debt which is defined as the ratio of debt payments (interest and principal) summed over a given number of years (usually five or ten years, according to banking conventions) to the total outstanding debt at a given date. Thus, the time-profile measure of the debt burden is a ratio of two stock items at a given date. Table 6.2 shows how it changed for NODCs between 1969 and 1972.

Table 6.2.   Time-profile Index of Debt Burden

	1969		1974	
	5-year ratio	10-year ratio	5-year ratio	10-year ratio
86 developing countries	48	84	52	90
a) Loan from government	39	71	38	71
b) Loan from international organization	38	75	31	69
c) Loan from private sources	75	106	79	124
Selected Regions				
Latin America and Caribbean	58	91	67	85
a) Loan from government	43	72	50	85
b) Loan from international organization	45	91	43	90
c) Loan from private sources	82	109	85	132
South Asia	34	63	30	55
a) Loan from government	30	61	31	60
b) Loan from international organization	26	50	16	31
c) Loan from private sources	78	116	78	106

Source: World Bank, World Debt Tables, Vol. 1 (EC-167/76), October 31, 1976, p. 18.

Table 6.2 makes two important points.   First, consequent upon an increase in the relative importance of private sources of credit, the terms and conditions of borrowing hardened considerably for NODCs.   Thus, the time-profile index of 5 years rose from 48 to 52 percent while the same 10 year-index rose from 84 to 90 percent.   This implies a shortening maturity period of the overall time structure of debt repayment, as more detailed country-wide study reveals.   Secondly, it will be seen that the overall time-profile index for Latin America and the Caribbean is considerably above the Third World average. This is partly due to the fact that, on an average, they obtain loans   on   less   concessional   terms   from   public   sources   and international organizations. But perhaps a more important reason is Latin America's heavier dependence on private sources of credit.

The other important index normally used to evaluate both the burden and the managability of debt is the debt service ratio, i.e., the ratio of annual servicing cost of debt (principal and interest) to annual export earnings from goods and nonfactor services. It will be noted that the debt service index is a ratio of two "flows" in a given period, while the time-profile index is a ratio of two "stocks" at a given date. Hence, both these ratios are simultaneously used to have an assessment of both the "stock" and the "flow" aspect of outstanding debt.

Table 6.3 tries to present a reasonably comprehensive picture of selected developing countries in accordance with their performance over time by the debt service index.

It is evident from table 6.3 that about one third of NODCs(1) have very significant debt service problems where something over 10 percent of their export proceeds are simply used to service debt. There are also several other alternative data to indicate the serious proportions which the servicing problem has reached in some Third World countries. According to World Bank estimates at the end of 1974, there were nineteen countries with an outstanding public debt exceeding 100 percent of their annual export proceeds. The servicing problem also is reflected in the ratio of net to gross assistance received by developing countries. Rough estimates suggest that annual debt servicing is already taking away about one-half of the new assistance they receive.(2) In a recent speech, the president of the World Bank broadly confirmed such an estimate by stating that by 1980, half of all gross borrowings will be needed for armotization payments.(3)

Quite apart from the problem of the growing volume of debt incurred by most Third World countries and its associated servicing burden, there is a somewhat different aspect to this whole question: the changing composition of debt by sources and its pattern of distribution among developing countries. It has already been pointed out that private sources of credit have increasingly come to dominate the scene so that well over 50 percent of the present outstanding debt is owed to private lenders. This, in turn, implies that commercial considerations of credit worthiness have also become increasingly important. There seem to be at least two important consequences of this. First, a relatively small subset of developing countries belonging to the middle-income group have been able to borrow on a significant scale from commercial banks and other private sources. This fact has added a new dimension to the problem: the ability of these countries to carry their debt without precipitating a generalized crisis in the international bank-ing system. Evidence on the issue is somewhat mixed, and

Table 6.3.   Debt Service Ratio of Selected
Developing Countries

	1967	1970	1973	1974
Group A: Countries with ratios over 20% in 1973 (6 countries)				
Egypt[a]	19.4	26.2	35.0	32.0
Mexico[c]	24.6	25.2	25.2	18.4
Pakistan[a]	18.5	27.8	21.9	15.3
Peru[a, c]	11.1	13.9	32.2[b]	25.6
Uruguay	17.0	19.2	29.2	21.8
Zambia	2.4	5.7	28.5	5.1
Group B: Countries with ratios 15-20% in 1973 (8 countries)				
Afganistan[a]	11.2	19.8	19.5	17.9
Algeria	2.0	3.7	15.1	14.4
Argentina[b]	25.9	21.0	17.8	16.2
Burma	6.4	16.0	18.7	14.4
India[a]	22.5	22.3	18.0	15.9
Iran	5.0	11.4	15.9[b]	6.8
Israel	15.7	18.6	17.7	18.7
Nicaragua	6.4	10.6	17.8	10.7
Group C: Countries with ratios 10-15% in 1973 (12 countries)				
Bolivia	5.9	10.9	15.0	11.6
Brazil[a, c]	15.6	15.1	13.1	15.2
Chile[a]	12.6	18.3	11.8	11.1
Colombia	14.2	11.9	13.6	16.7
Costa Rica	12.0	9.7	10.2	9.4
Gabon	4.7	5.4	14.7	4.4
S. Korea	6.2	21.0	10.3	10.5
Paraguay	7.4	11.2	10.3	7.8
Sri. Lanka	3.9	9.7	12.9	11.2
Sudan	5.6	9.2	10.9	11.7
Tunisia	20.6	19.5	12.0	7.2
Turkey[a]	16.4	22.5	13.1	12.2
Group D: Countries with ratio below 10% in 1973 but above 10% in 1974 (2 countries)				
Somalia	–	–	3.6	13.4
Zaire	–	–	8.5	11.7

[a]Debt service payments reduced in some years shown through debt relief arrangements.

[b]Debt service figures include prepayments.

[c]These ratios do not include service on private sector debt which is significant for the countries indicated.

Source: World Bank, World Debt Tables, Vol. 1 (EC-167/76), October 31, 1976, p. 19.

bankers, in their wisdom, can have more than one opinion.
But from the point of view of developing countries, the
question may even be judged as misleading. Suppose a country fails to satisfy some criterion of commercial credit
worthiness, in spite of its generally proved or expected
potentials for growth. Will this imply the sacrifice of growth
in the name of "sound finance"? In a different context,
Keynes had long ago warned against what he called the
"humbug of finance." The central problem of international
debt management today is to renegotiate and reorder the
pattern of debt in such a way as to accelerate economic
progress, particularly of the poorer countries, and not to
retard their process of development in the name of "financial
discipline." It is from this perspective that we will proceed
to analyze the nature of the rising debt problem.

INTERNATIONAL DEBT AND EXTERNAL ECONOMIC
RELATIONS OF THE THIRD WORLD

The external economic relations of the Third World are
overwhelmingly with the rich Western countries, rather than
with socialist countries or with one another. This is a pattern
which has hardly changed over the past two decades. The
predominance of the Western countries in shaping the external
economic relations of the developing countries is visible in
almost every important sphere, including trade, finance, and
technology. For example, about 75 percent of the external
trade of the Third World is with members of the OECD, 15 to
20 percent is among themselves, and only about 5 percent is
with centrally planned economies.(4) In the sphere of finance,
assets or exchange reserves of developing countries are held
almost exclusively in Western currencies. Given the pattern of
trade, this follows as a corollary, insofar as exchange reserves
are primarily held to settle trade deficits. But less
predictably, the pattern has remained almost unchanged in
spite of the emergence of massive and persistent surplus of oil
producing developing countries. Thus, although the pattern
of international trade surplus and deficits has undergone
considerable change since 1973 - with OPEC rather than the
OECD becoming the major net lender to the rest of the Third
World - this has not altered the fact that the exchange reserve
of the entire Third World continues to be held almost
exclusively in Western currencies through their commercial
banking systems.(5)
     In addition to trade and exchange reserves, foreign
private investment in the Third World derives almost
exclusively from Western sources. Such foreign
private investment not only has long-term "factor-payments"

implications for the balance of payments of developing
countries, but it usually also has implications in terms of
import of nonindigenous technology. Thus, regardless of their
internal economic and political institutions, the attractions of
trade, finance, and technology have usually been sufficient to
tie most Third World countries to the Western international
economic system.

Yet it can be said that, over time, such a pattern of
involvement has not been beneficial to the developing
countries. As is well known, one of the main reasons for this
is the extreme degree of commodity-concentration in the export
of the Third World to OECD countries. As a broad
generalization, it is valid to say that the main source of export
earnings for almost all developing countries is sales of primary
commodities, for which the world markets are unstable and
slow to expand, by and large experiencing declining trends in
price relative to industrial products. For primary commodities
other than oil, average prices relative to manufactures,
between the mid-1950s and the mid-1970s, fell between 10 and
20 percent. At the same time, the expansion of markets for
primary commodities has been much slower than that for
manufacturing - food items grew by about 5 percent a year,
raw materials other than oil by about 4 percent a year, while
market for manufactured goods grew about 10 percent.(6)
Thus, in terms of both price and quantity, the nonoil,
primary, commodity producers have been more or less
continuous losers over time in the international market. Yet,
for most developing countries, two or three such primary
products account for more than 60 percent of their total export
earnings.

Table 6.4 shows, in aggregate terms, the movements in
relative prices or terms of trade for broad commodity groups
over time.

Despite the highly aggregative nature of the data in table
6.4 and associated index-number problems, it seems to be valid
to say that the overall terms of trade have moved against
primary commodity producers by at least 10 percent over the
last two decades. But such aggregates tend to hide even more
serious problems being faced by some nations. For it is again
a broadly valid generalization to say that the poorest Third
World countries are relatively even more dependent on a few
primary commodities for their exports than the middle-income
developing countries. Table 6.5 gives some idea of the
extent of this dependence on a few commodities for the
poorest nations in the world.

Two points are worth noticing in table 6.5. First, the
poorest countries concentrate more on agricultural commodities
than on metals, minerals, and ores for their exports; and the
rate of decline in the relative price of agricultural goods has
been faster than that for metals and minerals. This can be

Table 6.4.   Terms of trade for producers of commodities*
(1974 = 100)

Year	Agriculture	Metals, minerals, and ores	34 commodities excluding petroleum
1950-54	108	85	103
1955-59	95	88	93
1960-64	81	78	80
1965-69	78	100	83
1970-74	83	85	83
1974-78**	84	89	N.A.

*Defined as an index of commodity prices in current US $, weighted by values of exports from developing countries (in 1967-69), divided by an index of the U.S. $ prices of exports of manufactures from developed countries to all destinations.
**Incomplete private calculation based on more limited data compared to the rest of the table.

Sources: Commodities and Export Projects Division, World Bank.   Based upon that data computed in Table 2, p. 208 in M. Abdel-Fadil et al., "A New International Economic Order." The last row is based upon private tentative calculation using incomplete OECD data for similar (but not identical) commodity groups.

Table 6.5.   Share of Poorest Countries (below per capita $200) in World Exports by Some of Their Principal Exported Commodities

Commodity	Percentage of world exports
Tea	73.7
Jute	68.4
Cocoa beans	63.1
Ground nuts	55.4
Palm kernel	39.8
Raw rubber	36.2
Raw cotton	18.6
Rice	12.5

Sources: FAO Trade Yearbook 1973;   FAO Monthly Bulletin of Agricultural Economics and Statistics, December 1974; Development Cooperation, 1975 Review, OECD p. 54.

seen by looking at the two corresponding price indexes in
table 6.4, where the relative price between agricultural
products and metals, minerals, and ores moved from a ratio of
about 1.27 in 1950-54 to about 0.98 in 1970-74 and less than
0.95 in 1974-78. This price ratio was most unfavorable against
agricultural commodities during 1965-69, when it reached a
ratio of 0.78. Secondly, it is probably true that the prices
of tea, jute, cocoa beans, and rubber have been even more
unfavorable compared to the other products in table 6.5.(7)
And still, the concentration of the poorest countries in
commodities such as tea, jute, and cocoa is among the highest.
It may not be an exaggeration to suggest that the larger the
share of the poorest countries in the world export of a
commodity, the more unfavorable is the price movement of that
commodity.(8) In brief, the present price structure of world
trade seems most heavily weighted against the poorest
countries, who can least afford to pay.

One problem deserving special attention in this connection
is that of price uncertainty for primary commodities and the
resulting fluctuations in export earnings. Indeed, the problem
seems to be compounded by the fact that years of relative
scarcity marked by somewhat higher prices in the international
market usually coincide with poor domestic production which
keeps down export earnings, while years of relative abundance
usually are accompanied by too sharp a decline in price to be
compensated by a greater volume of exports. Thus,
fluctuations take place around a low 'floor' of foreign exchange
earnings from exports, which makes financing of developmental
efforts almost a matter of chance. As a result, either the
financing of long-term development plans has to be drastically
reduced or, in the absence of enough foreign assistance,
external debt has to be contracted just to keep committed
expenditure programs going.

There is thus, a vicious circle in which the financial
management of these countries gets caught. A low rate of
growth of investment means relatively few new projects and a
correspondingly higher proportion of investment committed to
total developmental expenditure. This implies a lower degree
of flexibility in financing management, as expenditure on the
committed projects will have to be continued. A bad year of
lower export earnings, in the absence of much flexibility in
financial management, leads to debt which, in turn, reduces
available foreign exchange at the next round through higher
servicing costs and, perhaps, a still lower level of investment.
On the other hand, in a year of relatively easy foreign
exchange position, there are economic compulsions to raise the
level of fresh expenditure on development and, thus, lower the
proportion of committed expenditure in the total.

Much of the problem of mounting debt of the developing
countries is a reflection of the inherent imbalances in the

pattern of international trade; imbalances which arise from both the price structure and the regional distribution of trade. At the same time, even minor attempts at correcting such imbalances through diversification of exports - in terms of either range of commodities exported or the range of trading partners - have proved to be exceedingly difficult.

In this context, there are at least two serious problems faced by almost any Third World country. First, the decreasing dependence on primary products that increased export of manufactures makes possible is jeopardized by increasing competition from producers in highly industrialized Western countries. In such competition, the established industrial nations have a decided advantage on virtually every point, except for a few specialized products such as textiles and clothing where very low wages can yield comparative advantage to industries in the Third World. But, even so, the growth of sales of these few products to the West has systematically been encountered by trade restrictions imposed to protect industries within Western countries. According to one estimate, the post-Kennedy Round effective tariff rate on import of manufactures from developing countries was almost 24 percent in the United States, and 17 percent in the EEC, compared to an average of 10 percent.(9) In brief, the working of the market mechanism in the sphere of international trade, which heavily favors the Western nations on the whole, has been further manipulated by those very nations to gain still greater advantage from world trade at the cost of the developing countries. The import quota restriction on "cheap Asiatic textiles" imposed by many OECD countries is an example of this.

Since the 1973 rise in oil prices, a new possibility of trade diversification in terms of partners has emerged for the Third World. With the massive increase in the purchasing power of OPEC countries, some changes in the pattern of world trade should clearly be possible. As already pointed out, about 75 percent of the external trade of the Third World is with OECD countries, and only about 15 to 20 percent is among themselves. Along with trade creation through increased purchasing power of the OPEC countries, it should also be possible to divert some trade from OECD to the Third World itself. Two distinct issues are involved. First, trade creation in those particular commodities where low-wage developing countries have a distinct advantage; even on the basis of competition, the volume of trade among the Third World countries could be increased. Secondly, there is a question of trade diversion toward the Third World by giving preferential treatment to industries within it. This will be a kind of limited protectionism practiced by the developing countries, exactly along the lines shown by the European Economic Community, which perhaps, had far less justification.

Given the highly unfavorable international market in most primary commodities, as well as the many-sided problem of trade diversification in the Third World, the international payments situation could have been somewhat eased without getting into the problem of mounting debt, had grants and soft loans been forthcoming on a large enough scale. But the present picture is far from satisfactory.

Concessional aid from OECD nations has not increased in real terms. As a matter of fact, in 1976, the total official development assistance (ODA) was 6 percent below the estimates the previous year; and, in real terms, was actually less than it had been in 1975. More revealing is the fact that the ODA level, in real terms, has been more or less stationary over almost a decade, while during that same period, the real income of the OECD nations has increased by more than 40 percent. Consequently, ODA as a percentage of gross national product (GNP) fell from 0.42 in 1966 to 0.33 in 1976. Thus, the 1976 ratio of 0.33 is even less than one-half of the 0.70 percent goal acceptd by the United Nations General Assembly in 1970.

Not only has the overall level of developmental assistance been grossly insufficient and ungenerous (except for Norway, Sweden, and the Netherlands), but even that meager performance has typically tended to be distributed in an unfair and often politically motivated fashion. Very broadly speaking, one would have expected that, for the more advanced developing countries, adequate access to the international capital market on reasonable terms and expanding trade opportunities would be the more crucial issue, while, for the poorest countries in their very early stages of development, the 'grant' element in foreign assistance would have to be increased significantly, if such developmental process has to rely on foreign assistance at all. According to the present pattern of distribution of concessional assistance, the poorest nations having per capita income below $200 (geographically concentrated in South Asia and Sub-Saharan Africa) receive not more than half of the total concessional assistance. Table 6.6 gives a more detailed idea of the growth in net flow of total resources in nominal terms by broad regional groups from 1972 to 1975.

From table 6.6, it is clear that the developing countries in South America as well as Oceania have seen a considerably lower than average growth in the net flow of resources in their favor. At the same time, the developing countries of Europe and North and Central America have experienced the fastest growth of net resource flow in their favor, together with the Middle East. It appears, on the whole, that geographical proximity to the rich industrialized nations has been an important factor affecting the pattern of net resource flows. But, at the same time, it is also evident that the

Table 6.6. Net Flow of Resources to Developing
Regions from DAC Countries and Multilateral Agencies,
1972-75

	1972	(1972 = 100) 1973	1974	1975
Europe[a]	100	119	176	279
Africa total	100	121	150	264
North of Sahara[b]	100	84	158	289
South of Sahara	100	142	163	236
American North and Central[c]	100	208	338	277
South America[d]	100	130	161	154
Asia Total	100	144	139	202
Middle East	100	182	68	343
South Asia	100	119	199	258
Far East	100	140	141	160
Oceania	100	114	116	118
Total	100	131	157	212

[a]Includes Portugal, Cyprus, Gibraltar, Greece, Malta, Spain, Turkey and Yugoslavia.

[b]Includes Algeria, Libyan Arab Republic, Morocco, Tunisia, Egypt.

[c]Includes Bahamas, Barbados, Bermuda, Costa Rica, Cuba, Dominican Republic, El Salvador, Guadeloupe, Guatemala, Haiti, Honduras, Belize, Jamaica, Martinique, Mexico, Antilles, Nicaragua, Panama, Trinidad and Tobago, Anguilla, Dominica, West Indies Br, and Grenada.

[d]Argentina, Bolivia, Brazil, Chile, Colombia, Ecuador, Falkland, Islanas, Guyana, Guiana (Fr), Paraguay, Peru, Surinam, Uruguay, Venezuela.

Source: Compiled from Development Cooperation, 1976 Review, OECD. Based on tables 26, 27, and 28, pp. 242-47.

present international economic order has been incapable of
accelerating the net flow of resources to any significant extent
in favor of the poorest developing countries in South Asia and
Sub-Saharan Africa.

It can now be seen that the growing debt problem is the
result of several forces operating in the international market.
Relatively poor prospects of primary commodities, difficulties in
the diversification of Third World exports, and poor 'aid'
performance of the rich industrial countries have combined to
precipitate the growing problem of debt. In this sense, it is
a structural problem inherent in the present system of
international trade. This has two very important inplications
for renegotiation of Third World debt. First, renegotiation of
outstanding debt will merely solve the problem in the short
run, at best, unless the present structure of international
trade is altered in several ways. Secondly, renegotiation of
debt must proceed simultaneously with removing the three main
impediments to a better system of international trade.
Simultaneously with debt renegotiation, attempts must be made
1) to improve the commercial prospect of primary commodities,
2) to diversify exports from the Third World and, 3) to
improve the 'aid' performance of the rich industrial nations.
Except in this wider context, the issue of debt renegotiation
can have no radical or lasting solution.

ECONOMIC GROWTH OF DEVELOPING COUNTRIES AND MANAGEABILITY OF DEBT. DEVELOPMENT IMPERATIVE VS. FINANCIAL DISCIPLINE IN THE WORKING OF THE INTERNATIONAL FINANCIAL SYSTEM

While it is our view that an understanding of the structural
causes of mounting Third World debt is essential for any
lasting solution, the problem has become still more complicated
in recent years due to its serious implications for the working
of the international financial system.

There are two almost contradictory views which need to
be reconciled for any satisfactory resolution of the
international debt problem. On the one hand, it is clear that
sufficient inflow of resources must be guaranteed to non-oil
developing countries in their attempt to restructure the
pattern of world trade; rigid views about "financial discipline"
must not be allowed to interfere with their genuine longer-term
growth prospects. But, on the other, a certain degree of
financial stability has to be maintained in the international
system. Thus, debt renegotiation to assure an increased net
inflow through lower servicing cost for the Third World
has to be reconciled with a certain degree of international
financial stability, in which not only national governments and

international agencies, but also the international commercial banking system, have become increasingly involved. With sharply rising international debt in which an increasingly higher proportion is being financed by private sources, debt renegotiation is bound to affect the working of the transnational banking system in which the rich industrial nations have an enormous stake. The question of 'financial discipline' in terms of scheduled repayment is consequently counterposed to the imperative of faster economic development in the Third World.

Technical literature on the subject of debt managability has long been hinting at some of these aspects.(10) Assuming stable prices, it views the process as a race between two crucial variables growing at exponential rates: debt and income. Debt is assumed to be caused by the gap between investment and domestic savings and the interest accruing on growing debt. Thus, changes in reserves as well as noninterest-bearing capital inflows are ignored as a first approximation (particularly valid for private loans). At the same time, amortization of past debt is also ignored on the plausible assumption that, as long as a gap exists, scheduled repayments will continue to be outweighed by new borrowings. While higher investment entails a higher inflow of external finance, it also causes income to grow at a faster pace and, thereby, increases domestic savings capability in order to lower the requirements of external finance. Thus begins the race between growth rates of income and debt, which can be stylized in terms of simple algebraic models of the following sort:

From the definitional equation of the Harrod-Domar type,

$$g \equiv \frac{dY/dt}{Y(t)} = \frac{I(t)}{Y(t)} \cdot \frac{1}{v} \cdot \text{ where } v = \frac{dY/dt}{I(t)},$$

i.e., the incremental capital-output ratio.

Hence, $I(t) = g.vY(t) = g\ vY_o e^{gt}$ ....(1)

and assuming a constant savings propensity

$$S(t) = sY(t) = sY_o e^{gt} \dots\dots\dots\dots\dots\dots\dots\dots\dots(2)$$

The absolute growth in debt is consequently represented by the difference of the above two equations and accumulated debt at any point of time T including the interest charge which is given as,

$$D(T) = \int_o^T I(t) - S(t)\Big]\ e^{i(T-t)} dt \dots\dots\dots\dots\dots(3)$$

Substituting (1) and (2) in (3) and performing the integration, on simplification we obtain (given $g \neq i$),

$$D(T) = \frac{(gv-s)}{(g-i)} \, Y_o \, (e^{gT} - e^{iT}), \, g \neq i \dots\dots\dots\dots\dots(4)$$

Two interesting conclusions emerge from this algebra. First, the ratio of accumulated debt to national income is given as,

$$r(t) = \frac{D(T)}{Y(T)} = \frac{(gv-s)}{(g-i)} \, \frac{Y_o \, (e^{gT} - e^{iT})}{Y_o \, eg^T}$$

$$= \frac{(gv-s)}{(g-i)} \, \left[1-o^{(i-g)\,T} \right] \dots\dots\dots\dots(5)$$

Hence, taking a sufficiently long-term point of view,

$$T \xrightarrow{Lt} {}^a \quad r(T) = \frac{(gv-s)}{(g-i)} \text{ if } g > i \dots\dots\dots\dots(6)$$

But the same ratio of debt to national income $r(t)$ tends to infinity if $g < i$ in (6). Thus, so long as the growth rate of national income exceeds the average interest rate on external borrowing, the debt income ratio levels off at

$$\frac{(gv-s)}{(g-i)} \, .$$

Secondly, the maximum value of the debt-income ratio $r(T)$ is obtained by setting the first derivative with respect to T to zero (the second order condition is satisfied if $g > i$, so that there is a finite upper limit to this ratio, as already seen) to obtain

$$(gv-s) \, e^{(i-g)T} = \frac{(gv-s)}{e^{(g-i)T}} = 0 \dots\dots\dots\dots\dots\dots(7)$$

from which it is easy to see that the condition is satisfied for infinitely large values of T. In other words, the debt income ratio symptomatically approaches its upper limit

$$\frac{(gv-s)}{(g-i)} \text{ for } g - i,$$

through a gradual deceleration of this ratio over time.

It seems needles to point out that the above model is so utterly simple that it cannot be directly used for analyzing the international debt question. Significant amendments have to be made in at least three important aspects before it can even vaguely resemble an econometric exercise with estimated values of the relevant parameters. First, some of the parameters (i.e., savings ratio and incremental capital-output ratio) must be allowed to change with time. Secondly, noninterest-bearing capital inflows in the form of grants, changes in the international reserve position, as well as 'grace period' complications on softer terms have to be incorporated into the analysis. Finally, without looking at the effects of anticipated and unanticipated inflation on outstanding debt and real interest rates, such an analysis will not have much applicability for the post-1973 international scene.

Despite all these reservations, even this simple abstract model is useful for making at least one essential point on the practical question of debt renegotiation. Compatibility of financial stability for private lenders in the form of manageable debt without significant default, and the simultaneous requirements of growth in the Third World, compel one to judge the question of terms of new borrowings in relation to the actual growth performance of the borrowing countries. Traditional banking wisdom has looked upon this as a question of \ creditworthiness at given terms and conditions of borrowing. Indeed, lender's risk premiums have been increased when growth performance was poor. In the context of the renegotiation of Third World debt, the question must be reformulated: countries that have a lower growth performance over time and, consequently, are faced with a more serious debt problem are precisely the countries that should be able to obtain external finance on easier terms. This makes transnational banks' analyses of country-risk and creditworthiness invalid. But, from the point of view of longer term manageability (depending on the crucial condition $g > i$), the facts seem worthy of serious consideration.

Within a commercial banking system, this may not be possible because transnational banks must be assumed to be more interested in making their business profitable than in seeing the Third World develop rapidly. But this is precisely where international distribution of ODA has to play a compensating role. Third World countries with poorer growth performance, rather than being pushed to the wall, should be able to get a higher proportion of ODA or concessional finance, so that the 'weighted average' terms and conditions of obtaining external finance become cheaper for these countries while the debt ratio remains viable in the long run. Undoubtedly, such a system gives the impression of encouraging inefficiencies and rewarding slower growth. But it should be possible to find sufficient safeguards against this, in the form of monitoring of growth performance. Thus, in the absence of serious special conditions (such as sharp fall in terms of trade, or weather conditions beyond anyone's control) a continued, poor growth performance may be penalized with lower ODA inflow after a trial run of several years. However, it should be very clear that the rich industrial nations have no right today to even speak of such monitoring(11) without substantially improving their own dismal performance in ODA.

As far as the middle-income, faster growing, developing countries are concerned, their primary requirement must be

greater trade and wider access to the international credit
market on more reasonable terms. In their case, the
reasonableness of terms of borrowing has to be judged in
relation to their growth performance over a number of years,
and transnational banks must also pay adequate attention to
this growth factor in determining lending rates. But, in
addition to terms and conditions of borrowing, the whole issue
of debt renegotiation for these countries must proceed
simultaneously with trade negotiations relating to price support
for their primary commodities exported and diversification of
their exports. It is here that tariff and other trade barriers
against their export of manufactures to OECD countries ought
to be abolished as an integral part of debt negotiation. And,
surely, if removal of such trade barriers is unacceptable to
rich Western nations because they wish to protect domestic
employment, it should, at least, be possible to claim
compensation for such unfair trade practices.

The argument for linking ODA assistance, as well as
trade negotiations, with the debt question must be based, not
upon sentimental arguments of "rich helping poor," but upon
the emerging compulsions of the international financial scene.
Given the already accumulated surplus of OPEC countries, and
projected future annual surplus of 30 to 40 billion dollars, the
'recycling' of petrodollars has become one of the most crucial
issues in international finance to which the debt renegotiation
problem is linked. Since under the present international
monetary system, the dollar still is the 'reserve currency' of
highest importance, the massive current account deficits of all
non-oil countries have been, in effect, met continuously
through increased dollar liabilities of the United States. This
can be seen in a summary form from an analysis of the sources
of international reserve creation and its beneficiaries (1970-74)
presented in table 6.7.

Although rather outdated, table 6.7 is indicative of the
broad tendencies in the biased working of the international
monetary system. Concerted international decisions (row 2A)
accounted for only 7 percent of the growth of reserves in
1970-74 and, less than 0.5 per cent for physical additions to
the world monetary gold stock. The remaining contribution of
over 92 percent came from national currencies serving as
international reserves. With this tendency operating in the
world monetary system, reserve creation cannot be said to be
a collective decision, but to result from individual country
decisions. At the same time, row 2, columns 4 and 5, show
that about 97 percent of reserve credit (96.4 billion) of the
IMF benefited 27 rich, industrial nations, and only 3 percent
(3.2 billion) the 99 poorer, developing countries.

With the massive accumulation of OPEC surpluses, the
rich industrial nations had to face a simple choice. They
could have allowed OPEC countries to convert their financial

RENEGOTIATION OF THIRD WORLD DEBT 147

Table 6.7.   Sources and Beneficiaries of International
Reserve Creation, 1970-1974
(Unit: billions SDR = US $, until 1971)

	World	Industrial Countries			Third World Countries		
		U.S.	Other	Total	OPEC	Other	Total
Balance of payments change*	0.3	-66.2	22.5	-43.7	33.6	10.4	44.0
Beneficiaries of credit reserve creation:	99.6	62.4	34.0	96.4	0.2	2.9	3.2
Of concerted reserve creation:	7.3	1.2	2.9	4.2	0.2	2.9	3.2
SDR allocation	9.3	2.3	4.7	7.0	0.3	2.0	2.3
Net IMF lending**	-1.4	-1.0	-1.2	-2.2	-0.1	1.0	0.9
Net BIS-EF lending	-0.6	-	-0.6	-0.6	-	-	-
Of acceptance of national currencies as international reserve	92.3	61.1	31.2	92.3	-	-	-
Gross Reserves (row 1 plus row 2)	99.9	-3.9	56.5	52.7	33.9	13.3	47.2

*Balance of payments net charge (surpluses or deficits) is measured by the difference between the increase in the country's gross reserve in row 3 and their reserve liabilities in row 2 of the table. Their net total for the world as a whole is equal, by definition, to the increase in world gold reserve, including those of IMF, BIS (Bank for International Settlement) and EF (European Fund), shown in row 1, column 1.
**Net IMF lending is the sum of IMF "Gold deposits and investments" and "Use of Fund Credit" minus the undistributed profits of the IMF, allocated here pro rata of quotas: 23 percent to the US, 49 percent to other industrialized countries of the West, 5 percent to OPEC, and 23 percent to other Third World countries.

Source: Duncan Ndegwa and Robert Triffin, "The International Monetary Order" in Reshaping the International Order (RIO), ed. Jan Tinbergen (New York: E.P. Dutton, 1976), p. 201, Table 1 based upon international reserves tables published in the January 1969 and May 1975 issues of International Financial Statistics.   The table, due to lack of internation, excludes centrally planned economies.

claims (held in national currencies) to tangible assets in their countries, which would have meant OPEC's financial power getting rapidly converted to industrial power, through transfer of ownership rights.   OECD countries prevented such a natural "market solution" in very early stages after the oil price rise, so that, for the first time, the international economic system witnessed the uneasy, but at least partial, separation between industrial and financial power.   The massive petrodollar surplus held largely in transnational banks of OECD countries (and the United States, in particular) is a reflection of this uneasy separation.

Insofar as the "recycling of OPEC surplus" is taking place increasingly through the commercial banking system of the West, flushed with liquid surplus and, thereby, raising alarms of default and manageability of commercial debt in particular, it must be stressed that this is a direct conse- quence brought about almost entirely as a result of the decision of the OECD countries.   Under these circumstances, it seems not only a legitimate but small demand that at least official debts should be fully renegotiated.   This would in- volve renegotiation of the principal, terms, and condition of past as well as future borrowing of external finance by Third World countries in relation to their growth performance in a manner broadly outlined above.   It would also imply linking to ODA to commercial lending so that the poorest nations of the Third World are not left out.   For financial stability, this is probably more in the interest of the rich nations than of de- veloping countries.   It is also a very small price to pay for not surrendering even a part of their industrial power to OPEC.

SUMMARY OF FINDINGS AND RECOMMENDED
CHANGES FOR THE NIEO

The problem of the mounting debt of non-oil developing countries arises from structural imbalances in the international trade and monetary system.   On the one hand, it is the result of weak external economic relations of the Third World in the sphere of trade and finance; and on the other, a biased and outdated international monetary system with a few national currencies serving as "international reserves."   In the field of trade and finance, developing countries face three major types of obstacles: (1) decline in their terms of trade for primary commodities, excluding oil;   (2) difficulties in diversifying exports in face of competition from powerful nations and their protectionist policies toward manufacturers from the Third World;   and (3) absolutely dismal performance of most OECD countries in terms of ODA and other concessional finance.

The question of debt manageability has assumed new proportions, following the increased importance of private lenders, and has resulted in fear of large-scale default of commercial loans. This must be seen as an outcome of the partial separation of industrial from financial power among nations, following the oil-price rise in 1973. Such a separation is a deliberate decision of the West, reinforced by the working of the international monetary system. Hence, debt renegotiation for international financial stability is also in their own interest.

Revising a suggestion of the Pearson Commission, debt renegotiation on a world scale may proceed along the following four major lines:

1. All principal lent through official sources should be completely written off.
2. Terms and conditions of other outstanding debt should be revised in terms of the growth performance of borrowing countries. The logic behind using 'growth performance' rather than 'income level' as the dominant criterion is explained in this chapter. Similarly, for manageability of future debts, even transnational banks must take into account 'the growth performance criterion,' and lend generally on easier terms for development.
3. Concessional assistance from rich nations on an increased scale may be used to reduce the 'weighted average' rate of interest for commercial borrowing in poorer and slow-growing developing economies of the Third World.
4. There should be general agreement that during years of recession in rich nations, the volume of ODA and other assistance will be sharply increased with lower repayment from the Third World. During years of prosperity, repayment from the Third World (whose trade links with the OECD are the strongest) will be raised. This timing agreement will, at least partly, act as a "built-in-stabilizer" in international economic relations. The outstanding debt from official sources should also be linked to this general consideration of "demand management."

Writing off official outstanding debt will contribute to generating increased volume of world trade, as the servicing cost of debt can be diverted to importing goods.

The problem of debt will be a recurring question unless "structural changes" are carried out in the sphere of world trade. For primary commodities, all price-support schemes (including specific proposals such as the "common fund" and "integrated commodity scheme," indexation of commodity prices, and formation of producers association) must be thoroughly examined and proposals along those lines implemented as an integral part of the NIEO. OECD countries must agree not to follow a protectionist import policy toward Third World manufactures, and, in case of proved tariff or quota restriction, they must pay compensation to the developing countries trying to diversify their exports. Industrial development of the Third World cannot proceed without strong measures in this direction.

Most of these charges will turn out to be in the long-run interest of the world community. It is fair to expect that some of the shorter-term adjustment costs will be borne by the rich industrial nations of the West. Without some genuine sense of fairness on their part, a New International Economic Order cannot be implemented in any ordered manner; it will come about only through chaos and violence.

NOTES

(1) Excluding Iran as a special case, 27 out of a total of 86 countries are included here. They are: Afghanistan, Algeria, Argentina, Boliva, Brazil, Burma, Chile, Colombia, Costa Rica, Egypt, Gabon, India, Israel, Mexico, Nicaragua, Pakistan, Paraguay, Peru, Sri Lanka, Somalia, South Korea, Sudan, Tunisia, Turkey, Uruguay, Zaire, Zambia.

(2) James Grant and Mahbub Ul Haq, "Income Redistribution and the International financing of development," Annex 2 in RIO, Reshaping the International Order. Coordinated by Jan Tinbergen (New York: Dutton 1976), p. 215.

(3) Robert S. McNamara, "Economic Development: Past, Present and Future," Address to the World Bank and International Monetary Fund meeting in September 1977, reprinted in Economic Impact 1, No. 21 (1978): 82. The following table provides a rough estimate of amortization payments by developing countries from 1972 to 1974. (Source: Development Cooperation, 1975 Review, OECD, p. 122.)

Billion dollars

	1972	1973	1974
To DAC* for ODA** lending	1.2	1.2	1.1
To DAC* for other official flows	1.8	1.9	2.7
To Centrally Planned Economic	0.4	0.5	0.6
To OPEC countries	<0.1	<0.1	<0.1
To multilateral institutions	0.6	0.6	0.7
On private flows including Eurocurrency transactions	4.6	7.0	9.0
Total	8.7	11.3	14.2

 *) Development Assistance Committee
**) Official Development Assistance.

(4)   See M. Abdel-Padil, Francis Cripps, and John Wells, "A New International Economic Order?" Cambridge Journal of Economics 1, no. 2 (June 1977).

(5)   Minor signs of change since 1976 with commercial banks from the Middle East trying to enter the Asian credit market have been reported, e. g., in the Far Eastern Economic Review, April 8, 1977 (an issue devoted to banking in Asia, 1977).

(6)   M. Abdel-Padil, et al., "A New International Economic Order?" p. 207.

(7)   See UNCTAD monthly commodity price bulletins.

(8)   This conjecture needs to be statistically substantiated with price data for individual commodities. From a rough impression of available data, the conjecture seems worth further investigation.

(9)   B. Balassa, "The Structure of Protection in Industrial Countries and Its Effects on the Exports of Processed Goods From Developing Countries," in UNCTAD, The Kennedy Round Estimated Effects on Tariff Barriers, 1978.

(10) See Dragoslav Avramovic et al., Economic Growth and External Debt, (Baltimore: Johns Hopkins, 1964); Goran Ohlin, Aid and Indebtedness: The Relation Between Aid Requirements, Terms of Assistance and Indebtedness of Developing Countries (Paris: OECD, 1966); R. Solomon, "A Perspective on the Debt of Developing Countries," Brookings Papers on Economic Activity 2 (1977).

(11) The kind of operation suggested by Arthur F. Burns (Chairman of the Board of Governors of the Federal Reserve System, 1970-77) in his "Order Needed in International Finance," reprinted in Economic Impact, no. 21 (1978).

III

Private Bank
Financing

7 Financial Aid and Private Banking Institutions

A.K. Bhattacharya

Private bank lending through the international credit and capital markets (defined as foreign and international bond markets as well as publicized Eurocurrency credits) has assumed great significance in recent years in the external financing requirement of non-oil developing countries (NODCs). While much of the rapid growth in international bank lending to NODCs can be traced back to 1970-73, a period which coincided at once with high liquidity in the private banking sector and with booming developing-country exports due to higher commodity prices,(1) the involvement of private banks in NODCs became particularly pronounced after the oil-related crisis of late 1973. During 1974-76 alone, private bank lending provided nearly 40 percent of the annual net flow of financial resources from developed countries to NODCs, thus doubling the share provided by private banks during 1971-73.(2) Despite some changes in the direction of private bank lending overseas since 1976, the predominance of private banks in financial resource transfer to NODCs has remained relatively stable to date; and, barring some unlikely developments, such as a reduction in excess liquidity of the private banking sector or a turnaround in massive current account financing needs of NODCs, private bank financing of development will continue to play a major role in the years to come.

The steady transfer of external financing from the official to the private sector carries profound policy implications for international development strategies. There is no need for the pessimistic view prevailing in certain official circles that improving NODC access to international financial markets necessarily benefits only a limited number of deeply-entrenched "higher income" countries, and that, therefore, the issue is of marginal significance to the overall question of financial resource transfer to NODCs as a group.(3)

The past is not necessarily a foretaste of the future. Indeed, a number of market developments - high liquidity, declining interest spread, longer maturity - are likely to converge to bring private bank capital within the reach of less-creditworthy borrowers in the developing world, if certain key obstacles to improving the access of NODCs to the international financial markets are tackled by concerted action on the part of borrowers, lenders, and intergovernmental institutions. There is a great deal of potential in the private banking sector that can be tapped by those NODCs that traditionally have not been able to benefit adequately from this external financing route. Private bank financing is generally free from the political, military, or economic conditions that are usually associated with official financing. It is also available in much greater quantity (depending upon demand and supply of funds) at relatively favorable terms for creditworthy and not-so-creditworthy borrowers. Indeed, real interest rates on private bank loans, deflated for inflation and rate of return on investment projects, have recently been low, if not negative. In many cases, the maturities and interest rates on private bank loans compare favorably with those on nonconcessionary financing obtained from governmental and intergovernmental sources.

In any case, the amount of official financing that is available today is inadequate to finance the massive, albeit declining, current account deficit of NODCs as a group. The share of official financing in the total external financing requirement of NODCs has averaged slightly more than half since 1974, compared to two-thirds during 1971-73. During the critical years of 1974-76, for example, the IMF and the World Bank combined together to put up an amount that was only one fourth of that provided by private international banks.(4) Total official development assistance (ODA) is stagnant in real terms and is actually declining as a percentage of the combined GNP of developed countries belonging to the Development Assistance Committee (DAC) of the Organization for Economic Cooperation and Development (OECD).(5) In view of the domestic constraints facing major donor countries, no real progress on this front can be expected in the near future. And without a radical transformation of the Articles of Agreement of the IMF (permitting it to tap directly international financial markets for relending to NODCs), the paltry resources of the IMF could not be stretched substantially.

By contrast, international financial markets hold out good prospects for the external financing needs of NODCs. The list of "eligible" borrowers from the developing world is growing slowly but steadily. The Eurocurrency credit market witnessed the emergence of several "low income" newcomers in 1977 (e.g. India, Burma, Malawi), and 21 NODCs tapped the

international bond market in 1977 compared to 15 in 1976.(6)
The foreign bond market, however, continues to be highly
restrictive. The "low income" NODCs receive less than 2
percent of annual Eurocredits extended to NODCs as a group,
and obtain no bond financing at all.(7) The question of
improving the access of the majority of developing countries to
the international financial markets continues to be of critical
importance in future development strategies of the New
International Economic Order.

The purpose of this chapter is to (1) assess the
development impact of private bank lending to those NODCs
that have been able to tap the international financial markets;
and (2) suggest ways of improving the access of those NODCs
that have remained marginal borrowers or have not been able
to gain entry to the private financial markets.

AN OVERVIEW OF THE DIMENSIONS OF PRIVATE BANK
LENDING TO NODCS

Foreign lending, especially through the Eurocurrency markets,
has always been popular with large international banks, mainly
because it has historically provided handsome return by way of
spectacular net interest income, generated largely through
"maturity gapping" (that is, improving the contractual spread
by mismatching the maturities of bank assets and liabilities),
as well as through fee and commission-based income.(8) What
has changed in recent times is the geographical distribution of
international bank lending. The NODCs have dramatically
improved their share of both medium-term Eurocurrency credits
and foreign and international bonds, especially since 1975.
NODCs accounted for less than 25 percent of total borrowing
in international capital markets from 1972 to 1974; now, as
table 7.1 shows, they receive nearly 38 percent of gross sums
raised in such markets. Also worthy of note is the declining
share of Eurocurrency credits in total borrowing, implying
greater NODC participation in bond financing.

The clue to understanding the radically different pattern
of international bank lending lies in excess liquidity in the
private banking sector coupled with the massive current account financing needs of NODCs. The bank liquidity problem
has been heightened by tremendous inflows of petrodollars into
bank certificates of deposit on the liabilities side (a phenomenon that is being modified by the changing disposition of
OPEC current account surplus), and a lack of creditworthy
borrowers on the assets side in the face of global softness of
corporate demand for bank credit (once again, a phenomenon
that is changing slowly today in view of higher interest rates
in the United States).(9)

Table 7.1. NODC Borrowing in International Capital Markets
($ billions)

	1974	1975	1976	1977	1978 (first half)*
Total Borrowing by all customers	$40.8	$43.3	$63.0	$69.0	$46.4
-- of which NODC total	$ 9.8 (24%)	$13.2 (30.5%)	$19.4 (30.8%)	$23.1 (33.5%)	$17.4 (37.5%)
-- of which Publicized Eurocurrency Credits	$ 8.9 (21.8%)	$12.5 (28.9%)	$17.1 (27.1%)	$18.6 (27%)	$14.2 (30.6%)
Publicized Eurocurrency Credits as a percentage of total NODC borrowing	(90.8%)	(94.7%)	(88.1%)	(80.5%)	(81.6%)

*Preliminary data

Source: The World Bank, Borrowing in International Capital Markets, various issues; and Annual Report 1978, p. 109.

Regarding the NODC current account deficit, the issues involved are manifold and have been discussed by this author elsewhere.(10)   Essentially, partly as a result of higher oil import bills, NODCs have been running a staggering current account deficit, which increased from $11 billion in 1973 to an all-time high of $38 billion in 1975 before declining to $25 billion and $22 billion in 1976 and 1977 respectively (due primarily to effective domestic adjustment measures relating particularly to import control).   In 1978, this deficit increased to more than $30 billion, reflecting mainly the increased interest payments on external debt.   Between 1974 and 1976, NODCs obtained $60 billion from international commercial banks, or one half of their combined gross external financing requirement, $30 billion of which came from the Eurocurrency markets.(11)

Aside from increasing the size and share of their borrowing from the international financial markets, NODCs have also been able to benefit from the recent market trend toward longer maturities and shorter interest rate spreads. Table 7.2 shows that the average final maturities on Eurocurrency credits to NODCs increased from 5.1 years in the fourth quarter of 1976 to 8.3 years in the first quarter of 1978.   Also, table 7.2 shows that the average loan rate spread over the London Interbank Offered Rate (LIBOR) for NODCs declined from 1.87 percent in the fourth quarter of 1976 to 1.58 percent in the first quarter of 1978.   Although the latter figure is higher than that applicable to other groups of borrowers, individual developing countries such as India have been able to negotiate spreads of 1 percent over LIBOR.   In any case, the slightly higher interest rates on loans to NODCs have been offset by longer maturities for such loans.   In 1977, for example, 64 percent of Eurocredits carried an average maturity of 5 to 7 years compared with 31 percent in 1976.(12) Similarly, 27 percent of foreign bonds issued to NODCs in 1977 had an average maturity of 7 to 10 years compared to 7 percent in 1976, and 49 percent of international bonds issued to NODCs in 1977 carried an average maturity of 5 to 7 years as opposed to 28 percent in 1976.(13)   As for interest rates on bond financing, while NODC initial offering yields have been higher on the average than those offered by other groups of borrowers, there is substantial variation among individual issues, timing of issues, and markets of issues.(14)   Recent empirical studies suggest that the cost of bond financing through public offerings may not be more onerous than bilateral official loans or loans from international organizations, even for those NODCs that have not tapped this source of funds.   The grant element on bonds is about the same or better, compared to loans from bilateral and international official sources.(15)

Table 7.2. Interest Spreads and Maturities of Eurocurrency Credits to Selected Countries, Arranged by Category

	Q_4 1973		Q_4 1975		Q_4 1976		Q_3 1977		Q_4 1977		Q_1 1978	
	Average Spread (basis points)	Average Maturity (years)	Average Spread (basis points)	Average Maturity (years)	Average Spread (basis points)	Average Maturity (years)	Average Spread (basis points)	Average Maturity (years)	Average Spread (basis points)	Average Maturity (years)	Average Spread (basis points)	Average Maturity (years)
Non-oil LDCs[a]	121	10.9	165	5.4	187	5.1	179	4.6	177	7.3	158	8.3
OPEC[a]	129	7.3	167	5.7	133	7.0	132	5.6	159	5.5	104	8.5
Eastern Europe[a]	61	8.8	149	5.5	129	5.5	113[c]	7.0[c]	116[c]	6.0[c]	123	7.2
Small OECD Countries[a]	94	9.1	158	6.5	137	5.3	120	6.5	109	6.8	83	7.2
Range of spreads among country groups	(68)		(18)		(58)		(66)		(68)		(75)	
Average of individual countries: Weighted	111	9.5	163	5.7	161	5.6	153	5.3	155	7.0	132	8.2
(Unweighted)	(99)	(9.6)	(166)	(5.6)	(159)	(5.7)	(155)	(5.9)	(149)	(6.4)	(123)	(8.1)
Minimum spread for individual loans:[b]	56		125		113		88		88		57	

[a] Average spreads for individual countries weighted by total volume of borrowing by each country.

[b] Rate shown is lowest rate for syndicated Eurocurrency credit to all borrowers. To avoid extreme observations, rate reported is lowest rate for minimum of three credits.

[c] Observation from a single loan.

Source: IBRD, Borrowing in International Capital Markets, various issues.

The foregoing analysis is not meant to imply that the path to private bank borrowing is strewn with roses for NODCs. Two major problems continue to plague NODC use of the external private market borrowing alternative. First, although the private banking sector has remained highly liquid so far, the possibilities of a "credit crunch" and the consequent "crowding out" of NODCs from the international financial markets cannot be ruled out in the future. Secondly, the high degree of concentration of private bank funds limits their potential for greater use by newcomers from the developing world. Table 7.3 shows that nearly half of Eurocurrency

Table 7.3. Publicized Eurocurrency Bank Credits to NODCs
(Percentages)

	1975	1976	1977	1978 (first half)*
Total World	100.0	100.0	100.0	100.0
Total NODC	29.0	27.0	27.0	31.0
--				
Brazil	22.5	23.6	15.9	19.6
Mexico	23.0	15.3	19.6	9.9
Peru	4.6	2.5	1.0	--
Philippines	2.4	6.3	4.8	9.5
South Korea	3.5	7.3	5.4	5.2

*Preliminary

Source: Morgan Guaranty Trust, World Financial Markets, various issues; and IMF Survey, Report on International Lending, July 31, 1978, p. 232.

credits extended to NODCs are concentrated in a handful of countries, while table 7.4 shows that more than 70 per cent of U.S. commercial banks' claims on NODCs are held in Latin America, with Mexico and Brazil accounting for half of total claims. The foreign and international bond markets are similarly restricted to selected NODCs, with Brazil and Mexico historically obtaining more than half of the total NODC market share.

Table 7.4. Foreign Loans by major U.S. Banks to NODCs
(as of December 1977, $millions and percentages)

Country	Total claims	%	Claims on: Banks	%	Public borrowers	%	Other private	%	Maturity distribution of claims: One year and under	%	Over one to 5 years	%	Over 5 years	%
Asia														
China (Taiwan)	2,805	6.0	954	7.4	958	5.8	893	5.1	1,895	7.9	833	4.3	77	2.1
India	187	0.4	29	0.2	66	0.4	92	0.5	74	0.3	88	0.5	25	0.7
Israel	667	1.4	450	3.5	181	1.1	35	0.2	526	2.2	131	0.7	9	0.2
Jordan	101	0.2	7	--	79	0.5	15	--	22	0.1	44	0.2	35	1.0
Korea (South)	3,072	6.5	1,458	11.3	504	3.1	1,111	6.3	1,823	7.6	1,150	6.0	100	2.7
Malaysia	511	1.1	106	0.8	259	1.6	145	0.8	216	0.9	195	1.0	99	2.7
Pakistan	59	0.1	8	--	31	0.2	20	0.1	49	0.2	6	--	4	0.1
Philippines	2,049	4.4	611	4.7	505	3.1	933	5.3	1,250	5.2	603	3.1	196	5.4
Syria	97	0.2	72	0.6	21	0.1	3	--	84	0.3	13	--	0	0
Thailand	856	1.8	390	3.0	108	0.7	357	2.0	715	3.0	135	0.7	6	0.2
Other	555	1.2	125	1.0	111	0.7	319	1.8	331	1.4	188	1.0	34	0.9
Subtotal	10,959	23.3	4,210	32.5	2,823	17.2	3,923	22.3	6,985	29.0	3,386	17.5	585	16.1
Africa														
Cameroon	60	0.1	3	--	46	0.3	10	--	13	--	44	0.2	2	--
Egypt	427	0.9	205	1.6	170	1.0	50	0.3	343	1.4	77	0.4	6	--
Ghana	78	0.1	9	--	54	0.3	14	--	65	0.3	13	--	0	0
Ivory Coast	347	0.7	21	0.2	263	1.6	62	0.4	84	0.3	241	1.3	23	0.6
Kenya	39	--	4	--	14	--	20	0.1	20	0.1	17	0.1	1	--
Malawi	70	0.1	16	0.1	51	0.3	2	--	36	0.1	25	0.1	8	--
Morocco	462	1.0	24	0.2	407	2.5	30	0.2	64	0.3	338	1.8	58	1.6
Senegal	25	--	0	0	24	0.1	1	--	8	--	17	--	0	0
Sudan	219	0.5	20	0.2	181	1.1	18	0.1	119	0.5	89	0.5	11	0.3
Tunisia	95	0.2	6	--	80	0.5	8	--	38	0.2	48	0.2	8	--
Zaire	252	0.5	2	--	220	1.3	29	0.2	81	0.3	135	0.7	35	0.9
Zambia	182	0.4	15	0.1	135	0.8	31	0.2	107	0.4	70	0.4	4	--
Other	172	0.4	61	0.5	45	0.3	65	0.4	115	0.5	45	0.2	11	0.3
Subtotal	2,428	5.1	386	2.9	1,690	10.3	340	1.9	1,094	4.5	1,159	6.0	167	4.0

(continued)

Table 7.4. Continued

Country	Total claims	%	Claims on: Banks	%	Public borrowers	%	Other private	%	Maturity distribution of claims: One year and under	%	Over one to 5 years	%	Over 5 years	%
Latin American and Caribbean														
Argentina	2,639	5.6	598	4.6	1,238	7.6	803	4.6	1,669	6.9	900	4.7	69	0.7
Bolivia	446	1.0	50	0.4	194	1.2	200	1.1	233	1.0	183	1.0	27	36.5
Brazil	11,992	25.6	3,364	26.0	2,992	18.3	5,631	32.0	4,062	16.9	6,599	34.3	1,328	0.5
Chile	821	1.7	256	2.0	359	2.2	204	1.2	520	2.2	282	1.5	17	1.7
Colombia	1,293	2.8	464	3.6	366	2.2	461	.26	855	3.6	376	2.0	61	1.8
Costa Rica	424	0.9	54	0.4	148	0.9	221	1.3	227	0.9	166	0.9	30	0.8
Dominican Republic	283	0.6	29	0.2	145	0.9	109	0.6	116	0.5	143	0.7	23	0.6
El Salvador	188	0.4	51	0.4	52	0.3	84	0.5	141	0.6	42	0.2	4	---
Guatemala	226	0.5	24	0.2	13	---	188	1.1	143	0.6	76	0.4	7	---
Honduras	253	0.5	64	0.5	41	0.2	147	0.8	145	0.6	100	0.5	7	---
Jamaica	247	0.5	16	0.1	147	0.9	84	0.5	92	0.4	134	0.7	21	0.6
Mexico	11,213	23.9	1,982	15.3	4,801	29.3	4,434	25.2	5,418	22.5	4,697	24.4	1,097	30.2
Nicaragua	562	1.2	174	1.3	204	1.2	183	1.0	360	1.5	154	0.8	46	1.3
Paraguay	33	.07	1	---	1	---	30	0.2	26	0.1	7	0.4	0	0
Peru	1,831	3.9	450	3.5	995	6.1	383	2.2	1,021	4.2	686	3.6	123	3.4
Trinidad and Tobago	44	.09	1	---	37	0.2	5	---	22	0.1	10	0.1	11	0.3
Uruguay	203	.04	53	0.4	85	0.5	65	0.4	134	0.6	66	0.3	1	---
Other	830	1.7	710	5.5	38	0.2	81	0.5	793	3.2	35	0.2	2	---
Subtotal	33,534	71.4	8,341	64.4	11,856	72.4	13,313	75.7	15,977	66.4	14,656	76.3	2,874	79.2
TOTAL	46,921	100	12,937	100	16,369	100	17,576	100	24,056	100	19,201	100	3,626	100

Source: Federal Reserve Bank of Chicago, International Letter, No. 372 (June 23, 1978).

Overall, however, the international financial markets hold out good prospects for the external financing needs of NODCs as a group, as well as for a further extension of the list of eligible borrowers. The markets continue to remain highly liquid, interest spreads are declining, and maturities are lengthening. From the NODC viewpoint, two issues will loom large in deciding the wisdom of selecting the private bank financing route. First, the development impact of such lending has to be assessed, especially in those NODCs that have been able to tap private bank capital. Second, ways must be found to improve the access of those NODCs that have remained on the sidelines or have been bypassed altogether by private lenders.

THE DEVELOPMENT IMPACT OF PRIVATE BANK LENDING

In assessing the development impact of private bank lending, it is important to bear in mind the fact that, as financial intermediaries, private banks simply channel funds from capital-rich to capital-poor areas, and that they may not have the capacity and/or responsibility to solve the economic ills of the developing world. The contribution of private bank financing to economic development depends largely on the uses to which such funds are put by the borrower.

Private bank financing has contributed to the economic development of NODCs in several ways. To begin with, such financing has supplemented NODC domestic saving, thus reducing the burden of adjustment that typically falls on deficit countries. Many NODCs were able to maintain high real GDP growth rates (averaging 5 percent) during 1973-76 despite rising oil prices and depressed world economy. Thanks partly to their access to private borrowing, the "higher income" NODCs could proceed with their development plans and record even higher real growth rates. As stated earlier, bank financing funded half of NODC gross external financing requirements (that is, amortization plus other capital outflow and current account deficit), mitigating, to a larger extent, severe restrictive policies in the short run (IMF "conditionality" style) that generally lead to higher unemployment and possibly higher inflation.(16) Secondly, bank financing has contributed to a rather substantial increase in NODC reserves during 1976-77 that totaled some $20 billion in surplus. It should be noted, however, that much of this surplus more or less equals NODC gross borrowing from international financial markets. Essentially, many NODCs borrowed from such markets in order to redeposit the funds into their reserves.(17) Finally, international bank involvement in certain NODCs has attracted sizable non-bank net capital inflows, as evidenced by the clear success of Singapore in this regard. While the prestige factor associated with international banking is not quantifiable, the massive presence of large international banks has certainly contributed to the enhanced status of Singapore and Panama as regional financing centers.(18)

In terms of the Asia-Pacific region, the area as a whole has traditionally been a net taker of Eurocurrency funds, which have provided precious foreign currencies that have been used for industrialization or development purposes. Thus, as table 7.5 shows, while the area provides less than 50 percent of offshore funds to the Asian dollar market (based in Singapore but also operating out of Hong Kong and the Philippines), nearly 80 percent of such funds are utilized in the region itself. To the extent offshore funds are supplied for capital project financing (for example, agriculture, mass transit, oil exploration, mining, steel, electricity, chemicals and petrochemicals), bank lending contributes to the economic development of the area by either improving the export competitiveness of industries or by assisting import substitution policies of countries in the region. The existence of the offshore banking market in the region itself is of particular significance to the majority of local businesses that find it difficult to gain access to the European market due to problems relating to size, ownership pattern, bookkeeping practices, and lack of familiarity with international investors.(19).

The other major net taker of international bank funds is Latin America, and here, too, the development impact of private bank financing has been substantial. The local sector in Panama is a net taker of Eurodollar funds that have been put to use in trade financing, cattle raising, sugar production, construction, and the like. Table 7.6 shows that, in 1976, the local sector in Panama provided a mere 5 percent of total Panamanian bank liabilities, but local loans absorbed more than 16 percent of total bank assets. Offshore banking in Panama plays a crucial role in reducing the country's traditionally high dependence on domestic monetary policies in the United States (the U.S. dollar is the legal tender in Panama), and in providing a major source of external financing for both capital projects expenditure and automatic adjustment of balance of payments deficits. Table 7.7 shows that the Latin American region (broadly defined to include South and Central America as well as the Caribbean basin) is the chief beneficiary of external credits extended by Panamanian banks, and South America alone receives nearly half of such credits.(20)

International capital market borrowing has brought tangible benefits to NODCs, but the development impact of

Table 7.5.   Assets and Liabilities of Asian Currency Units
by Geographical Distribution, 1973-1977
(Percentages)

	1973	1974	1975	1976	1977
Total Liabilities	100	100	100	100	100
Asia*	58	53	49	43	44
Europe	33	36	37	42	38
Other	9	11	14	15	18
Total Claims	100	100	100	100	100
Asia*	76	79	81	83	78
Europe	17	11	11	8	11
Other	7	10	8	9	11

*includes Australia

Source: IMF Survey (July 17, 1978), p. 218.

Table 7.6.   Consolidated Balance Sheet of Panamanian
Banking System, 1976
(Percentages)

ASSETS	100.0
Liquid Assets	31.7
Local Loans	16.5
Foreign Loans	48.1
Local Securities	0.3
Foreign Securities	0.9
Other assets	2.5
LIABILITIES	100.0
Local Demand Deposits	2.4
Local Time Deposits	5.1
Foreign Demand Deposits	3.2
Foreign Time Deposits	78.2
Other Deposits	11.1

Source: Comision Bancaria Nacional, Boletin Estadistico, no. 7
(Diciembre de 1976), pp. 115-16.

Table 7.7.   Geographical Distribution of the External Sector
Credit Portfolio of the Panamanian Banking System, 1976
(Percentages)

North America	27.8
Central America	10.0
South America	48.4
Caribbean Zone	1.4
Asia	1.0
Africa	2.3
Europe	9.1
Total	100.0

Source: Comision Bancaria Nacional, Boletin Estadistico, no. 7
(Diciembre de 1976), p. 19.

such borrowing has not been entirely beneficial.   On the
negative side, questions have been raised about the impact of
the "easy" availability of bank credit on domestic inflation.
During 1972-75, for example, both Hong Kong and Singapore
were flooded with a massive influx of speculative foreign
currencies, which were later swapped for local currency, and
relent at a higher rate for speculative investment in local stock
and real estate markets.   While such activities can, indeed,
bring about "imported" inflation and threaten vital exports,
they can be checked by swift official action, as demonstrated
by the floating of both Singapore and Hong Kong currencies,
the imposition of special deposit ratios on interbank swap
arrangements in Singapore, and the passing of a Securities
Ordinance and Deposit-Taking Ordinance in Hong Kong.(21)
     A second negative impact of private bank financing on the
development process relates to the external debt situation of
NODCs.   In nominal terms, NODC total external debt reached
more than $200 billion in 1977 - double the figure for 1973 - at
least 40 percent of which was owed to private banks.
However, deflated by an index of export or import prices, the
real level of external debt rose by only a fifth during 1973-77.
Allowing for inflation, NODC external debt is of the same
order of magnitude as it was prior to the oil crisis, in con-
formity with the historical pattern of capital imports.   But individual countries have disturbingly high debt-service ratios.
Ironically, the debt-service payment issue (that is, amortization
and interest payments) is all the more acute for precisely those
higher income and middle income NODCs that have made exten-
sive use of private credit facilities.   Over one half of total
external debt of NODCs is held by 10 countries, with Brazil

and Mexico alone accounting for a third of total external debt.
Many low income NODCs, by contrast, have little commercial
debt to worry about and are, in fact, net suppliers of funds
to the international financial markets.   Five of the top six
NODCs in debt-service ratios are in Latin America (Mexico,
Brazil, Chile, Argentina, and Peru), and Mexico ranks first in
real debt growth.   Still, the main issue in NODC indebtedness
is not debt itself, which is somewhat insignificant relative to
growth potential, but debt-service burden in a stagnant economy.   The biggest bank debtors (Brazil, Mexico, South Korea,
and   Taiwan)   have   pursued   successful   restrictive   domestic
policies, thereby reducing their current account deficits; while
Zaire, Peru, Turkey, and Argentina have either defaulted or
renegotiated their existing commercial debt.(22)

NODC ACCESS TO BOND FINANCING

By far the most serious constraint on private bank lending to
NODCs lies in thier restricted access to the foreign and
international bond markets.   The latter markets provide limited
access to a handful of NODCs, and regional capital markets in
NODCs are not sufficiently developed to make a difference.
Table 7.8 shows that in 1977, for example, NODCs raised
a meager $5 billion in bond financing, more than half of which
was obtained by high and upper middle income countries.   The
low income countries have historically obtained next to nothing
in bonds.   Although the list of eligible borrowers from the
bond markets has been growing lately, this segment of the
international capital markets continues to remain highly
restrictive.   As table 7.1 showed, bond issues comprise less
than 20 percent of total funds raised by NODCs in the
international capital markets; and whatever financing is
available is dominated by a handful of NODCs (Brazil, Mexico,
South Korea, the Philippines, and Singapore particularly).
Moreover,   all   bond   borrowings   were   undertaken   by
governments or government agencies, and the private sector
did not play any role in such financing.(23)
    Basically, the reasons for the limited NODC access to
bond markets are twofold: (1) national regulations limiting
foreign access to bond markets; and (2) relative unfamiliarity
of NODC borrowers in bond markets where country risk
assessment standards are substantially different from those
prevailing in the medium - term credit markets.
    As far as national regulations on capital markets are
concerned, there is no deliberate discrimination against NODCs
in   general.   As   carefully   documented   by   the   IBRD-IMF
Development   Committee,   such   regulations   cover   a   broad
spectrum,   including   limitations   on   investments   in   foreign

Table 7.8. Borrowing in International Capital Markets by Type of Loan and Category of Borrowing Country 1974 to Second Quarter, 1978
(US$ millions or equivalent)

CATEGORY OF BORROWING COUNTRY	FOREIGN BONDS PUBLIC	PRIVATE	TOTAL	INTERNATIONAL BONDS PUBLIC	PRIVATE	TOTAL	TOTAL BONDS PUBLIC	PRIVATE	TOTAL	EURO-CURRENCY TOTAL CREDITS	TOTAL BONDS AND CREDITS
HIGH & UPPER MIDDLE											
1974*	259.7	387.7	647.4	92.2	4.0	96.2	351.9	391.7	743.6	4,884.0	5,627.6
1975*	242.8	51.0	293.8	190.4	85.6	276.0	433.2	136.6	569.8	5,382.6	5,952.4
1976*	300.0	141.2	441.2	616.7	39.2	655.9	916.7	180.4	1,097.1	9,474.0	10,571.1
1977*	968.6	182.1	1,150.7	1,396.4	44.8	1,441.2	2,365.0	226.9	2,591.9	9,803.0	12,394.9
1977-I	136.9	67.7	204.6	328.4	–	328.4	465.3	67.7	533.0	2,404.4	2,937.4
1977-II	151.7	61.6	213.3	448.4	–	448.4	600.1	61.6	661.7	1,954.4	2,616.1
1977-III	128.4	37.4	165.8	345.1	21.6	366.7	473.5	59.0	532.5	2,132.3	2,664.8
1977-IV	551.6	15.4	567.0	274.5	23.2	297.7	826.1	38.6	864.7	3,311.9	4,176.6
1978-I	90.9	156.0	246.9	509.5	248.8	758.3	600.4	404.8	1,005.2	4,403.2	5,408.4
1978-II	387.3	118.4	505.7	226.5	33.3	259.8	613.8	151.7	765.5	2,897.0	3,662.5
INTER. & LOWER MIDDLE											
1974*	16.2	155.2	171.4	17.2	–	17.2	33.4	155.2	188.6	4,007.3	4,195.9
1975*	75.0	161.5	236.5	155.8	28.3	184.1	230.8	189.8	420.6	5,393.9	5,814.5
1976*	400.6	118.2	518.8	481.8	154.0	635.8	882.4	272.2	1,154.6	6,943.7	8,098.4
1977*	257.8	309.8	567.6	998.8	196.5	1,195.3	1,256.6	506.3	1,762.9	8,330.8	10,093.7
1977-I	–	78.7	78.7	87.0	39.7	126.7	87.0	118.4	205.4	1,859.0	2,064.4
1977-II	60.0	64.3	124.3	259.8	45.5	305.3	319.8	109.8	429.6	1,072.1	1,501.7
1977-III	42.1	54.1	96.2	277.4	73.4	350.8	319.5	127.5	447.0	2,174.1	2,621.1
1977-IV	155.7	112.7	268.4	374.6	37.9	412.5	530.3	150.6	680.9	3,225.6	3,906.5
1978-I	106.3	291.6	397.9	259.5	24.6	284.1	365.8	316.2	682.0	3,443.8	4,125.8
1978-II	67.7	58.7	126.4	208.2	216.5	424.7	275.9	275.2	551.1	4,689.3	5,240.4
LOW											
1974*	–	–	–	–	–	–	–	–	–	669.0	669.0
1975*	–	17.5	17.5	–	–	–	–	17.5	17.5	1,680.7	1,698.2
1976*	–	–	–	–	–	–	–	–	–	642.1	642.1
1977*	–	–	–	–	–	–	–	–	–	555.6	555.6
1977-I	–	–	–	–	–	–	–	–	–	12.5	12.5
1977-II	–	–	–	–	–	–	–	–	–	303.8	303.8
1977-III	–	–	–	–	–	–	–	–	–	111.6	111.6
1977-IV	–	–	–	–	–	–	–	–	–	127.7	127.7
1978-I	–	–	–	–	–	–	–	–	–	676.5	676.5
1978-II	–	–	–	–	–	–	–	–	–	528.2	528.2

*Includes loans which have not been allocated to a specific month

Source: World Bank, Borrowing in International Capital Markets, Second Quarter, 1978, p. 17.

securities by institutional investors, government authorization
for foreign public issues, ceilings on foreign issues, and a
queue system that favors the domestic sector.(24)   The
Eurobond market, by virtue of its "offshore" character, is
relatively unregulated but, in practice, is hampered by the
reluctance of surplus countries to encourage Euroissues
denominated in their own currencies.(25)   There is, clearly,
ample room for improvements in national regulations along the
lines of the latest Japanese government decision to ease the
requirement regarding previous market exposure.(26)
      The real issue inhibiting NODC access to capital markets
is, however, attitudinal rather than institutional.   Even if
national regulations on foreign access were liberalized, it is
unlikely that NODCs would be able to increase their market
share substantially.   Conversely, if there were sufficient
market interest in NODCs, institutional investors would
certainly make sure that investment limitation laws were
changed overnight.   As fiduciaries of other people's funds,
institutional investors tend to be over cautious in assessing
the quality of foreign debt obligations, and the "retail"
character of the Eurobond market imparts a special kind of
risk assessment for investors.   Both the foreign bond markets
and the Eurobond market evaluate country risk much more
conservatively   than   the   syndicated,   Eurocurrency,
medium-term credit market.(27)   Even in the absence of
country risk, the differential between U.S. government bonds
and A-rated utilities in the U.S. bond market is generally
around 2 percent, whereas in the medium-term Eurocurrency
credit market the spread over LIBOR has rarely been that
high, even for less-creditworthy customers.(28)   As noted
earlier, the spread over LIBOR has actually been declining in
recent years in the Eurocurrency credit market.   The
declining spread has caused a great deal of concern in the
international banking community about covering the banks' cost
of capital, not to mention the risk premium.(29)
      The major obstacle to greater NODC access to capital
markets is relative unfamiliarity coupled with "high risk" image.
While investor resistance to NODC issues permeates all bond
markets, it assumes a critical importance in the U.S. foreign
bond market (the "Yankee" bond market, as it is popularly
called).   The U.S. capital market is not only the largest in the
world in terms of volume of transactions, but it also carries, in
the specialized terminology of financial analysts, depth,
breadth, and resiliency (that is, ability to absorb large issues
at reasonable rates, longer maturity schedules, and so
on).(30)   At the same time, the yield premium over comparable
domestic issues and the elimination of the Interest Equalization
Tax make foreign bonds (including NODC bonds) an attractive
proposition today from the investors' viewpoint.   As the
experience of the Asian Development Bank shows, with proper

protection afforded to investors in the form of guarantees,
sound projects, and appropriate financial ratios, lending to
NODCs may, indeed, be highly attractive to the international
capital market community.(31)

Regional capital markets in NODCs are either nonexistent
or are not sufficiently developed to provide the needed
external financing. Being secondary centers of international
finance, such markets typically rely on recycled funds from
primary centers, and such funds have not been forthcoming in
sufficient amounts for a variety of reasons: cumbersome
foreign exchange restrictions, high taxes and duties, the lack
of an active secondary market, and the "high risk" image of
NODC borrowers. Domestic investors have historically stayed
away from capital markets, primarily because of their narrow,
government-dominated client base that sponsors issues carrying
artificially low interest rates well below market rates of interest
on short-term bank deposits or other investment instruments.
The upshot has been highly predictable. The offshore banking
market in the Caribbean does no bond financing in Latin
America, and the Asian dollar bond market is miniscule in size,
rarely catering to the financing needs of non-Singapore entities
in the developing world of the Asia-Pacific region. South
American investors prefer to deal with Miami or New York than
with Panama. Venezuela and Ecuador - two regional members
of the Organization of Petroleum Exporting Countries (OPEC) -
supplied a mere 5 percent and 1.5 percent respectively of the
total paid-up capital of the Panamanian banking system in 1976,
while the Middle East OPEC members provided less than 2
percent of such funds. Even when Venezuela provides long-
term capital to the area, it prefers to do so through intergovernmental organizations than through the regional financing
centers. As regards the Asian dollar bond market, there have
been only about 30 bond issues so far, with a meager dollar
value that amounts to less than $1 billion; except for the
Korean Development Bank and the Republic of Panama, no
other non-Singapore-based NODC has tapped this market. The
more developed NODCs in the Asia-Pacific region (Hong Kong,
Malaysia, the Phillippines) prefer to borrow from the Eurobond
market rather than the Asian dollar bond market for reasons
that have already been discussed--larger issues, longer
maturities, and lower cost, while the less-creditworthy borrowers in the region have difficulty gaining access due to the
unfamiliarity-cum-risk image syndrome referred to above.(32)

To sum up, the restricted access of NODCs to
international capital markets, coupled with the absence of
active regional long-term capital markets within NODCs
themselves, presents a formidable problem for the external
financing requirements of NODCs. The process of economic
development calls for truly long-term financing through either

equity or debt routes, and it is precisely in this area that a
great deal could be accomplished through concerted action by
private banks and governmental or intergovernmental agencies.

CONCLUSIONS AND POLICY RECOMMENDATIONS

The very nature of economic development demands long-term
financing, and international financial markets can play a
significant role in providing NODCs with substantial amounts of
such finance at reasonable market terms. A continued
extension of the eligibility list of borrowers can respond to
additional market penetration needs of private banks and
financial institutions within the framework of risk-evaluation
constraints, which can be lessened by appropriate action on
the part of borrowers, lenders, and international institutions.
Within the developing world, there ought to be a conscious
recognition of the potential economic benefits of long-term
private bank financing in the development process, and a
"political will" to implement measures facilitating the inflow of
such capital, particularly from the securities markets. In this
context, careful note should be taken of the massive
availability of private bank capital relative to official capital,
the declining trend in the concessionary elements of offical
finance, the currently favorable borrowing terms on private
bank capital, the relatively nonpolitical nature of private
finance, the proven existence of debt-relief measures in the
world of private finance as opposed to official finance, and the
irrelevance of the external debt issue to economic growth
potential.
        Assuming that there is political agreement on the
congeniality of the private bank financing route, a series of
measures need to be undertaken to improve the access of
NODCs to the international financial markets. To begin with,
governmental and intergovernmental action is called for to
initiate and sustain NODC access to the securities markets in
the short run. Such action could take the form of interest
subsidies, guarantee schemes, cofinancing projects,
international investment and insurance trust funds, technical
assistance, and relaxation of national and local restrictions on
acquisition of foreign investment instruments by resident
investors.(33)
        Secondly, since investor unfamiliarity with NODC
borrowers is a barrier, a massive educational effort should be
launched. This could be accomplished by retaining financial
public relations firms; organizing visits, seminars, and
conferences on investment opportunities in the developing
world; listing of NODC securities in major financial markets;
and accepting issue ratings by independent rating agencies in

order to allay investor fears of lack of disclosure of adequate information. On the last point, it should be noted that a rating of less than triple-A does not necessarily affect entry into the U.S. capital markets (after all, many major U.S. corporations and local governments carry such ratings), although it will affect the yield premium.(34) Also, investor attention should be drawn to the fact that international diversification offers significant risk reduction to the financial community; and, in order to minimize country exposure and loan concentration in a handful of manufacturing NODCs, it may be advisable to inject risk capital in agricultural and primary-good exporting NODCs, which face low income elasticity of demand for their products and, thus, are less vulnerable to world aggregate demand.(35)

Finally, and most important, NODCs need to undertake sound domestic management of those economic-financial variables that impinge on private foreign investment. In view of the difficulty of pinpointing an international risk-free rate, the risk-free rate will vary from country to country and so will gains from international diversification for the investors' point of view. In order to minimize their "high risk" image, NODCs ought to adopt certain domestic adjustment measures (relating particularly to monetary restraint, economic growth targets, and exchange rate changes), liberalize certain administrative controls (e.g., release foreign exhange for "impact" loans, permit resident investment in "offshore" securities, streamline diverse accounting procedures), and offer certain incentives (e.g., waive taxes on interest accruing to nonresidents, reduce corporate income taxes on "offshore" transactions, eliminate stamp and other kinds of duties for nonresidents). Indeed in the absence of long-range plans for substituting national savings for external savings, and in view of the continuing need for external financing of the massive current account deficit of the developing world, a voluntary adoption of a plan of self-imposed discipline and a "minimum regulation-maximum incentive" package may very well be preferable to relying on declining volume of official handouts or to mortgaging national economic policy to the IMF. At the same time, considerable thought needs to be given to the issue of private bank financing and its possible effects upon patterns of production, allocation of resources at the margin, exports and investment, and social change and income redistribution.

NOTES

(1) Lending to developing countries became popular in the late 1960s and gathered momentum in the early 1970s. Medium and long-term lending to developing countries increased from an annual average of less than $1 billion in the late 1960s to nearly $10 billion in 1973. The period also witnessed the introduction of syndicated Eurocurrency loans. See Federal Reserve Bank of New York, Quarterly Review (Summer 1977), p. 2; Ishan Kapur, "The Supply of Eurocurrency Finance to Developing Countries," Finance and Development 14, no. 3 (September 1977): 32-33; and Antoine W. van Agtmael, "Evaluating the Risks of Lending to Developing Countries," Euromoney (April 1976), p. 16.

(2) Morgan Guaranty Trust, World Financial Markets (January 1977), p. 4.

(3) For an exposition of this pessimistic view see Joint Ministerial Committee of the Boards of Governors of the Bank and the Fund on the Transfer of Real Resources to Developing Countries, Developing Country Access to Capital Markets (November 1978), p. 3.

(4) Morgan Guaranty Trust, World Financial Markets (January 1977), pp. 1-7; and Speech by the Governor of the Bank of England in Bank of England, Quarterly Bulletin 17, no. 2 (June 1977): 207.

(5) While the net flows of total financial resources from DAC countries has been increasing every year in nominal terms, they have remained virtually unchanged in real terms since 1974. Also, ODA as a proportion of DAC aggregate GNP has been declining, reaching 0.31 percent in 1977. See World Bank, Annual Report 1978, pp. 35-36; and Federal Reserve Bank of Chicago, International Letter, No. 375 (August 4, 1978).

(6) World Bank, Annual Report 1978, p. 109; Bank for International Settlements, 48th Annual Report (April 1, 1977-March 31, 1978), pp. 88, 91 (referred to hereafter as BIS); and Morgan Guaranty Trust, World Financial Markets (June 1977), pp. 1-12.

(7) Morgan Guaranty Trust, World Financial Markets (June 1978), pp. 2-3.

(8) Overseas earnings have generally accounted for between 50 and 75 percent of total after-tax operating income of major U.S. international banks. Also, U.S. bank earnings have been the greatest in areas with the lowest assets, i.e., the NODCs. See IMF Survey, Supplement on International Lending (June 1976), pp. 180-81; and Speech by G.A. Costanzo, Vice Chairman of Citibank, in Diversification in International Banking (New York: Citicorp, 1977), pp. 4-12.

(9)   A.K. Bhattacharya, The Myth of Petropower (Lexington,
      Mass.: Lexington Books, 1977), pp. 65-69.
(10) A.K.   Bhattacharya,   Foreign Trade and International
      Development (Lexington, Mass.: Lexington Books, 1976),
      pp. 26-28.
(11) IMF, Annual Report 1978, pp. 18, 24-25; BIS, 48th
      Annual Report (April 1, 1977-March 31, 1978), pp. 64,
      84-85, 91-92; and Federal Reserve Bank of New York,
      Quarterly Review (Summer 1977), p. 4.
(12) Morgan Guaranty Trust, World Financial Markets (June
      1978), pp. 4-5; and World Bank. Borrowing in Inter-
      national Capital Markets, various issues.
(13) World Bank, Borrowing in International Capital Markets,
      (Fourth Quarter 1977), pp. 85, 90, 96.
(14) Ibid., p. 111; and World Bank, Annual Report 1978, pp.
      108-11.
(15) R.S. Koundinya, "Financing the Economic Development of
      Developing Nations: The External Market Borrowing
      Alternative," Proceedings of the Academy of International
      Business Studies (1977).
(16) Federal Reserve Bank of New York, Quarterly Review,
      (Summer 1977), p. 1; and Speech by the Governor of the
      Bank of England, p. 206.
(17) BIS, p. 85.
(18) A.K.   Bhattacharya,   The Asian Dollar Market: Inter-
      national Offshore Financing (New York: Praeger, 1977),
      p. 69; and "Offshore Banking in the Caribbean," Journal
      of International Business Studies (forthcoming).
(19) Bhattacharya, The Asian Dollar Market, pp. 55-86.
(20) Bhattacharya, "Offshore Banking in the Caribbean."
(21) Bhattacharya, The Asian Dollar Market, pp. 69-70.
(22) Federal Reserve Bank of New York, Quarterly Review,
      (Summer 1977), pp. 1-8; Morgan Guaranty Trust, World
      Financial Markets (June 1977), pp. 9, 11; and IMF
      Survey (May 16, 1977), p. 149.
(23) World Bank, Annual Report 1978; pp. 106-12; and
      Morgan Guaranty Trust, World Financial Markets (June
      1978), pp. 2-3.
(24) Joint Ministerial Committee of the Boards of Governors of
      the Bank and the Fund on the Transfer of Real Resources
      to Developing Countries, Developing Country Access to
      Capital Markets (November 1978). Details of national
      regulations on capital transactions can also be found in
      Bank of England, Quarterly Bulletin 18, no. 3 (September
      1978): 390-94; Deutsche Bundesbank, Monthly Report 30,
      no. 5 (May 1978): 18-24; OECD, Financial Market Trends
      0 (June 1977): 49-53; U.S. Chamber of Commerce, Joint
      Report on Investment Obstacles in the OECD Countries
      (December 1975); U.S. Treasury Department, Foreign
      Portfolio Investment in the United States: Report to the

Congress (August 1976); and New York Stock Exchange, Recommendations on Access and Membership by Foreign-Controlled Brokers-Dealers to the U.S. Securities Markets (June 1974).

(25)   M.M. Ahmad, "The Developing Countries and Access to Capital Markets," Finance and Development 13, no. 4 (December 1976): 26-30.

(26)   Morgan Guaranty Trust, World Financial Markets (June 1978), p. 8.

(27)   Joint Ministerial Committee, Developing Country Access, p. 30; and Remarks by Nicholas A. Rey, Managing Director of Merrill Lynch Capital Markets Group, at IBRD/IMF Development Committee Seminar on Access to Capital Markets, Paris, October 11, 1978.

(28)   "International Lending and the Euromarkets," Remarks by Henry C. Wallich, Member of the Board of Governors of the Federal Reserve System, at the 1978 Euromarkets Conference sponsored by the Financial Times (London), May 9, 1978.

(29)   But, of course, Eurobanks offset much of the decline in the spread by liability management as well as by fee-based income. Ibid.; and Morgan Guaranty Trust, World Financial Markets (December 1977), p. 6.

(30)   The Morgan Guaranty Survey (June 1977), pp. 9-10.

(31)   David Ilyas, "How a Bookful of LDC Loans Equates with a Triple-A Rating," Euromoney (April 1978), p. 131.

(32)   Bhattacharya, The Asian Dollar Market, pp. 55-61; Bhattacharya, "Offshore Banking in the Caribbean"; The Monetary Authority of Singapore, Annual Report 1977/78, pp. 29-30; and Comision Bancaria Nacional de Panama, Informativo Mensual, no. 7 (July 1977). On the related problem of the Arab Currency bond market, see Institutional Investor (August 1977), pp. 149-52.

(33)   For details on such proposals, see IBRD-IMF Joint Ministerial Committee, Developing Country Access; Robert G. Hawkins, Walter L. Ness, Jr., Il Sakong, "Improving the Access of Developing Countries to the U.S. Capital Market," New York University Bulletin, 1975; Morgan Guaranty Trust, World Financial Markets (January 1977), pp. 4-7; and Xenophon Zolotas, "A Proposal for a New Fund to Insure Against Euromarket Defaults," Euromoney (April 1978), pp. 77-83.

(34)   Speech by Nicholas A. Ray.

(35)   "Current Trends in International Risk Analysis," Speech by A.K. Bhattacharya at the Chase Manhattan Bank World Forum on International Risk/Opportunity, Rye, New York, November 14, 1978.

8 Changing Patterns in International Liquidity and Eurocurrency Multipliers
Agustin Caso

MONETARY REFORM AND INTERNATIONAL LIQUIDITY

Achieving a more equitable and balanced New International Economic Order will require profound changes in the existing international society, now dominated by the world's major powers. This will decrease the exercise of hegemony over smaller nations by the superpowers, and alter the general attitude of the world's major powers with respect to the growth and development possibilities of Third World countries.

In this context, the evolution of the International Monetary System - from the postwar period up to the present - accurately reflects the scheme of power relationships which results in problems of excess liquidity, inequitable allocation of international currencies, severe balance of payments deficits, and growing difficulties in the attainment of national economic objectives.

This situation has reached a point of high tension with the consolidation of a global economy, consisting not only of the sum total of the various national economies, but also, of a joint economy made up of blocs of interdependent countries. Commerce, production, and labor mobility have become international activities, and present monetary relationships have been, at the same time, both the result and the catalyst of world economic patterns.

Bretton Woods: A Monetary System with Entropy

The principal changes in international monetary relationships in the last few years have come about as a result of the progressive break-up of the Bretton Woods system, and not as a result of a deliberate reform. This makes them seem to be a necessary but insufficient condition for achieving world economic equilibrium. National government officials, pressed by problems of payments, internal control of liquidity and inflation, and by disequilibria in the exchange markets, have been forced to stop abiding by the special rules of the system.(1) The result of this is that international monetary obligations have been reduced to a minimum and, in place of the set of explicit rights and obligations which constituted the Bretton Woods system, the present-day world has been functioning by a set of practices that has evolved from a mixture of customs and crises.

The Articles of Agreement of the International Monetary Fund (IMF) had, as a principal component, a set of rules and restrictions concerning the behavior of adjustable rates of exchange, as well as a system of support for member countries for the financing of their balance of payments deficits. Nevertheless, the system contained several flaws that were observed over the long run: (a) no mechanism existed for influencing member countries to change their parities when they were substantially out of balance; (b) the agreement focused on the behavior of member countries, and failed to strive for greater consistency regarding national monetary policies, the exchange system, and international liquidity. This problem assumed especially severe proportions in the developing countries. The structural deficit in their balance of payments, and the carrying out of inflationary public expenditure policies, with restrictions in the rate of exchange, generated recurring internal and external disequilibrium.(2)

First of all, problems of adjustment became apparent in the Bretton Woods system. Fixed exchange rates coexisted with constantly more severe international financial outflows, showing up in the form of accumulative distortions. In addition, fixed and overvalued rates of exchange offered a great opportunity for speculation, since both the magnitude and direction of the foreign exchange were highly predictable. This resulted in a growing cost of social programs for countries with a chronic balance of payments deficit, who were forced to maintain international reserves in an effort to finance the rate of exchange.

Secondly, the most serious problem in the International Monetary System was its implicit entropy. Contrasting to the expansionary shift in the world economy, the lack of mechanisms for generating international liquidity during the 1950s and 1960s created excessive demand. This situation was aggravated by the scarcity of gold, stemming from problems of profitability in its production. The supply of dollars and of other important reserve currencies was increased as an expedient to satisfy the need for international liquidity. The immediate effect was to subject their behavior to the dynamics of the U.S. economy.

In retrospect, the American economy constituted the keystone of the 1944 International Monetary System. The war led banks, companies, and individuals to erect control barriers - the exception being the United States - and short-term movements of capital did not represent an immediate threat to establishing fixed rates of exchange. The United States, the great creditor, was willing to undertake the correction of internal and external imbalances, since it was supposed that its economy would continue to generate surpluses for many years to come.

From 1965 on, however, the U.S. economy started to show a growing balance of payments deficit. Excess dollars that accumulated in countries with balance of payments surpluses, together with the disequilibria that occurred in the U.S. economy, eventually led to the substitution of dollars for gold. This put pressure on the gold/dollar relationship, resulting finally in the declaration of inconvertability of dollars to gold (August 15, 1971) and, subsequently, to the de facto floating of the strong currencies (see table 8.1).

Table 8.1.   International-Liquidity

Year	(G) U.S. Gold (In billions of dollars)	(D) Foreign Liabilities of the U.S. (In billions of dollars)	G/D
1950	22.82	7.89	2.89
1955	21.75	12.53	1.73
1959	19.51	16.05	1.21
1960	17.80	16.35	1.08
1961	16.95	17.44	0.97
1965	14.06	26.86	0.52
1966	13.23	27.86	0.47
1967	12.06	31.41	0.38
1968	10.89	31.86	0.34
1969	11.86	40.35	0.29

Source: Graham   Walshe,   International Monetary Reform (London: Macmillan, 1971).   Data from International Financial Statistics, IMF.

In this way, two of the basic principles of the IMF
Articles of Agreement - the system of fixed parities, and the
convertibility of dollars to gold - became inoperable, giving
way to monetary relationships characterized by the coexistence
of various systems of exchange(3) and an about-face in the
problems of international liquidity, i.e., from an excess of
demand to an excess of supply. The suspension of
convertibility of dollars to gold was a unilateral action that had
detrimental effects on developing countries with structural
payments imbalances and with a portfolio of international
reserves, predominantly in dollars.

The Excess International Liquidity Controversy

The search for a solution that would satisfy the international
needs for liquidity, without bringing about greater instability
in the process of international monetary adjustment, has been
a difficult one. An analysis of the factors that determine a
level of surplus liquidity has given rise to diverse positions.
On the one hand, countries with a payments surplus
assert that (a) excess liquidity has been caused by the
behavior of the U.S. economy, and (b) in identifying the
relationship between the U.S. payments deficit and the dollar
surplus, solutions should be sought which would exercise
greater control over the external sector of the U.S. economy,
in order to even out the liquidity level and prevent
subsequent revaluations of strong currencies.(4) According to
the Bank for International Settlements, the liquidity problem in
the Bretton Woods system (and its vestiges) did not lie in the
overall scarcity of reserves, but rather in the scarcity of gold
at the official price set in 1934, and in a growing excess of
dollars convertible to gold up to August 1971.(5) At present,
under floating rates of exchange, a "Policy for the Dollar" has
been proposed, based on the need to substantially reduce the
current account deficit, thus solving the current main cause of
that deficit: the energy crisis. Otherwise, adjustments in
rates of exchange greater than needed to achieve a balance of
medium and longterm payments will continue.
On the other hand, there are arguments that go beyond
the simplistic position of supposing that the problems of
international liquidity have been caused exclusively by the
U.S. payments deficit, and which focus more on the working
of the world economy as a whole and, particularly, on
mechanisms which independently generate additional means of
payment.(6)

1. Growing economic interdependence has added to both the
    number and magnitude of the disequilibria to which
    balances of payments are subject. This indicates the

need to direct economic policy toward the goal of achieving greater external equilibrium with a high cost in terms of the speed of adjustment of the economy and the attainment of national objectives.(7) In the monetary context, disequilibria in the money market quickly affect the external sector of the economy. With fixed rates of exchange, a chronic current account deficit in the balance of payments, and a rise in internal liquidity caused by the internal components of the monetary base (direct financing of the government and commercial banks by the central bank), there is a drain on international reserves, forcing monetary authorities to acquire compensatory reserves to finance the rate of exchange.(8)

2. The growth of international reserves since the late 1960s and during the 1970s has been reinforced by the expansion of the Special Drawing Rights, which have gradually been taking the place of dollars as reserve assets, and which deal with "the problem of long-range confidence," resulting from the gradual erosion of the position of U.S. liquidity, and from the expansion of other reserve assets (see table 8.2).

3. The deficit on current account of the U.S. economy stems not only from the process of internal expansion but, also, from the growth and expansion possibilities of the OECD countries and Japan. At the present time, these countries are experiencing problems, mainly of structural origin, that prevent accelerated growth. Moreover, restoring a satisfactory rate of economic recovery would require a more efficient and symmetrical operation of the international adjustment process. The expansion of countries with a surplus has not been enough to attain a rate of growth in world commerce which would help debtor countries in their efforts to adjust.

4. The process of internationalizing financial flows has given rise to autonomous mechanisms for generating additional liquidity, since the Eurocurrency markets have been firming up as systems that are exempt from monetary regulation and control in their process of growth. The Eurocurrency market has been growing at an accelerated rate as a result of various factors. Among the most important factors, the following should be noted: the U.S. Interest Equalization Tax (1963), the Voluntary Foreign Credit Restriction (1965), the Regulation of Reserve Requirements and Limitations on Interest Rates Charged on Liabilities (1967) (these changes affected the structure of international interest rates by putting mechanisms of financial arbitration to work, which directed ever-larger flows of dollars beyond the control of the Federal Reserve), the massive accumulation of dollars and other reserve assets by central banks in the form of

Table 8.2.   Changes in global reserves, 1974 to 1976*

Areas and periods	Gold	Foreign exchange	IMF reserve positions	SDRs	Total
			In millions of US dollars		
Group of Ten + Switzerland					
1974	+ 520	+ 1,735	+ 1,745	+ 390	+ 4,390
1975	- 1,605	+ 945	+ 1,620	- 230	+ 730
1976	- 260	+ 5,650	+ 4,340	+ 15	+ 9,745
Amounts outstanding at end-1976	33,555	70,535	12,715	7,775	124,580
Other developed countries					
1974	+ 55	- 2,590	- 145	- 215	- 2,895
1975	- 220	- 1,335	- 355	- 90	- 2,000
1976	- 240	+ 690	+ 400	- 125	+ 725
Amounts outstanding at end-1976	3,965	21,695	1,065	740	27,465
Developing countries other than oil-exporting countries					
1974	- 50	+ 3,075	- 155	+ 5	+ 2,875
1975	- 80	- 1,430	- 100	- 215	- 1,825
1976	- 10	+ 11,030	- 130	- 110	+ 10,780
Amounts outstanding at end-1976	2,100	35,500	480	1,140	39,220
Total oil-importing countries					
1974	+ 525	+ 2,220	+ 1,445	+ 160	+ 4,370
1975	- 1,905	- 1,620	+ 1,165	- 535	- 3,095
1976	- 510	+ 17,370	+ 4,610	- 220	+ 21,250
Amounts outstanding at end-1976	39,620	127,730	14,260	9,655	191,265
Oil-exporting countries					
1974	+ 50	+ 31,040	+ 1,945	+ 40	+ 33,075
1975	- 50	+ 7,310	+ 2,785	- 50	+ 9,995
1976	+ 55	+ 8,010	+ 1,215	+ 20	+ 9,300
Amounts outstanding at end-1976	1,505	59,050	6,350	400	67,305
All countries					
1974	+ 575	+ 33,260	+ 3,390	+ 220	+ 37,445
1975	- 1,955	+ 5,490	+ 3,950	- 585	+ 6,900
1976	- 455	+ 25,380	+ 5,825	- 200	+ 30,550
Amounts outstanding at end-1976	41,125	186,780	20,610	10,055	258,570

*Including valuation changes.

Source: Bank for International Settlements, <u>Forty-Seventh Annual Report</u>, April 1, 1976-March 31, 1977. (Basle, June 13, 1977), p. 139.

deposits in Eurodollars, and the placing of reserves of multinational companies in deposits of Eurocurrencies offering higher rates of interest. On the other hand, the key factor in the growth and expansion of the Eurocurrency market has been the recycling of petrocurrencies. The partial deposits in the Eurocurrency market by central banks of the international reserves of the OPEC member countries with balance of payments surpluses are explained by the opportunity to obtain higher yields from their petroleum surpluses, and to find alternative ways to channel these funds, given the difficulties facing these countries in putting their economies to work in a socially useful and productive way.

In short, the Eurocurrency market, whose practical significance lies in the fact that it provides a broad range of resources and an immense variety of uses, has played a very important role in expanding international reserves and liquidity. If the central banks of the rest of the world were to place their reserve assets in the Eurocurrency market, however, the result could be a multiple expansion of liquidity which, because it is unregulated, would be beyond the reach of the traditional approach of monetary policies.

EUROCURRENCY MULTIPLIERS

The Eurobanks and the International Intermediation

Eurobanks have been in a position to generate, within a short time, impressive increments in their liabilities in dollars and other currencies, by offering investment facilities and interest rates that are more attractive than those offered by national financial markets that have drained the reserves in local currencies from innumerable banks and nonbanking enterprises. In addition, several central banks have deposited large amounts of their monetary reserves in Eurobanks, in response to complex national and international monetary policy situations.

This process of financial intermediation has been unfolding in an atmosphere of uncertainty arising from futures in exchange rates, the nature of international export and import transactions, and the ownership of net assets. Besides adding to the cost of such transactions, uncertainty has led to the development of a varied financial technology to cover spot and future risks. It has also had great repercussions on the growth of Eurocurrency markets and, in fact, constitutes one of the basic reasons for their existence.

A further dimension to the normal processes of financial intermediation is added by the fact that each country lists its transactions in a particular currency, different from the others; and, in this way, the opportunities for international intermediation are greater. At the same tme, it becomes advantageous to keep large balances in "working currency" or "vehicle currency" of which, in international practice, only a few are considered to be quasimoney. If the rates of exchange were fixed and unavoidable, the only risk involved in holding assets in these currencies would be the one associated with the nature of the assets. Under the Bretton Woods system, there was always the possibility of infrequent but sweeping adjustments in the value of parties, with subsequent changes in their wake. At the present time, the fluctuations based on daily changes are such as to add great uncertainty to currency transactions. A "working currency" is identified by: (a) its high and stable purchasing power; (b) it broad markets which are not affected by isolated transactions; (c) its low operating costs as compared to other currencies; and (d) the fact that it is subject to small predictable fluctuations.(10)

Finally, international financial intermediaries are in a position to internalize certain economies of scale by carrying out wholesale transactions and working only with certain "vehicle-currencies" which allow different degrees of specialization. Taken together, these characteristics of the system make it possible to obtain substantial reductions in costs as the volume of transactions increases.

Nonetheless, there are good reasons to assert that the growth of the Eurocurrency market and its relative contribution to the generation of large amounts of liquidity lies not only in the important process of international financial intermediation, but also in the existence of a multiplier of deposits in Eurocurrency of considerable magnitude.

The Empirical Evidence over the Multiplier

The Eurocurrency market and, particularly, its impact on the world supply of liquidity is one of the most controversial and important topics in international finance.(11) The growing importance of the market and the levels of international liquidity observed are a source of concern to the international community from several standpoints: (a) the process of restructuring the International Monetary System; (b) the effectiveness of national economic policies and timely decision-making; (c) the attainment of a New International Economic Order; and (d) world economic stability.

To date, there have been different attempts to understand more clearly the multiple processes of deposits in

Eurocurrencies, but the great number of variables affecting the size of the market has made this quite difficult. The controversy has been developing along the following lines.

The existence of a credit creation process based on a multiple of primary deposit flows

According to Friedman, "the Eurocurrency market is the latest example of the mystical quality of money creation" where the expansion of deposits in Eurocurrencies can be explained by a process that is completely analogous to that which occurs in commercial banks.(12)   Under the observation of extremely small precautionary reserve requirements that exist in Euro-banks, and the almost total absence of monetary control instru-ments, it is to be expected that multipliers greater than unit (M > I) will be observed.

In this respect, it is argued that the credit creation process is explained more by the close relationship existing between the balance of payments deficit and other sources of the Eurocurrency market, on the one hand, and additional deposits in Eurocurrencies, on the other.   In this context, Eurobanks, as a behavior group, are able to recover only a small fraction of the credits granted.   Therefore, the flight of Eurobank deposits indicates the existence of a process of multiple expansion of limited dimensions.(13)   According to Hewson and Sakakibara, this would mean the existence of multipliers in the approximate range of 0.50 to 0.90.(14)

Open banking circuits vs. closed banking circuits

In addition to the extremely small reserve requirements existing under a typical commerical banking system in developed countries, flights from the system are small, and the autonomous process of credit creation in the banking system is of considerable magnitude. Credit expansion by banks helps to increase current demand and the circulation of income which in turn, feed back into the banking system, thus closing the circle of credit expansion.   By contrast, the liabilities of the Eurocurrency market do not constitute a close monetary circuit, and the holders of Eurodollars are scattered throughout the world.   Although it is possible that dollars allocated by the market are converted into national currencies and then reconverted into dollars - and first deposited in the Eurocurrency market - the very nature of their uses (such as loans to developing countries) renders the process difficult. Therefore, a genuine multiplier effect will take place only to the extent that the use of the credits is added to the circulation of income.(15)   This argument against the existence of a multiplier of considerable magnitude is based principally on the fact that Eurobanks are essentially deposit and savings institutions and that, consequently, the contribution of the market to credit creation (juxtaposed to intermediation) is very small.

Interbanking operations and Eurocurrency multipliers

Toward the end of the 1960s, the controversy about the existence of a multiplier in Eurocurrency deposits and its causes was represented, on the one hand, by the position of Friedman and others, whose main assumptions were that the process of credit expansion in the Eurocurrency market was similar to the process observed in the closed banking systems, and that the proportion of Eurobank assets kept as reserves was small, due to the absence of legal reserve requirements. Therefore, flights or outflows from the banking system were small, and the multiplier showed great values. On the other hand, it was argued that the banking system of Eurocurrencies behaved like an "open circuit" with a high level of flights that determined a multiplier with values close to one, and even less.

Subsequently, other explanations arose maintaining that the process of credit expansion came about through a mechanism of interbanking operations, inducing a chain of pyramid-like interbank deposits. Each bank in the chain of intermediation kept a small proportion of its assets in the form of reserves for the purpose of minimizing the profits of intermediation. The tendency to maintain a certain level of reserves meant that, as the number of intermediary operations increased, interbank loans diminished proportionally, coming down to a final operation of intermediation between a banking surplus unit and nonbanking deficit unit resulting in subsequent repercussions on a real economic activity.(16)

Swoboda deserves the credit for having developed a general multiplier for the Eurocurrency market, where the expansionist effects deriving from a fractional banking system and the interbank chain operations are linked together. Swoboda's multiple expansion parameters were conceived under the criterion of fixed reserve coefficients. Nonetheless, it was necessary to consider that interbank pyramiding depended on the cost of intermediation; that the proportion of deposits kept as precautionary reserves depended upon the preferences for assets over liabilities on the part of the banks; and that the redeposit of loans made to nonbanking units did not necessarily occur. Again, doubts arose as to the advisability of using fixed flight coefficients, and as to the degree of "opening" of the system.

Redeposit of central bank reserves

The arguments advanced by Mayer on the concept of the
Eurocurrency market as an open circuit brought forth a series
of attempts to prove that a large-scale multiplier exists, by
analyzing the sources of the Eurocurrency market.(17)   In
essence, the alternative incorporates the behavior of central
bank reserves and their process of redeposit in the
Eurocurrency market. According to Clendenning, if central
banks do not deposit part of their reserves in the market,
only a low-value multiplier is obtained whereas, if they are
redeposited in the market, a multiplier with a higher value is
obtained, since "flights" or "outflows" from the system are,
thereby, considerably reduced.
    According to Hewson and Sakakibara, however, the
empirical evidence from other authors, with respect to
Clendenning's hypothesis, shows substantially dissimilar results
regarding the absolute value of the multiplier in Eurocurrency
deposits, even when redeposits of central bank reserves are
included, and when similar time periods are being dealt
with.(18)

Eurocurrency multipliers with variable coefficients

The process of obtaining a multiplier in Eurocurrency deposits
has followed a course similar to the development of monetary
multipliers. At the outset, the monetary multiplier was merely
a fixed coefficient which, together with the monetary base,
determined a level of monetary supply. Subsequently, it was
found that the monetary multiplier was determined by fixed
reserve and cash coefficients.   This mechanistic conception was
later abandoned to make way for a new theory which would
explicitly include policy variables under the direct control of
monetary authorities.   It would also establish a regular link
between the control variables and the monetary aggregates
and explain, to a greater degree, the variations in the quantity of money resulting from actions and reactions on the part
of the monetary authorities, the financial system, and the lay
public.
    Similarly, in recent years, efforts have been centered on
developing multipliers in the Eurocurrency deposits which
would take into account the preferences of both lenders and
borrowers with respect to the composition of their assets and
liabilities, in order to explain more precisely the changes in
the liquidity of the Eurocurrency market, derived from the
multiplication of deposits.   An argument has, therefore, been
advanced in favor of a theory of the supply of Eurocurrencies
based on a multiplier with variable flight coefficients, as a
reflection of the process of choosing portfolio on the part of
economic units that comprise the market.

In its development, such a reorientation of the theory takes the following factors into consideration: (1) the dynamic arbitration process which is engendered in the international financial context, and its effects on the term structure of the interest rates existing in the market, as well as the effects the changes of these variables produce in the composition of the portfolio of financial intermediaries and of the lay public; (2) the net supply of Eurocurrencies and their fluctuations; (3) the control of variables, such as the regulatory measures and reserves requirements of U.S. commercial banks in Eurocurrencies; (4) restrictions such as variables in income and wealth; and (5) speculative variables such as futures in the strong currencies or "vehicle-currencies."

As one can see, the concept of a Eurocurrency multiplier that includes such parameters makes it possible to deal effectively with a number of worrisome aspects surrounding the multiplier controversy. According to McKenzie, perhaps the most outstanding attempt to explain the expansion of the Eurocurrency system based on a multiplication process has been made by Hewson and Sakakibara, who have worked out a model of behavior for the portfolio of lenders and borrowers in Eurocurrencies, that arrives at the following conclusions:(19)

- The multiplier with fixed coefficients is relevant and useful for approximating the process of monetary supply in a domestic banking system, where important regulations on banking practices usually exist. Nonetheless, their application is not appropriate in unregulated competitive markets such as the Eurocurrency market.
- The use of a portfolio model of general balance made it possible to derive an expression for the Eurocurrency multiplier. Taking into consideration the primary influx of Eurocurrencies, the multiplier registers values that fluctuate between zero and one, in the absence of central bank redeposits in the market.
- When central banks kept part of their reserves in the form of deposits in Eurocurrencies, the multiplier showed values substantially above one (1.4) during the 1968-72 period.
- This estimate for the multiplier should be considered to be the maximum, owing to the possibility that redeposits of central banks are reaching their highest rate of expansion.

As can be shown, the present state of empirical evidence points to the existence of a multiplier for deposits in Eurocurrencies with values substantially greater than one, where there are redeposits of central bank reserves in the Eurocurrency market. It would seem, then, that the variable which dynamically marks the existence of a multiplier of deposits in the Eurocurrencies is the reserves of central banks, especially of those countries with a payments surplus

such as the OPEC members, some members of the OECD, and
Japan.

EXCESS LIQUIDITY IN THE EUROCURRENCY
MARKET: CONTROL ALTERNATIVES

Excess Liquidity and Inflation

There are two basic sources of change in the process that
creates excess international liquidity: (1) the accelerated
growth that has been registered in the base of liquidity
expansion, brought about by an excess of vehicle currencies
and conversions made between them by Specal Drawing Rights,
payments surpluses, and redeposits of central bank reserves;
and (2) the existence proved by empirical evidence of a
multiplier of deposits in Eurocurrencies of considerable
magnitude.

Such factors play a very important role in the growth and
stability of the world economy. Achieving optimal international
liquidity would also, in a general way, help attain a world
economic growth balanced by optimal rates of inflation and, in
particular, the expansion of international trade. In contrast,
the two extremes – lack of liquidity and excess liquidity –
have characterized global economic development over the past
twenty years.

Both situations of disequilibrium have advantages and
disadvantages for international economic activity. Since
worldwide distribution of wealth is uneven and inequitable, and
the gap in per capita income between industrial and developing
countries is getting wider, a situation in which there is a lack
of international liquidity tends to lead the global economy into
a situation of stagnant growth. This happens because the
scant resources for financing are mainly absorbed by developed
countries, which slow down their rate of growth in the face of
financial restrictions. This has important repercussions on
developing countries, since it imposes restrictions on economic
growth that derive not only from the scarcity of resources for
financing the internal and external deficits, but also from the
decline in foreign aid, the gradual elimination of growth via
the foreign sector, and a considerable lag in capital formation.
In contrast, the trend towards no growth brings with it a
lowering of the deficit on current account, and a lower rate of
external indebtedness.

On the other hand, a situation of excess liquidity acts as
a necessary condition for achieving higher growth rates in
developed countries which, in turn, positively affects the
growth of developing countries, stimulates the growth of the
export sector, and helps development financing in various

way, although with higher costs in terms of more external
indebtedness and greater disequilibrium on current account of
the balance of payments.

Nonetheless, Heller and others have correctly pointed out
the detrimental effects of excess liquidity on the behavior of
prices.(20) Surveys of 126 member countries of the International Monetary Fund for the 1951-74 period indicate an
annual shortfall between the percentile changes in the value of
overall monetary reserves, and the growth rate of the world
monetary supply.   At the same time, there is a direct
relationship between the percentile changes in the world
monetary supply and the rate of increase in world inflation,
with one lagging about 18 months behind the other.

In this process, one should not forget the importance
already examined, of a "pool" of international funds (the
Eurocurrency market) with its own multiplier elements for
deposits.

Other Effects of Excess Liquidity:
The Availability of International Financing
and Banking Practices of Granting Credits

In the discussion of the positive effects of excess
liquidity derived from the process of creating international
means of payments in the Eurocurrency market, the argument
for financial advantages assumes a certain importance: (21)

1.   The development of the Eurocurrency system constitutes a
      big improvement in monetary mechanisms, signifying an
      important means of overcoming national barriers.
2.   Under the system, the conditions of deposit and financing
      are much more flexible, as compared to the conditions
      prevailing in domestic markets.
3.   The system improves international financial transactions
      by reducing the friction that often prevents market
      mechanisms from being effective.

The existence of an interest rate structure in an international
money market leads to automatic correction of imbalances
between supply and demand.

From the point of view of developing countries, more and
more of them have been making ever-larger loans, a situation
which partially confirms the advantages of the Eurocurrency
system.   A very high proportion of these loans, however, has
been made through medium-term syndicated credits with
floating interest rates and, in fact, the bulk of the
indebtedness has been concentrated in a few medium-income
countries - notably, Brazil, Mexico, Argentina, and Peru.
Actually 85 percent of all medium and long-term foreign debt

that is negotiated in Eurobanks is accounted for by 15 developing countries, which have relatively high per capita incomes, export earnings, and overall growth rates.(22)

The high rate of foreign indebtedness of the countries mentioned has been due fundamentally to the development of the syndicated loan market (in consortium). This has facilitated access to funds in Eurocurrencies, created systems of renewable credit with periodically adjustable interest rates and, in fact, has spread out the risk of default among a large number of banks. This also has had a pronounced effect on the removal of tolerance "levels," and on introducing important amounts of credit in Eurocurrencies into markets considered to be marginal under the other circumstances.

The events of 1974 and 1975, characterized by the inability of certain countries to meet their short-term obligations, have introduced into the international scene important measures of selectivity concerning borrowers, coverage of risks due to default, and rationing of credit. According to research done by Kapur, banks determine the credit capacity of a country in accordance with its liquidity, economic growth, foreign debt, degree of export activity, and existing level of banking obligations. In addition, the political risk is evaluated. Based on empirical evidence, the variables that have the most weight are (besides political stability): the present level and expected growth of exports; the projected variation in the medium-term foreign debt burden; the existing level of net obligations; and the level of income.

In addition to these factors, which cause credit to be directed only to a few, privileged, developing countries, there are other elements tending to ration the international supply of Eurocurrencies, especially with respect to the systems of control that Eurobanks have been setting up internally, in order to "cover" their position in the Eurocurrency market.

A Strong Case for Monetary Regulation

In recent years, there have been many proposals for monetary reform such as the Triffin Plan, the Stamp Plan, the Modigliani-Kenen Plan, the Roosa Plan, and the Hart-Kaldor-Tinbergen Plan. As Harry G. Johnson sees it, such plans commonly focus on only one part of the solution for international monetary conflicts. They either offer solutions to the overall requirements of international monetary reform, or they seek ways to earmark additional financial resources and other types of aid to developing countries.(23) Within the overall pattern of monetary reform, Eurobanks may be considered to be a strong case for regulation because of the following circumstances:

1.   It is necessary to establish mechanisms of monetary regulation that act directly on short-term deposits in Eurocurrencies, with the purpose of preventing circumstantial problems of excess of liquidity or shortage of liquidity, as well as avoiding adjustment problems in segments of the short-term market. This would go far toward stabilizing the multiplier of deposits in Eurocurrencies by acting upon the reserve coefficient and by side-stepping seasonal fluctuations in the market.

2.   Achieving more control over the volatile behavior of international liquidity requires an International System of Prevention of Financial Crises, which would make known, with relative dispatch, the amounts of credit extended in Eurocurrencies by type of institution and by user, in relation to the limits of risk established. Such a system would help to control the growth of the market with relative flexibility, and would prevent unwise credit expansion over and above the limits indicated for each institution. In this context, one might also give thought to a system of reciprocal assistance between central banks and treasuries for the purpose of averting large loans in those vehicle-currencies that are subject to adverse pressures, and which might eventually introduce unfavorable effects into the process of financial intermediation.(24)

3.   It can also be argued that the system of prevention of financial crises, currently used by several private international financial institutions, should have the authority to intervene opportunely in cases where Eurobanks have granted credits in Eurocurrencies above the limits of risk coverage.(25)

4.   It is felt that the IMF itself, or possibly a new central banking organization of international scope, could implement these instruments of surveillance, monetary control, and channeling of surpluses. An interesting alternative which would redound to the greater benefit of developing countries would be a plan whereby liquid resources in Eurocurrencies, absorbed in the form of precautionary deposits, would be earmarked for the creation of a fund to stabilize, and make more profitable, the production of exportable raw materials. Such a mechanism would represent a suitable way to affect positively the monetary surpluses accumulated in the Eurocurrency market.

5.   As far as the demand for Eurocurrencies is concerned, there is an urgent need for a juridico-financial framework of international scope which would regulate the use of credit on the part of developing countries. In other words, there should be a law of public debt which would permit the governments and their institutions to have

orderly access to the Eurocurrency and Eurobond markets, in order to help stabilize these markets, and to prevent the introduction of elements of risk in the process of international financial intermediation.

6. Such juridico-financial framework should give priority to the preparation by the governments of a financial program to manage the public debt, anticipating the currencies needed for handling external demand. Similarly, it would channel resources from the public debt into projects, activities, and enterprises favoring plans of economic and social development.

7. This would also involve the auditing of the paying capacity of the economic units that negotiate resources in Eurocurrencies for the purpose of meeting obligations, and the supervision of optimal amortization of the principal and interest. It would avoid the authorizing of external financing that might generate obligations beyond the capacity of payment, and it would also centralize the authorization of credits for the state negotiated abroad. Lastly, it would favor the use of external financing of projects that would produce sufficient resources for their amortization and the obligations assumed, and check the use of external financing for current expenditures.

It is felt that, if the international community in general were to adopt these juridico-financial instruments, not only could future problems be averted, but it would also be possible to monitor external resources to assure their use in a more productive and efficient manner. Such a measure, in conjunction with a system of prevention of international financial crises, instruments for the monetary regulation of liquid deposits in Eurocurrencies, and the reinvestment of the monetary surpluses obtained, would make it possible to reorder and regulate international monetary relationships to a greater degree than has so far been possible.

NOTES

(1) Tom de Vries, "Reforming International Monetary Relations: An Analysis in Changing Patterns in Foreign Trade and Payments," in Changing Patterns in Foreign Trade and Payments, ed. Bella Balassa. (New York: W.W. Norton, 1978), p. 250.

(2) See William R. Cline, International Monetary Reform and the Developing Countries (Washington: The Brookings Institution, 1977), p. 2.

(3) The Jamaica Accord (January 1976) guarantees each country the right to determine and modify its exchange

system, without simultaneously trying to control and improve the quality of international liquidity.

(4) World Financial Markets, In Search of a Dollar Policy, (New York: Morgan Guaranty Trust Co., January 1978), pp. 1-9.

(5) In this respect, countries such as Switzerland, France, the Netherlands, and Belgium strongly preferred international reserve holdings mainly in gold and, therefore, supported a freeing of its price. Bank for International Settlements, Forty-Seventh Annual Report (Basle, June 13, 1977), p. 140.

(6) See in this regard Robert Heller, "International Reserves. Money and Global Inflation" in Balassa, Changing Patterns p. 242.

(7) Richard N. Cooper, "National Economic Policy in an Interdependent World Economy," in Ballassa, Changing Patterns, p. 222.

(8) Antonio Caso and Alberto Mayoral, Politica Monetaria, Inflacion y Crecimiento Economico; El Caso de Mexico (Mexico: Limusa, 1979), p. 20.

(9) Talat M. Othman, "How Foreign Exchange Markets Work" in Foreign Exchange Trading Techniques and Controls, ed. D. R. Man Rich (American Bankers Association, 1977), pp. 6-11.

(10) George W. McKenzie, The Economics of the Euro-Economy System (London: Macmillan, 1977), p. 49.

(11) Helmut Mayer, "Multiplier Effects and Credit Creation in the Euro-Dollar Market," Banca Nazionale del Lavoro Quarterly Review (September 1971), p. 3.

(12) Milton Friedman, "The Euro-Dollar Market: Some First Principles" in Recent Advances in Economics, ed. Fels and J.J. Siegfried (Homewood, Illinois: R.A. Irwin, 1974), p. 166.

(13) Fred H. Klopstock, "Money Creation in the Euro-Dollar Markets: A Note on Professor Friedman's Views," in Fels and Siegfried Recent Advances, p. 180.

(14) J. Hewson and E. Sakakibara, "The Euro-Dollar Deposit Multiplier: A Portfolio Approach," International Monetary Fund Staff Papers 22 (March 1975): 308.

(15) Mayer, "Multiplier Effects and Credit Creation", p. 243.

(16) McKenzie, The Economics of the Euro-Economy System, pp. 79-80.

(17) See: Wayne E. Clendenning, "Euro-Dollars and Credit Creation," International Currency Review 3 (March/April 1971): 12-19. Boyden E. Lee, "The Euro-Dollar Multiplier," Journal of Finance 23 (September 1963): 867-74; and John H. Maken, "Demand and Supply Functions for Stocks of Euro-Dollar Deposits: An Empirical Study," Review of Economics and Statistics 54 (November 1972): 381-91.

(18) See: Lee, "The Euro-Dollar Multiplier", pp. 867-74.
      Maken, "Demand and Supply," pp. 381-91.
(19) Hewson and Sakakibara, "The Euro-Dollar Deposit
      Multiplier," pp. 326-27.
(20) Heller, "International Reserves," p. 245.
(21) Paul Einzing, The Euro-Dollar System (New York: St.
      Martin's Press, 1973), pp. 169-71.
(22) Ishan Kapur, "Fondos en Eurodivisas para los Paises en
      Desarrollo," Revista Bancaria 25, (no. 11, November
      1977): 15-21.
(23) Harry G. Johnson, Essays in Monetary Economics,
      (London: Union University, 1974), pp. 306-07.
(24) See Einzing, The Euro-Dollar System, p. 175.
(25) See Edward I. Altman and Arnold W. Sametz, Financial
      Crisis: Institutions and Markets in a Fragile Environment
      (New York: John Wiley & Sons, 1977).

IV
OPEC Funds

9 The Use of OPEC Funds for Promoting Collective Self-Reliance Among Developing Countries*
Rehman Sobhan

THE IMPLICATIONS OF THE OPEC SURPLUS

The Ramadan War of 1973 precipitated action by the collective of oil exporters, acting through the Organization of Petroleum Exporting Countries (OPEC), to raise the posted price of crude oil from $3.00 per barrel to $5.12 as of October 16, 1973. When the world market price of oil began to climb in the wake of actual and anticipated scarcities, precipitated by interruption of oil exports from the Middle East, OPEC once again raised the price of crude as of January 1, 1974 to $11.65 per barrel.

The recent Iranian revolution which led to the overthrow of the monarchy has produced a constellation of forces similar to the oil embargo of 1973. This time, however, it was the collective action of the Iranian oil workers to suspend production which led to an enforced suspension of exports from Iran. Iran being the second largest exporter of oil in the world, suspension of exports and expectation that eventual resumption would be at levels well below prerevolution volume led, again, to actual and anticipated scarcity of stocks in the importing countries. This, in turn, led to an increase in the market price of oil. OPEC took advantage of the changed market situation and raised oil prices as of April 1979 from $12.70 to $14.50 per barrel. The possibility that the market

---

*This paper is derived from a broader study scheduled for completion by the end of 1979. The presentation and argument are, therefore, highly tentative. The author wishes to acknowledge the valuable contribution in research assistance from Ashfag Hai.

situation will perpetuate the upward pressure on prices makes it inevitable that OPEC will raise prices yet again. As it stands, individual producers are already selling their oil at its scarcity price rather than the price fixed by OPEC.

This initial comment on OPEC pricing policy is relevant to our discussion because it has reaffirmed that the critical factor in realizing an upward movement in prices and a resulting favorable move in terms of trade of the commodity producers was the capacity of producers to not only act collectively but to sustain their unity over nearly a decade. The action to work collectively to raise prices was not the result of protracted negotiations within a North-South dialogue, but came from the unilateral action of a group of Third World developing countries to reverse the historic alignment of economic power and control over the benefits from their national resources. The investment of political effort to realize and then maintain, in the face of severe external pressure, this unity of purpose has yielded unimaginable dividends to OPEC and has opened up an entirely new perspective on the balance of power in the world economy.

The implications of the OPEC action were immediately realized within the Third World. Collection action was not only seen to be profitable, but, for the first time, a group of Third World countries had control over a large volume of investable resources to back up their bargaining power. The idea of realizing a New International Economic Order (NIEO), which sought to restructure the pattern of international economic relations in favor of the Third World, was given substance by the achievements of OPEC. At that stage it was envisioned that OPEC would use the price of oil as a bargaining counter on behalf of the Third World to extract concessions from the developed North on the spectrum of issues which made up the North-South Dialogue. This expectation reached its high point in the Conference of International Economic Cooperation at Paris between December 1975 and June 1977, when the oil exporting countries, for the last time, played a leading role in the North-South Dialogue.(1)

Almost five years separated UNCTAD IV (Nairobi, 1975) from UNCTAD V (Manila, 1979) and perspectives within the Third World appear to have changed subtly but significantly. Neither at Arusha in the preparatory meeting of the Group of 77 prior to UNCTAD V nor at Manila was there any further reference to the use of OPEC resources as a negotiating asset in the North-South Dialogue.(2) This reflects the failure of the South to evaluate the true meaning of the OPEC action after the Ramadan War, and to realize the enormous potential implicit in the gains which accrued to OPEC from those events. As a result, five years later, the North-South Dialogue has yielded only modest gains to the South in the way of a watered-down Common Fund, and a limited amount of debt has been written off.

In contrast, the pattern of domination and dependence on the North, which characterized the old economic order, appears virtually unchanged. A major part of the gains from the oil price increase have been recycled back to the North in the way of imports and investments, so that, today at least, the 'surplus' oil exporters appear as dependent on the North as before. In the process, OPEC surpluses are rapidly diminishing, having fallen from $64 billion in 1974 to $9 billion in 1978.(3)

Within the OPEC countries, only four currently have a surplus, three have surpluses of a billion dollars or less, and the rest are in the deficit. The capacity of the rest of the countries to realize sufficient structural changes in their economy to change the pattern of dependence on the North is coming increasingly into question.

In view of this course of events, the idea of the developing countries working together to transform the prevailing pattern of the world economy would appear to be little more than an abstraction. The gains realized by OPEC could be seen to be unique to the nature of the commodity which brought them together.

The significant feature of the OPEC action does not, however, limit itself merely to the virtues of collective action by commodity producers. More significant to the developing countries is the fact that OPEC action brought about a historic transfer in the ownership of investable resources from the industrial world to a group of developing countries. Between January 1, 1974 and the end of 1978, an additional $459 billion of resources accrued to the OPEC countries.(4) Of this, 83 percent, or $381 billion, was, in effect, a transfer of resources from the developed world to these countries.(5) This transfer of resources to the oil exporters gave them the potential not only to transform their own economies but, in the process, to transform the entire balance of world economic power. The very process of economic transformation in these countries opened up hitherto unimagined possibilities for building up economic ties within the South by diverting these resources to the import of goods, services, manpower, capital, and technology from within the region.

The capacity of the developing countries to respond to the needs of the OPEC countries was obviously not unlimited; the industrial countries would have played an important role in the development process of the oil exporters. However, had the development plans of the oil exporters been purposefully directed toward the Third World, the potential for a major realignment in the external economic relations of the oil exporters would have been accompanied by a quantum change in the development potential of these countries. This change in the development prospects would not have been entirely at the expense of the industrial countries, because it would have led to an accelerated flow of imports of capital and intermediate goods catering to the needs of the oil exporters.

Apart from the development potential inherent in a realigment of the current trading patterns of the South, the investable resources surplus to the development needs of the oil exporters could have been used as a major political resource for the South. The surpluses opened up a whole range of options to the South which could enable the Third World to break out of the impasse imposed on it by the North-South Dialogue. OPEC surpluses could have been used to commercially underwrite a series of collective 'Southern' projects designed to strengthen the economies of developing countries, and consequently to improve their bargaining strength within the North-South Dialogue. It is argued here that such projects should have preceded, or at least moved concurrent with, the attempt to seek mutual accommodation with the North.

Prior to the Ramadan War, the bulk of the world's investable surpluses originated in the developed world. In 1973, virtually all capital transfers to developing countries originated from the industrial nations, with the residual coming from the socialist bloc. Some oil exporters had accumulated surpluses, but these were mostly invested in the money markets of the West, with only an insignificant amount used as aid or commercial investment in the Third World. This meant that the very process of development within the developing countries was dependent on the volume and pattern of capital transfers from the North, and the concomitant technology package which went with this transfer. In many cases, the pattern of dependence was reinforced by the tendency of such transfers to be accompanied by ownership and control of assets created in the developing countries by multinational corporations, by dependence on the markest of the developed world for the products of these investments, and by an ongoing flow of technology, spares, and intermediate imports from these same countries. International development institutions (such as the World Bank and the private commercial banks and financial institutions of the developed world) merely perpetuated this pattern of dependency, that could hardly be divorced from political dependency and the consequent constraints on sovereignty. The capacity to act collectively with other developing countries to seek a redress in the balance of power was correspondingly diminished by this pattern of economic dependence and constraints on political sovereignty.

The accrual of $459 billion in additional resources to the oil exporters meant that, for the first time in contemporary history, one developing country could look to another for markets and capital. In 1977, 12 percent of global exports went to the oil exporters, compared to 5 percent in 1972.

However, of this big increment in imports by the oil exporters between 1972 and 1977 only 12.4 percent came from non-oil developing countries.(6) If one looks at the actual increment in annual imports by OPEC between 1972 and 1977, only 13.4 percent came from non-oil developing countries.(7) In contrast, the developed countries accounted for 84.5 percent of the increment in imports by the oil exporters.(8)

Apart from the market potential of the oil exporters, between 1974 and 1978 they disposed of $185 billion in investable surpluses. Of this amount, $128 billion, or 69 percent, of the investable surpluses went into commercial investments in the Western world compared to $147 billion, or 25 percent, of concessional and non-concessional transfers to developing countries.(9) This vast increment in investable funds is, of course, well below what had initially been projected in 1974, but it is still a sizeable sum, and it will continue to increase for some years. This volume of investable funds constituted a major commercial as well as political resource for the developing contries, and it could well have been invested in reducing the pattern of external dependence. The oil exporters have earned negative returns from their investment in the developed world. An estimate derived from our wider study indicates an aggregative return of 5 to 5.5 percent for 1976 and 1977, which was below the current rate of inflation on export prices of the industrialized countries, and very much below the increase in import prices for OPEC. In the process OPEC has become even more dependent on the stability of the capital markets and external currency values of the developed countries, on their level of economic activity and, most important, on their political good will. Threats from the developed world of expropriation of assets constitute a perpetual sanction on the freedom of action of oil exporters.

The surpluses which accrued to the oil exporters could have provided commercially profitable possibilities for investment, trade, cooperation, technology and labor transfers, and commodity price stabilization, which could have been predicated on mutual benefit and cooperation among developing countries, rather than on perpetuation of political dependence of one group of countries on another. Had these ideals eventually been realized, a genuine realignment in the international economic order would have been entirely possible.

In actual practice, however, it was the developed world which, in many ways, proved much more responsive to the threat posed by the transfer of resources to the oil exporters. Ever since this historic development, the collective strategy of the industrial countries has been directed toward redressing this dramatic reallocation of the world resources. A major part of the OPEC surplus has been successfully appropriated through the escalation in prices as well as through the export of goods and services, participation in the development projects of the oil exporters, and sales of arms. A major part of the residual has also been captured by short and long-term investments directed to the developed world. As a result, the potential negative effects on the economies of the industrial world of the major accrual of resources by the oil-exporting countries has been minimized, and the real costs have effectively been shifted to the oil-importing developing countries, who are, today, paying higher prices for both oil and imports.

This successful recycling of the OPEC surpluses back to the developed world has perpetuated the traditional pattern of economic relations, but it has also extracted a price from the world economy. The slow revival of economic activity in the West reflects the importance of price increases in realizing a net increment in the export of goods. As a result, increments in export earnings have gone hand-in-hand with underutilized export capacity in the developed economies. A slow-down in economic activity in many developing countries has not been compensated for by the conspicuous success of some of them in responding to the crisis.

The perpetuation of the old order in a stagnant world economy appears to be the direct consequence of the failure of the Third World to respond effectively to the historic opportunities opened up to it after the Ramadan War. In trying to elaborate more fully on the potential which still exists for using these surpluses, it becomes essential to understand how, in effect, they were recycled into the world economy over the last five years. In this process we can come to a more realistic appraisal of the nature of the constraints that inhibit collective self-reliance within the Third World and serve to perpetuate the old order.

THE RECYCLING OF THE SURPLUS FUNDS

Much of the current literature on OPEC surpluses projects the progressive erosion of the surplus, and points out that, in effect, there are now only five surplus countries left within OPEC. This conclusion derives from the notion that the surplus is really a residual financial estimate derived from the balance of payments, and represents the revenues available for commercial investment. By this measure, even concessional transfers to developing countries are deducted from the estimates. The concept of surplus, in effect, is derived from the needs of Western investment bankers who need to estimate the flow of investable funds into the money market from OPEC sources, and to evaluate its placement in terms of countries, currencies, and composition. The most widely used estimates of the surplus are prepared by the U.S. Treasury, Morgan

Guaranty Trust, and the Bank of England.(10) Though various other sources (such as Chase Manhattan and the OECD) prepare their own estimates, all of them inevitably see the surplus in terms of the needs of the Western money market.

This particular conceptualization is important for our assessment of resources directly available for non-concessional lending to developing countries, but is clearly inadequate as a measure of the potential scope for OPEC's economic interaction with them.(11) As defined by the bankers, the surplus is a residual figure dependent on any number of policy variables within individual oil exporting countries. A checklist of such policy measures would begin with the collective decision to raise prices. However, within this, the decision to sell some oil at the market price above the fixed price, or at concessional prices, would obviously affect revenues, depending on the policy defining how much oil to sell, to whom, and at what price.

More critical than the price of oil is, in fact, the actual production and export decision. The decision of the oil producers to progressively nationalize the oil companies was of special significance to the resumption of sovereignty over production and mrketing decisions. Previously, it was the international oil companies, dominated by the "Majors" or "Seven Sisters," who decided how much oil would be extracted and sold and at what price. Crucial to any policy of collective price-setting was the capacity to regulate output, so that production policy could be used as the main variable to give practical effect to pricing policy. The nature of the product is such that a producer has complete freedom over his decision to produce during any one year, or even within shorter time periods.

To the extent that the production decision can effectively determine the size of the surplus, that decision becomes a part of the investment strategy of the oil producers. In effect, by deciding to cut back production to the level of domestic needs for both oil consumption and revenues, an oil producer is taking an investment decision to keep oil in the ground rather than to build up an investable surplus. This derives from the fact that oil is a nonrenewable resource, which is directly convertible into capital investments either at home or abroad. Every barrel of oil so produced has an opportunity cost which can be estimated in terms of projections of the appreciation in the price of oil in comparison with returns on domestic and foreign investment of revenues earned from the sale of the oil. The Iranian decision to cut back oil production from six million to four million barrels a day can, in this context, be evaluated as a rational investment decision rather than an act of bloody-mindedness. Unlike the production of cocoa or other cash crops, oil production foregone is not lost forever, but merely retained for future use. Producers, thus, have com-

plete freedom to choose between current and future need
for revenue.

A number of oil producers have narrowed their options by
committing themselves to programs of accelerated development.
Algeria, Indonesia, Nigeria, Venezuela, and Ecuador are
pushing their production of oil to the limits of capacity in
order to sustain the development targets they have set for the
economy. Others (such as Iran, Iraq, and Libya) have tended
to tailor their production decisions to the needs of their
development plans, with sufficient flexibility to step up or cut
back output depending upon their decision to discount current
over future consumption. It is, thus, only in Saudi Arabia,
the United Arab Emirates, Kuwait, and Qatar that a situation
arises where current production decisions are dictated by the
compulsions of the major oil consuming countries. Here, the
size of the surplus is determined by the gap between the
market needs and the absorptive capacity of the producers.
For the Gulf States, given their small population and limited
resource base, this figure is low, but for Saudi Arabia the
growth potential is much greater. The current Saudi
development plan to spend $140 billion, at current levels of
production and trends in import prices, could exhaust the
Saudi investable surplus by the mid-1980s.(12) Beyond this,
surpluses can be realized by further price increases and/or
greater production. However, as is the case of Libya and
Iraq, the "surplus" countries retain complete freedom to trade
using their surplus funds for keeping their investments in the
ground.

Any investment model for the oil producers has to take
"production foregone" as a definite policy option, which merits
evaluation in terms of its earning potential and the needs of
future generations. Such a decision will, however, have to
take cognizance of the hazards of nonproduction. These may
range from the extreme hazard of military action by Western oil
consuming countries threatened by the shortage of oil, to the
threat related to the future earning capacity of oil. The latter
hazard may arise from an accelerated search for new sources
of energy and/or programs for conserving energy. Neither
of these possibilities is, however, likely to prejudice the
position of oil producers, unless it actually leads to a fall or
stabilization in the price of oil. Most available projections,
under the most optimistic assumptions about substituting oil
imports, predict a fall in the dependence on OPEC oil, rather
than any reversal in the upward trend of prices.(13) In such
a situation a fall-off in the rate of growth of demand for OPEC
oil would not be inimical to the interests of oil exporters, since
it would enable them to prolong the use of depletable asset
while seeing its value appreciate over time.

The policy option to produce more or less oil is, however,
dependent on the domestic development plans of the oil pro-

ducers. There has been some tendency to take the investment plans as policy parameters.(14) This stems from the compulsion to realize certain domestic policy goals within a particular time period. These goals range from policy decisions common to all countries to attain certain standards of education, health, sanitation, housing, and social welfare, to decisions in some countries to restructure the domestic economy sufficiently to enable them to maintain a rising level of consumption when their oil wealth has eventually become exhausted. To sustain these development objectives, and to provide for a rising level of current consumption, large investments to create an infrastructure of modern communications, water resources, land development, and administrative modernization have also been put into operation.

Within this perspective, investments in social capital and development infrastructure remain inflexible, so that all countries must produce enough oil revenues to realize their development goals. However, even here, the production decision is subordinated to both the time frame of the policy decisions and the wide spectrum of technological options to realize the policy goals. Thus, if the policy goal is to provide health care to the entire population, this may be realized through investments to create facilities currently catering to rich Americans in California, or at a level equivalent to that provided by the National Health System in the United Kingdom, or even at a lower level. Similarly, education policy decisions may aim at building universities that are modern even by the U.S. standards, or at creating functionally efficient institutions by Third World standards, with the same objective of producing an educated and technically qualified populace. This wide range of technological choices will determine whether $5 billion or $1 billion is spent on a particular set of development programs. The choice will again reflect a trade-off between alternative investment options: oil in the ground, and the current investment package.

Investment decisions to diversify the production structure of the economy, again reflect a wide range of choices not only between alternative technologies but between different sets of investment options. These may range from investments in highly capital intensive industries designed to substitute imports and capture hypothetical export markets, to policy goals which put a premium on realizing full employment of the active labor force and greater self reliance in terms of technology and resource use. Outside of the domestic economy, policy options may range from investments in earning assets located to the West, to equity investments in developing countries as a means of widening the resource base of oil producers and diversifying the revenue sources for the future.

The investment decisions (in terms of investment strategy, choice of techniques, and location of investment) have to be set against trade - derived from current investment. A policy which permits unrestrained imports of luxury goods, foreign travel, and luxury housing construction has implications for the surplus. The decision to accelerate defense procurements must, within the prevailing strategic options open to the region, be seen, at least for some countries, as a consumption decison as opposed to a decision dictated by geopolitical necessity.

The size and composition of the surplus is, however, not just a function of the mix of policies pursued within each of the oil exporting countries. The developed countries have resorted to the tactics of the hard sell to induce a demand for luxury imports and projects of the most capital-intensive and technologically sophisticated variety. Defense sales have been similarly induced.(15) Once the demand was created, pricing policy has and is being used as an instrument to move the commodity and project terms of trade against the oil producers so that a reverse flow of the surplus can be put into effect.(16) The residual surplus was attracted back to the West through the initiative of the Western-based monetary institutions.

Within this framework of analysis, the surplus of the oil producers (as estimated by Western bankers) and the disguised surplus concealed within the policy decisions of the oil producers and the marketing policies of the developed countries are conceptually and quantitatively very different measurements. The underlying assumption behind this redefinition of the surplus indicates that the current patterns of consumption, investment, and imports into the oil producing countries carry a substantial element of surplus which has been effectively recycled to the industrial countries through exporting inflation and the techniques of the hard-sell. This surplus represents investments foregone for future generations in terms of oil production, and production foregone in terms of wasteful current consumption and inappropriate investment decisions. It would appear to be a major research imperative to review the investment policies of every oil producer with a view to estimating this concealed surplus. Such a task would not only be relevant to understand the true logic of the current recycling of the surplus to the West, but would provide a basis for reviewing current and future development policies and the wider relationship of these policies to restructuring the prevailing international economic order. To the extent that the surpluses represent not just the assets of future generations within the oil producing countries, but constitute a potent political and economic resource for the Third World as a whole, such an exercise not only deserves a major investment in resources but should be carried out on a priority basis.

   In the absence of such a full-scale review of the
investment strategies of individual oil producers, no
quantitative measure of the surplus appears feasible. All that
can be attempted is to review the end product of the
expenditure policies of the oil exporters in terms of imports,
development expenditure, and defense procurement to see
where the expenditures and, by implication, the surpluses
have gone. This component of OPEC expenditures may be
termed primary recycling. The actual placement of "bankers"
surpluses may be classified as the secondary recycling of the
surplus.(17)

   In trying to see how far surpluses can be channeled
toward the developing countries, one needs to review the
options in terms of both primary and secondary recycling. In
attempting this exercise, the emphasis will be on identifying
the commercially viable investment options within the Third
World. To put the problem in perspective, the flow of
concessional resources to the developing countries will be
briefly reviewed. But this will really be seen as part of the
phenomenon of primary recycling and cannot be viewed as
long-term policy option. The oil exporters must, in the final
analysis, use their surpluses to promote collective self-reliance
not just as an end in itself but to mutually benefit all
developing countries. It is central to this analysis that the
long-term political and economic interests of the oil exporters
lie in the creation of a New International Economic Order
realized through a policy of collective self-reliance. By
implication, such an order will also serve to benefit the
industrial nations, and, hence, will contribute to both growth
and stability in the world economy.

THE LOGIC OF A NEW INVESTMENT STRATEGY

The current pattern of recycling has not worked to the
advantage of the OPEC countries. Table 9.1 gives a summary
of how, in effect, the OPEC revenues have been recycled.
This indicates that 38.9 percent of OPEC revenues have been
spent not in the import of real goods and services but in the
import of inflation. Since 83 percent of commodity imports,
the bulk of service imports, and defense purchases come from
the West, the main beneficiary had been the developed world
of the West. Non-oil developing countries have, so far,
received only 5.9 percent of the recycling of the OPEC
revenues in terms of concessionary and nonconcessionary
transfers, and 13.2 percent through commodity imports.
There is no independent estimate for developing countries
shares from service imports, though it may be assumed that
this is relatively lower than their share in commodity trade.

Table 9.1 Recycling of OPEC Export Earnings
(in billions of $)

		1974	1975	1976	1977	1978	1974-78	%
Goods	Real imports of	29.6	32.8	32.2	29.5	30.3	154.4	22.5
	Inflationary component	7.4	22.6	36.0	52.6	66.7	185.3	26.9
Services	Real imports of	17.3	13.7	14.4	13.6	12.8	71.8	10.4
	Inflationary component	4.3	9.5	16.1	24.2	28.2	82.3	12.0
Imports of goods & services (nominal value)		58.6	78.6	98.7	119.9	138.0	493.8	71.8
Transfers to LDC's	Concessionary	2.8	4.0	3.8	4.6			
	Nonconcessionary	3.7	5.25	4.95	5.4			
Total Transfers to LDC's		6.5	9.25	8.75	10.0	6.0	40.5	5.9
Commercial Investments in developed countries (incl. investments in multilateral agencies)		52.28	29.22	32.07	30.55	9.0	153.12	22.3
Grand Total of Exports		117.38	117.07	139.52	160.45	153.0	687.42	100.00
Defense Imports		2.38	2.80	3.98	4.4	4.54	18.10	

Notes: i) The inflationary and real components of imports of goods and services were separated by using the OPEC deflator for imports cited in Abdel Kader Sid Ahmed, Mobilisation of Domestic Resources, Development & the members of OPEC, UNCTAD, October 1978. These figures are different from other OPEC import deflators derived from figures of export prices and inflation in developed countries used by IMF and OECD.

ii) Figures for nominal imports of goods and services are obtained from Economic Groups Report, Chase Manhattan, Nov. 1978.

iii) Transfers to developing countries are based on Chase Manhattan estimates, but figures for concessionary transfers are derived from an UNCTAD report on concessionary transfers to developing countries from OPEC.

iv) Commercial investment figures derived from Chase Manhattan and include investments in multilateral institutions. The figure used for revaluating commercial investments in industrialized countries excludes investments in multilateral institutions which are directed to developing countries.

v) The figure for the grand total of exports includes earnings from oil and non-oil exports and investment income, but is not netted for private capital transfers.

vi) Defense imports are cited as a separate entry outside the table because it has not been possible to incorporate them in balance of payments accounts derived from the IMF tables. There is no reference in commodity or service imports or any other entry to indicate expenditures on defense. To the extent that such expenditures may be concealed under some other head, we have presented this figure separately to avoid double counting. For some countries, however, this may well constitute a net addition to outpayments.

vii) Figures for defense imports are obtained for the period 1974-76 from Arms Control and Disarment Agency, World Military Expenditures and Transfers 1967-76 by U.S. Washington, July 1978. Figures for 1977 and 1978 only relate to arms deliveries to OPEC from the United States, Foreign Military Sales and Military Assistance Pacts. Published by Data Management Division DSAA, Department of Defense, Washington, D.C., 1978. These figures are, thus, an underestimate of total defense procurements.

211

We may assume, arbitrarily, that 10 percent of service imports derive from developing countries. Over and above this, developing countries have gained from migrant remittances. Our study indicates that remittance to developing countries from migrants in the OPEC countries was in the region of $10 billion between 1974 and 1978.

The secondary recycling process indicates that, between 1974 and 1978, 25 percent of the surplus was directly, and indirectly via multilateral institutions, channeled toward the developing countries, while the balance went to the industrial countries in the form of commercial investments.

This indicates a better record than for primary recycling, and reflects the rising share of concessionary transfers, a large part of which, however, find their way back to the industrial countries in the way of imports. It must, however, be kept in mind that the pattern of concessionary transfers is heavily biased toward the Arab bloc who between 1974 and 1976 received 67.6 percent of all concessionary aid commitments from OPEC.(18)

While fellow Arabs have, to some extent, become immediate beneficiaries of OPEC secondary recycling, the overwhelming share of both primary and secondary recycling of OPEC revenues has been directed to the industrial world. This has been dictated by the compulsions of the market where the industrial countries have been best equipped to respond to the growth and prevailing pattern of OPEC import demand to supply the needs of its development plans, to equip its defense needs, and to provide a secure outlet for its commercial investments. However, our contention here has been that this commitment to the industrial countries has extracted a heavy cost from OPEC in the way of imported inflation, inappropriate choice of technology, overcommitment of defense expenditures, and, finally, negative rates of return on commercial investments. Estimates of the revenues from these commercial investments indicate a rate of return on capital well below the current rate of inflation in the developed world. These inflationary trends have been compounded by the depreciation in the external value of the dollar against other strong currencies. This has further depreciated the real value of OPEC assets held abroad which today are estimated at $188 billion. Our study has indicated that, had OPEC left in the ground the equivalent in barrels of oil that it took to generate the $128 billion invested in the industrial world between 1974 and 1978, its capital value at $20 per barrel would have been $294 billion. This implies that the depreciation in the real value of its current investment portfolio is in the region of $109 billion or 37 percent.

The more serious problem for OPEC has been that its past investment strategy has tied it to the industrial world to the point where any precipitate attempt to diversify its investment

is likely to lead to a further depreciation in its capital value
due to a threat to the exchange value of the U.S. dollar,
which is the currency in which the bulk of its investments are
denominated. Furthermore, in the trade and development
sector, a whole class of intermediaries has grown up within
OPEC with a vested interest in promoting industrial country
exports and participation in OPEC development projects. This
means that, at each stage when OPEC seeks to compensate
itself against its declining purchasing power by raising oil
prices, the industrial countries can expect to recycle the surpluses back into their economies through raising export prices
and retaining the surplus as commercial investment. The
capacity for OPEC to effect a real transfer of resources to its
members through the use of the price mechanism has, thus,
substantially dissipated itself, and they will now be hard put
to even protect their current purchasing power. As we have
seen, their terms of trade have deteriorated compared to 1973
from a high of 346 in 1974 to 157 in 1978.(19) The current
round of price increases in terms of OPEC's purchasing power
over imports in 1973 indicates that, even if oil is priced at $20
per barrel, it will, in effect, be worth $5.7(20). Since OPEC
is cutting back on oil exports, its earnings will be less than
might have been expected at such high prices. It has already
built up a large development program with heavy import commitments. If one further allows for a continuing upward movement in import prices, the increment in the surplus from the
recent oil price rises will be much less dramatic than they
were in 1974.

Given OPEC's experience with the recycling process, it
would appear that a review of its options is very much in
order now that it has moved to protect itself against the erosion of surplus. Such a review would need to focus on the
scope for redirecting the primary recycling toward the developing countries, to make some readjustment in the placement of
their current surpluses. Such a reappraisal would need to
take into account certain critical concerns which constrict OPEC
expenditure and investment strategies. These primarily relate
to the need to obtain alternative sources of earnings in the
future by judicious investment of the current surpluses.

If OPEC is to redirect its investment strategy toward the
developing countries it needs to do so in terms of mutual self
interest. Its humanitarian impulses have been adequately reflected in the absolute and relative rise in its contributions
to concessionary resource transfers to the Third World. Its
capacity to sustain its earlier pattern of commitments is, however, fast eroding and may well disappear if its policy of
cutting back exports is supplemented by greater diversion of
expenditure to domestic development. For the future, therefore, it must more clearly focus its relations with other developing countries in the context of its past, unsatisfactory

relations with the industrial countries and the potential relative economic and political advantage of extending its interaction with the Third World.

Concessional transfers, obviously, remain attractive, particularly for the least developed countries. However, if opportunities could be opened up for them to both expand exports to OPEC and attract investments from OPEC which could improve their general development and export potential, they would no longer be dependent on the narcotic of concessional transfers. In these circumstances, rather than respond to every round of price increases from OPEC by sending around delegations with begging bowls, there should be a built-in mechanism in their relationship to expand trade and investments.

The building up of economic relations with the developing countries has a variety of advantages for OPEC. In the first place, it diversifies its procurement options. The need to do so has already been apparent to OPEC which has been responding to the inflation in import costs and project bids from the developed world by turning to South Korea, Brazil, India, and Pakistan to play a bigger role in their development efforts. There is, as yet, no direct evidence of the price competitiveness of developing countries' exports to OPEC. One study indicates that export price trends for manufactures have increased more slowly in developing countries compared to the industrial world.(21) The ratio of prices moved in favor of developing countries from 100 in 1975 to 90.7 in 1976. This, of course, does not say much for the specific situation in OPEC where the general index of import prices has risen much more steeply than the IMF export price index for industrialized countries.(22) From this, one may deduce evidence of price discrimination against OPEC by the industrial countries who are the principal exporters. Since we have no evidence of developing countries' pricing policy to OPEC, one can only deduce on a priori grounds, and some casual empiricism, that they are less prone to discriminate against OPEC compared to other markets.

A corresponding diversion of investments into the developing countries would again need to be justified in terms of a more attractive rate of return, compared to the negative rates being currently realized by OPEC in the West. These returns would also have to be hedged against the greater uncertainty of the return and apparent insecurity of the investment project. However, the apparent security of the OPEC commercial stake in the West has to be set against the inflexibility imposed on OPEC by their current commitments. If every attempt to readjust their investment portfolios carries a risk of capital loss, then the investment is less secure. More seriously, such a strategy makes them hostage to the economic and political fortunes of the West. Economic recession in the

West has contributed to loss of stock values and declining returns on OPEC equity investment in the United States.(23)
Furthermore, its capacity to use its oil wealth as a political
resource to realize collective Arab interests in the Middle East
is, today, constrained by implied threats to the security of
their investments in the West. While suggestions such as food
and capital goods embargoes, and the freezing of OPEC assets
have been articulated through unoffical sources in the West,
OPEC's exposure in the West lends itself to such retaliatory
measures. The big investors (such as Saudi Arabia) will obviously have to think many times before they play the oil card.
Their defense involvement with the United States amounts to
some $18 billion in equipment, and 50,000 personnel to train,
service, and secure this equipment, and this imposes a major
constraint on the Saudis' freedom of action. In contrast, the
dimensions of the OPEC economic stake in the West are no
longer significant. For example, in the United States, their
holdings do not exceed 11.6 percent of all foreign holdings,(24) while in relation to domestic holdings, their share is
negligible. In the Eurocurrency market their surpluses account for only 10 percent of the claims on the market.(25)
Since the price of oil has ceased to create the fears it did in
the post-1973 period when the industrial world used its own
price weapon with equal effectiveness, OPEC's economic leverage is much less than that exercised by the industrial world
on the imports, development needs, and investment holdings
of OPEC.
    Given the fact the OPEC oil and gas is a depleting
resource, a strategy which exchanges nonrenewable resource
for financial claims on the developed world appears to be
questionable, both politically and economically.
    In the world economy, where even such powerful com-
modity producers as OPEC remain as dependent on the industrial world as they were before 1973, such a strategy serves
merely to perpetuate the ancien regime. If, therefore, the
assertion of sovereignty by OPEC which threatened the balance
of power in the world economy in 1973 is not to lose its force
in the next generation of citizens in these countries, but is to
effectively reorder the world system, a major reappraisal of
OPEC's expenditure strategies is necessary. OPEC must realize
that its own strength and position in the world must depend
on a reordering of the international economic system by
strengthening the relative position of the developing countries
through collective action. The developing countries have a
vast reservoir of manpower including a growing pool of skilled
and professional labor with considerable managerial and administrative expertise. They have large natural resources, many
of which remain unexploited. Their capacity to exploit these
human and material resources remains constrained by lack of
capital and dependency on the industrial world. OPEC has the
liquid capital to link up with the resources of the developing

countries. Such a union would, in effect, serve to greatly enhance the collective wealth of the developing countries, to diversify OPEC's own resource base beyond its dependence on oil, and, in the process, contribute to a readjustment in the economic balance of power in the world.

MEASURES FOR COLLECTIVE SELF-RELIANCE USING OPEC SURPLUSES

Some of the principal areas where OPEC's current surplus could be immediately employed may be identified as follows:

Exploitation and Processing of Mineral Wealth Including Energy Resources

Ironically, such a possibility was suggested by the United States at UNCTAD IV in Nairobi in 1975, when it was proposed that a mineral development bank be set up.(26) This proposal was largely designed to open up the developing countries to further exploitation by multinational corporations. In practice, however, if the bank were initially capitalized by using OPEC surpluses, it could serve to give OPEC a stake in the exploitation of the mineral wealth of the developing countries. Such a possibility was recently suggested at the Annual Meeting of the Board of Governors of the Asian Development Bank in Manila, where it was proposed that the ADB seek OPEC funds to support projects for oil exploration in Asia. The venture could initially focus on the known resources in order to minimize the risks attendant on mineral exploration. A mineral development program should carry with it a processing component and, eventually, a marketing program. To the extent that the OPEC-supported mineral bank could provede loan capital, OPEC could also take out an equity stake in partnership with the concerned country. This would enable the project to bring in capital and technology from the industrial world on a contractual or junior partner basis.
      Apart from a multilateral initiative, there is much scope for bilateral actions as in the case of the Kudremukh project in India.(27) Iranian capital was used to develop Indian iron ore deposits for export in pelletized form to Iran for use in a steel mill. Capital, technology, and markets were internalized within the two countries.

Food Production

The developing countries and OPEC remain heavily dependent on a few industrial countries for import of food grains. This has held out the prospect of the United States using its grain exports as a political bargaining weapon directed at OPEC and at dividing an aid-dependent Third World from OPEC. The Arab members of OPEC have already perceived this threat, and have sought to invest heavily in Sudan in the hope of creating an indigenous source of foodgrains and livestock within the Arab world.(28) The perceptions of the Arabs and their concrete steps appear to be a promising response to the problem. Nevertheless, OPEC should realize that Sudan is not the only option open to them on the food front. Pakistan, for example, has become a big exporter of long, staple rice to the Middle East, within a program that has moved forward largely on Pakistan's initiative. It may be worth exploring the prospects of OPEC initiating a long-term commercial program, in partnership with the government of Pakistan, to provide a guaranteed market for rice, the proceeds from which should then be passed on to rice growers in Pakistan in the form of purchase contracts and investments in irrigation, equipment, seed, fertilizer, pesticide, and storage facilities. The prospect of a guaranteed market sustained by capital to secure modernizing inputs could not only transform the prospects of many farmers in Pakistan but provide a secure source of supply to OPEC.

A similar program wth both India and Pakistan on cattle farming and poultry would aim at augmenting the productive wealth of both these countries rather than to cut into the local market with its impact on domestic consumers. Similar programs for development of tropical fruit farming on a commercial basis could take place in Bangladesh, Thailand, and the Philippines, to supply fresh and canned tropical fruits through production and marketing joint ventures between local growers and OPEC traders.

Forest Resources

The as yet untapped forest resources of Africa, Latin America, and South East Asia could also be opened up by OPEC investments for both exploitation and industries based on forest products. These, again, would be directed to markets in OPEC and in other developing countries.

Manufacturing Industry

OPEC imports of manufactures in 1975 amounted to 16.7 percent of the world import of manufactures. However, only 10.8

218   FINANCIAL ISSUES OF THE NIEO

percent of exports from developing countries went to OPEC in
that period, which amounts to 4 percent of OPEC's import of
manufactures. If one considers that the Third World was already exporting $43.8 billion worth of manufactures by 1976,
there would appear to be considerable scope for raising exports to OPEC, whose import of manufactures today is substantially higher than in 1975, given the rise in the total of
imports from $51 billion in 1975 to $97 billion in 1978.(29) A
program to build up developing countries' exports of manufactures to meet a growing share of OPEC's needs should not aim
at diverting their current exports, but at augmenting their
export capacity. This again could be realized by investments
by OPEC in the manufacturing sector of selected developing
countries. The critical ingredient would be to package the
investment and marketing program together, so that OPEC
could have an equity stake in meeting its own import needs.

A considerable emphasis would need to be put on multinational joint ventures incorporating a wider spectrum of developing countries. If marketing is to be an integral part of
the package, then it will not be enough to rely on the OPEC
market but must be tied in to other developing countries. For
example, a proposal to set up a urea fertilizer plant in Bangladesh, using local natural gas, could be financed by OPEC
capital, based on a guaranteed, long-term market in India.

Investment in the building up of an OPEC shipping fleet
should not be limited to the current Arab multinational shipping venture. The scope of this project could be widened to
include the creation of a confederation with the state shipping
lines of South Asia, which would provide a wider and more
balanced market. The project could give a stake to India,
South Korea, Singapore, and Hong Kong by placing orders in
shipyards of these countries as long as they provide a part of
their carriage to the fleet. A program could be worked out
with Bangladesh, India, and Pakistan to secure manpower.

In each case, countries would be contributing a resource
where they already have some comparative advantage, while
their collective involvement could be sustained by a program of
market sharing.

Financial Flows

In the field of banking and finance, OPEC is already making
some headway in developing a local financial capability to invest its surpluses. The growth of such banks, mostly with
Arab capital, has played a growing role in syndications of
Eurocredits and bond issues to selected Third World countries.(30) Here, again, there is considerable scope for tying
these banking ventures to the already-established private and
state banking sectors of Asia.

Such an effort should not be limited to syndications, but should aim at creating multinational Third World banks in order to widen the network of commercial financing beyond the hallowed circle of middle income developing countries, which dominate the Third World market for commercial loans. The movement of both finance capital and equity investment would be facilitated by the growth of a secondary market in debt instruments. Kuwait has made some headway in this area, but a more purposeful collective effort, built around money markets in Hong Kong, Singapore, Kuwait, and Bahrain, would need to be developed, by bringing in some of the bigger economies such as India, South Korea, and Pakistan, and even Brazil or Mexico.

In seeking to build up regional capital markets, much more effective use could be made of regional multilateral financial institutions such as the Asian Development Bank, The African Development Bank and the Islamic Development Bank. OPEC has already been given a capital stake in the African Development Bank and dominates the Islamic Development Bank. It should now contribute to greatly expanding the capital base of the Asian Development Bank in exchange for a stake in its management. This could provide the basis for a new program of commerical lending to the ADB, and for the expansion of cofinancing programs involving OPEC multilateral and bilateral loan agencies. To the extent that OPEC investments in these institutions would be based on commercial considerations, they should be used for commmercial loans. In order to accomodate the least developed countries, OPEC could contribute to an interest subsidy account.

Any escalated OPEC involvement in the financing of the Third World on a nonconcessional basis should provide a commercially viable program for OPEC, and a sense of security. The attraction of the Western money market to OPEC lay in the fact that the risks attendent on lending to small countries was carried by the Banks, while OPEC only had to depend on the long-term viability of Citibank or the Chase Manhattan. In their minds even a negative rate of return was acceptable to ensure security for their capital. Though this capital stake is fast eroding, there must be some price to the search for security.

Any program of OPEC investments in developing countries needs to build up a secure mechanism to guarantee transfers by pooling risks and using established multilateral institutions to underwrite them. While the threat to such investments in developing countries has been overstated, it cannot be ignored. It must be realized that the threat of political expropriation has been manifest in situations of political dependency, largely related to relations between colonial powers and their satellites. A transformation in the domestic political balance puts the stake of the dominant power at risk. Since OPEC is

not seeking political hegemony as the price of its commerical
stake, this type of threat is greatly reduced. Where it does
emerge, however, OPEC has the most powerful of sanctions
through its monoply of oil supplies. To the extent that it can
introduce the oil weapon against politically induced default, the
risk will be minimized. The possibility of default by developing countries due to the fortunes of the world market or their
own domestic problems is a more real hazard which, in part,
needs to be reduced by creating conditions where the effect of
such random jolts to the economy can be mitigated.

Commodity Price Stabilization

In order to create conditions where developing countries are
not faced with periodic crises in their external accounts, one
of the first areas of action would need to relate to their commodity exports.

For a large number of developing countries, the health,
not just of their balance of payments but also of their domestic
economy, rests on the volume and value of exports of a limited
number of primary commodities. The initiatives of the South
to realize a program for stabilizing prices and income of commodity producers through the Integrated Programme of Commodities and the Common Fund has been one of the central
themes of the North South Dialogue. Implicit in these programs has been the search for a collective initiative among
commodity producers in the hope of duplicating the success of
OPEC. The nature of the negotiating process has, however,
obviated the prospect of emulating OPEC, since it seeks to
help commodity producers through a consensus with consumers
from the industrial world. Since, by definition, the interests
of producers and consumers are contradictory, very little progress has been made in the pursuit of these goals. After four
years of protracted negotiation, agreement, in principle, has
been reached for only one commodity out of a list of eighteen.
A watered down Common Fund has been set up with resources
well below what had been projected, and without a Second
Window to support programs for commodity development.

It is in this area that OPEC can come forward to play a
major role. To the extent that the search for consensus with
the North has been the main constraint in setting up these
programs, the emphasis should be diverted to seeking an
agreement among producers to realize the objectives implicit in
these programs. Since the program initially has to rest on a
Southern initiative, it may, in the first phase, be advisable to
limit action to those commodities which are overwhelmingly produced by developing countries, such as jute, rubber, tea,
coffee, cocoa, and bananas.

The main lines of the strategy should be to set up buffer
stocking arrangements for each commodity. These should be

built around producers' cartels, perhaps set up as a multinational marketing venture. OPEC could be given an equity stake in this entity. The idea would be to settle a fund, underwritten by a Common Fund supported by OPEC, to buy up and stock commodities when the price falls below an agreed floor, and to market the product when prices rise. In contrast to the UNCTAD IPC's, this program would not seek to enforce a ceiling on prices, but only a floor price which, at least for those commodities not threatened with competition from synthetics, could be progressively raised. OPEC's commercial stake could be kept viable by the prospects of selling on a rising market, while the prospect for collective action would aim at realizing long-term real gains for the producer. For the program to remain viable, however, it should also invest in yield improvements, the search for new uses, and new methods for processing the raw material.

A Southern Common Fund underwritten by OPEC could then finance each IPC through commercial loans. The assumption would be that, once the producers' cartel came into existence, the industrial countries would be much more inclined to come to terms with commodity producers, and would provide scope for stable earnings to producers. At this stage, however, the successful IPC's would, perhaps, prefer to depend on their own collective efforts. By investing in the development and marketing of a whole range of commodities, OPEC would have made an important step away from its dependence on a single commodity to assure its future.

Other Suggested Measures

An alternative proposal, derived frm a suggestion by I. Gulati,(31) would use the accumulated reserves of some $60 billion of the non-oil developing countries to float a Southern Common Fund that could be assisted in its initial capitalization by OPEC on a concessionary basis. Through the Fund's borrowing on the capital market, as proposed by Gulati, OPEC could collectively agree to underwrite the amounts required on commercial terms. This would provide an alternative outlet for OPEC's current holding of assets in the West with a lower risk threshold than for our initial proposal of an equity stake in the Fund.

A variety of other possibilities exist for using OPEC surpluses. They range from using OPEC funds to underwrite programs to create or to transmit technology within and between developing countries, to investments in programs for setting up purchasers' cartels and the creation of Third World stockpiles of key commodities. All such programs must, however, be premised on the realization that the present international economic order has to be transformed, and that

OPEC's own material and political interests lie in identifying
with the contributing to this process. While there can be little
doubt that the collective perception of the peoples of these
countries will seek such an identity with the Third World to
secure the future for coming generations, the short-term
interests of certain elements in some of these countries may
certainly be inimical to any such redirection of OPEC
expenditure strategies. The current material stake of these
interests has been built around inducting Western bankers and
suppliers of capital and defense equipment into OPEC, so they
have a decided stake in preserving the old order. In this
task, they would be assisted by the mistaken notion
entertained by the governments of some industrial countries
that the old order is viable and can be sustained. To this
end, the responses within OPEC to the prospects suggested in
this paper are as likely to be contingent on the political
dialectic within these countries, as they are to the intrinsic
worth of the proposals. Any meaningful assessment of the use
of OPEC surpluses as an instrument for collective self-reliance
can, therefore, no more than identify opportunities. To seek
to transform them into programs of action would not only
demand more detailed investigation and working out of each
program but would require a review of the domestic balance of
forces within each oil exporting country and its interaction
with the strategic interests of the major powers in the world
system.

NOTES

(1) K. G. Vaiyda, "The Paris Episode in the North-South
    Dialogue" (Paper presented at the Seminar on North-
    South Negotiations in the Conference on International
    Economic Cooperation [CIEC], Queen Elizabeth House,
    Oxford, June 1979, mimeographed).

(2) Interim Progress Report of the Preparatory Committee
    for the Fourth Ministerial Meeting of the Group of 77,
    Arusha, Tanzania, Feb. 5-16, 1979; and Draft Reports
    of Senior Officials, Arusha, Tanzania, Feb. 6-12, 1979,
    mimeographed.

(3) Figures derived from Report of the Economics Group,
    Chase Manhattan Bank, New York, prepared from data
    published by the U.S. Treasury Department (hereafter
    referred to as Chase Manhattan Report).

(4) Export revenue figures for 1973 and 1974 were derived
    from Bank of England Quarterly Bulletin, December 1974
    and March 1975. Figures for 1975 to 1978 are from Chase
    Manhattan Report. The incremental earnings figure is
    computed from the differential in the earnings figure from

oil exports actually realized by OPEC between 1974 and
1978 and a hypothetical earnings figure based on actual
export between 1974 and 1978 but priced at the 1973
average unit take of $2.1 per barrel. This differential,
in practice, may have been an underestimate of oil
revenues, since a lower price may have increased the
offtake of oil.

(5)   This figure is derived from estimating the share of the
value of OPEC commodity exports directed to the industrialized developed countries between 1974 and 1977 and
assumes that an equivalent proportion of the incremental
earnings from oil exports was derived from these countries.   Figures for destination of exports were obtained
from Direction of Trade, Annual 1971-77 published by the
IMF, Washington, D.C.

(6)   This figure is derived from IMF, Direction of Trade,
various issues, and includes the People's Republic of
China as well as Taiwan.

(7)   Ibid.

(8)   Ibid.   The developed countries are here defined to
include "Industrial Countries," "Other Europe," Australia,
New Zealand, and South Africa as categorized in Direction
of Trade.

(9)   Derived from Chase Manhattan Report.

(10) See various issues of U.S. Treasury Bulletin; Bank
of England Quarterly Reports; and World Financial
Markets, Morgan Guaranty Trust Company, New York.

(11) There is a large literature related to the conceptualization of the nature of the OPEC surplus.   Of these,
special reference may be made to the work of Yoon S.
Park, Oil Money and the World Economy (London: Wilton
House, 1976); and Abdelkader Sid Ahmed, Mobilisation of
Domestic Resources - Development and the Members of
OPEC (Paper prepared for UNCTAD, Trade and Development Board, Committee on Invisibles and Financing related
to Trade, Oct. 1978, mimeographed).

(12) This perspective on the current prospects of the Saudi
development plan is derived from T.H. Moran, "Oil Prices
and the Future of OPEC" Research paper R-8, Resources
for the Future, Washington D.C., March 1978.

(13) Chapter on Energy, Intermediate Result Interfutures
Research Project OECD, August 1977.

(14) For a discussion of OPEC development plans see Moran,
"Oil Prices and the Future of OPEC."

(15) See Anthony Sampson, The Arms Bazaar, (London:
Penguin Books, 1978) for a discussion of how demand for
arms was induced.

(16) Sid Ahmed, Mobilisation of Domestic Resources, for a
discussion of the manipulation of prices by developed
countries.

(17) The term primary and secondary recycling has also been used by Yoon S. Park but with a rather different connotation.

(18) This estimate has been calculated from data compiled by the UNCTAD, Division for Economic Cooperation among developing countries for their forthcoming Report on concessionary and nonconcessionary transfers to developing countries from OPEC.

(19) Calculated from import price indexes computed by OPEC for 1975-77 and cited by Sid Ahmed, Mobilisation of Domestic Resources. Figures for 1978 are extrapolated from price indexes of export of manufactures from industrialized countries cited in World Financial Markets, Morgan Guaranty Trust, December 1978.

(20) Estimated by using OPEC import price indexes.

(21) "World Trade and Output of Manufactures: Structural Trends and Developing Countries' Exports," World Bank Staff Working Paper No. 316, January 1979.

(22) Derived from International Financial Statistics, published annually by IMF.

(23) See Russell B. Scholl, "The International Investment Position of the United States: Developments in 1977," Survey of Current Business (August 1978).

(24) Ibid.

(25) The figure is derived from BIS estimates of assets and liabilities of reporting banks of the BIS as of September 1978. The tables are presented in Bank of England Quarterly Bulletin, March 1979.

(26) See the World Bank's Minerals and Energy in the Developing Countries, May 4, 1977.

(27) See Deepak Lal, Industrial Co-operation Agreements, in Co-operation for Accellerating Industrialisation, Commonwealth Secretariat, July 1978.

(28) Ibrahim Shihata, Joint Ventures Among Arab Countries, Group of Experts on Economic Cooperation Among Developing Countries, UNCTAD, October, 1975.

(29) World Bank, Minerals and Energy in the Developing Countries.

(30) Arab Banking survey, Euromoney, April 1979.

(31) I.S. Gulati, "International Monetary Developments in the Third World: A Proposal to Redress the Imbalance," Working Paper No. 86, Centre for Development Studies, Trivandrum, Feb. 1979.

Index

About the Editors and Contributors

JORGE A. LOZOYA - Project Co-director for the NIEO at CEESTEM.

A. K. BHATTACHARYA - Principal Research Associate for the NIEO Project at UNITAR, Assistant Professor of International Business, Pace University, New York.

AMIT BHADURI - Jawaharlal Nehru University, New Delhi.

AGUSTIN CASO - Interamerican Development Bank, Washington, D.C.

JAIME ESTEVEZ - Project Research Coordinator at CEESTEM.

ROSARIO GREEN - El Colegio de Mexico.

PEDRO PAZ - Universidad Nacional Autonoma de Mexico.

V.K.R.V. RAO - Institute for Social and Economic Change, Bangalore.

REHMAN SOBHAN - Centre for Research on the New International Economic Order, Oxford.

RENE VILLARREAL - El Colegio de Mexico.